AF589182

The Honesty Crisis

The Honesty Crisis

Preserving Our Most Treasured Virtue in an Increasingly Dishonest World

Christian B. Miller

OXFORD
UNIVERSITY PRESS

Oxford University Press is a department of the University of Oxford.
It furthers the University's objective of excellence in research, scholarship,
and education by publishing worldwide. Oxford is a registered trade mark of
Oxford University Press in the UK and in certain other countries.

Published in the United States of America by Oxford University Press
198 Madison Avenue, New York, NY 10016, United States of America.

CIP data is on file at the Library of Congress

ISBN 9780197840801

DOI: 10.1093/9780197840801.001.0001

Printed by Integrated Books International, United States of America

The manufacturer's authorized representative in the EU for product safety is
Oxford University Press España S.A. of Parque Empresarial San Fernando de Henares,
Avenida de Castilla, 2 – 28830 Madrid (www.oup.es/en or product.safety@oup.com).
OUP España S.A. also acts as importer into Spain of products made by the manufacturer.

To the Wake Forest Philosophy Department,

my home for the past 20 years,

and to my department chairs

Dr. Ralph Kennedy, Dr. Win-chiat Lee, Dr. Stavroula Glezakos,
Dr. Emily Austin, and Dr. Patrick Toner,

for your tremendous support and friendship

Contents

Preface

A Real-Life Example

Nineteen-year-old José Nuñez Romaniz from Albuquerque, New Mexico, was helping his grandfather buy some clothes online, and needed to deposit money into his account to complete the transaction. So José drove to his bank's ATM, where he saw something unusual—a large plastic bag on the ground next to the machine. When he looked inside, he found that the bag was packed with $20 and $50 bills. The grand total: $135,000 in cash.

José faced a choice. He could take the bag, or at least some of the cash in it, and no one would ever know what happened. The money could have been put to good use—José's family was not well-off, and José was helping raise his two younger siblings while working part-time as a store clerk and getting his college degree in criminal justice. But he says he never gave this option a moment's thought. Instead, he immediately called the police to report the lost money which, it turned out, had been accidentally left behind by the company which refills ATMs with cash.

"In the back of my head, I was just thinking about my parents, especially my mom," he later said. "What she would do if I came home with the money and what she would do with her chancla [flip flop] to hit me," he laughed. "I did the right thing and I know my parents are proud and my family is proud as well."[1]

José's honest action did not go unnoticed. He was lauded by the community, and given a plaque by the mayor, gift cards by local businesses, free tickets to football games, and even an invitation to apply for a job with the local police department. After all, José's dream was to work as a criminal investigator.

As the mayor of Albuquerque confessed in a moment of honesty himself, "Man, we all know that temptation—even just take a little, just one of those bundles off the top, I mean that had to be really hard."[2]

José's example vividly reminds us of the power of honesty in our world today.[3]

Main Themes of the Book

Honesty is indeed valuable. In fact, out of all the virtues, honesty is arguably the *most* valuable. It helps to show respect for others, to treat them as persons with dignity, and to demonstrate that we value their autonomy. Honesty promotes trust and credibility, and prevents harm. It also fosters healthy relationships, and strengthens organizations and societies. Empirically, increased honesty is related to decreased aggression, higher GPA, and increased performance, among other benefits.[4] Without honesty, communication would break down, relationships would fail, and businesses would crumble. Competitive athletics, financial investing, and academic assessments would all cease to exist.

Fortunately, people tend to recognize just how important honesty is. Indeed, there is actual data which suggests that we care about honesty *more than any other quality a person might possess*. For instance, our team at Wake Forest University ran a study in which participants were given 60 different names of traits, like being forgiving, intelligent, mature, kind, lazy, needy, and humble.[5] Honesty was on the list too. Then participants in the study were asked to consider three questions:

> Your task is to group these words into those that are most characteristic of a person you would like . . .
>
> Your task is to group these words into those that are most characteristic of a person you would respect . . .
>
> Your task is to group these words into those that are most informative toward feeling like you understand who someone really is . . .

Which trait emerged in first place out of the 60 on the list? Surely it would be something like being compassionate or kind or maybe fair, right? No, it was honesty *in all three cases*. More than all the other traits, people rated honesty as central to what they liked, respected, and wanted to know about other people.

This resonates with our own experience too. It is often deeply upsetting to find out that a friend has been lying to us, a spouse has been cheating on us, or a sibling has been stealing from us. We care about others treating us in an honest way, and when they don't, it usually hurts. A lot.

So honesty matters, and people care a great deal about it. Yet we are facing an unprecedented erosion of honesty today—what I call an *honesty crisis*. Indeed, we are facing not just one crisis, but a variety of honesty crises in different parts of our society. In this book, I reveal how deception has become easier than ever and why there needs to be a collective effort to address these honesty crises head-on. Fortunately, in many cases, there are concrete steps we can take to try to turn the tide.

For the past 10 years, I have been studying both what honesty is and the state of honesty in the world today. Thanks to one of the largest grants in the history of the humanities for something we called "The Honesty Project," I was able to lead a group of academics from across the globe to advance our understanding in an area where we know so little. In this book, I share where this journey has taken me, and why I am so worried about the prospects for honesty in the coming years.[6]

As a result of this research, we can now bring honesty into much clearer focus. From my perspective as an ethics professor, honesty is an excellence of someone's character. It helps us to avoid behaving badly in a wide variety of circumstances (the courtroom, the office, the party, at home, and so on) and allows us to maintain this standard of behavior consistently over time. In particular, an honest person will avoid intentionally distorting or misrepresenting the world as she sees it—whether that is by telling a lie, stealing, cheating, breaking a promise, acting hypocritically, or BSing.

This framework will be developed in Chapter 1, and with it in place, we will have a better idea of what honesty is and why it is important. We will also be able to more readily spot the honesty crises in our society today. An honesty crisis occurs when there is a significant surge in dishonest behavior due to two factors: (i) dishonesty becoming easier to get away with than it was before, and (ii) dishonesty becoming more enticing or appealing to engage in. When we are in such a crisis, everything dishonest accelerates.

There are many areas of society facing honesty crises. In this book, I focus on six in particular:

In online spaces, the frequency of deepfakes has skyrocketed, now that they are simple to make and basically untraceable. Distributing these recordings is often dishonest, and undermines our ability to trust what we see and hear online.

With the easy availability of pornography, anonymous chatrooms, and infidelity websites like Ashley Madison, cheating in a relationship has never been easier.

In education, many students are using AI to complete their writing assignments for them with little chance of being detected by their professors.

In politics, social media helps with the dissemination of fake news, and polarization reduces our tendency to condemn political dishonesty if it aligns with our own views.

In public spaces, it is easier to become a celebrity than it has ever been in human history, and the allure of celebrity might be stronger than ever before too. Yet celebrity encourages greater dishonesty, since celebrity tends to be insatiable, to be closely guarded, to erode moral safeguards, and to create greater opportunities to be dishonest.

Religious leaders are increasingly confronted by pressures to be dishonest that arise in different areas of their lives, including pressures to engage in sermon plagiarism, have inappropriate emotional and sexual relationships, and fall into the trappings of celebrity.

In each of these cases, I show how there are more frequent opportunities for dishonesty to mold our characters in a direction further and further away from virtue. This would be a tremendous loss not just for us as individuals, but for society at large.

So honesty is extremely important, and people care a great deal about it. Yet we are facing the frightening reality of a number of honesty crises in our society. There needs to be a collective effort to confront these crises head-on.

The main purpose of the book is to highlight this sobering reality. But in addition, we will see that in many cases we are not powerless in the face of these crises. There are both individual and institutional strategies available to help us push back. Individually, for instance, role models of honesty can inspire us to be better, and perspective-taking has been found to reduce temptation to cheat in certain circumstances. Institutionally, cultures where cheating or stealing are prevalent make it very hard to resist joining in such behavior. Cultures committed to honor, integrity, and truthfulness can curb temptation to cheat.

However, to be very clear from the start, I do not have any quick fixes, easy remedies, or simple solutions. At times, I will enthusiastically support more nuanced strategies for resisting an honesty crisis. But, to be honest (which seems appropriate for this book), there will be times where I will just admit that I do not see a way to move forward constructively.

The Honesty Crisis is a wakeup call to pay attention to the many ways in which it is becoming easier to act deceptively, and to do what we can to protect our most treasured virtue.

Intended Audience

Over the course of my career, I have written many books and articles for academic audiences. But after a while I grew dissatisfied with that kind of writing, and in 2017 published a book called *The Character Gap: How Good Are We?* for a general audience with no background in philosophy.

This book is written with the same audience in mind. No familiarity with philosophy is presupposed, only an interest in engaging with matters of honesty and dishonesty. Academics will no doubt want more details, arguments, and distinctions, and in the endnotes I cite some resources to explore for further engagement. But this book is not written for my fellow academics. These are issues which, I believe, we all need to be confronting today.

Notes

1. Burkhart 2020.
2. Ibid.
3. This account drew on Burkhart 2020 and Padilla 2020.
4. See Park and Peterson 2008 and Sosik et al. 2012.
5. Hartley et al. 2016.
6. To read more about The Honesty Project, see https://honestyproject.philosophy.wfu.edu/.

Acknowledgments

This book arose from my work leading the Honesty Project, a five-year initiative here at Wake Forest University funded by the John Templeton Foundation. Initially I wrote an academic monograph, *Honesty: The Philosophy and Psychology of a Neglected Virtue*, which was published by Oxford in 2021. This was very important for me in being able to work out the details of my theory of honesty, and also dive deeply into the empirical literature. But I was not content to just write for an academic audience, and so at the end of the Honesty Project I turned my attention to a book for a popular audience. This is the book before you.

I am grateful to Sarah Clement and Richard Bollinger at the Templeton Foundation for their support of the Honesty Project. The opinions expressed here are those of the author and do not necessarily reflect the views of the foundation.

Most of the work on this book was done during a research leave generously supported by the Wake Forest University Reynolds leave program and the Thomas J. Lynch Fund. Thanks to my department chair, Stavroula Glezakos, for her support of this project.

Peter Ohlin at Oxford University Press was my editor for this book, and it has been a joy to work with him on many projects over the years. I am very appreciative of his support of this book. Many thanks as well to Meridith Murray for preparing the index so carefully. I am also most grateful to the two reviewers for Oxford who provided very helpful comments.

Many thanks to the following for the opportunity to share some of my ideas in these pages: Wake Forest University Honesty Project Final Conference, Coastal Carolina University, Princeton University, Learning and the Brain Conference, American Philosophical Association Central Division Meeting, Parr Center for Ethics at UNC Chapel Hill, Highlands Center for Life Enrichment,

Hampden-Sydney College, and the Poteat Lecture at Wake Forest University. Jackson Miller provided helpful written comments on Chapters 1 and 5, as did Christian Hart on Chapter 2. My mother as always was amazingly helpful with her editing suggestions, spending hours looking over the entire manuscript.

Chapter 3 on deepfakes makes use of ideas first published in Tobias Flattery and Christian B. Miller, "Deepfakes and Dishonesty," *Philosophy & Technology* 27 (2024), with permission from Springer under the terms of the Creative Commons CC BY license (http://creativecommons.org/licenses/by/4.0/). My colleague and friend Tobias is the one who deserves most of the credit for developing the framework for thinking about how dishonesty plays a role in deepfakes. Chapter 7 on fame is adapted from my paper, "Celebrity and Dishonesty: Do They Go Hand in Hand?" *The Philosophy of Fame and Celebrity*, Eds. Alfred Archer, Catherine Robb, and Matthew Dennis, Bloomsbury, 2024, and is used with permission of Bloomsbury Press.

As I do with every book, I want to save my deepest appreciation and gratitude to my family: my parents Bill and Joyous Miller; my mother-in-law Eileen Smith; my children Jackson, William, and Lillian; and most of all my wife Jessie Lee Miller. She has taught me more about honesty than anyone else. While I teach ethics, she does a much better job of actually living it out.

One of my children insisted on writing the author's bio for this book, and I could not say no. So here it is: "Dr. Christian Basil Koban Miller was born in a large house in Maryland and soon moved to a house on one side of Florida, where he helped thousands of sea turtles. Christian is now a philosophy professor at Wake Forest. He enjoys reading, spending time with his wife and three kids (ages 13, 11, and 9), and playing video games." This sums it up pretty well.

1 Honesty Is a Lot More Interesting Than You Might Think

"We hardly need a chapter on what honesty is. That's simple—honesty is just telling the truth. Don't tell any lies, and you are honest. That's it!"

Ah, if only it were that easy. The honest truth is that honesty is way more complicated than this. It involves lots of other kinds of behavior. It also makes a big difference what lies behind our behavior, that is, what's going on in our heart and mind.

In this chapter, we will bust the myth that honesty is just the same as plain old truth-telling, by exploring some of the complexity involved in being an honest person. In doing so, we will discover that honesty is far from boring. It is actually a fascinating topic concerning how to live our lives.

Busting a Myth: Honesty and Lying

When I ask what honest people do, I always get the same answer. "They tell the truth." Or if I say, "What's a good sign that someone is not honest?," the answer comes back as, "Lying."

Now surely honesty *does* have to do with truth-telling and preventing lies. No one disputes that. But what is striking about honesty is how much more there is to it.

To see this, consider some examples of other failures of honesty that do not involve lies:

The Honesty Crisis. Christian B. Miller, Oxford University Press. © Oxford University Press 2026.
DOI: 10.1093/9780197840801.003.0001

Misleading. Wife: "Why did you come home so late last night?"

> Husband: "I was at the bar with the guys."
> Wife: "Oh, okay."

Here is what the husband should have said if he was completely honest:

> "I was at the bar with the guys and then I went back to the apartment of a girl I met there."

In withholding this additional information, he is being dishonest. Note, though, that he is not lying. He did in fact go to the bar with the guys. But by answering in the very misleading way he did, he is hoping that his wife will come to the false conclusion that he was *only* at the bar with the guys.

Giving misleading answers that are true but aimed at getting your audience to arrive at a false conclusion is dishonest. Honest people would not do that.

Cheating. Suppose I include very explicitly on my paper assignment for my philosophy class:

> The use of any AI programs like ChatGPT to help in any way with the writing of this paper is prohibited and will be considered a violation of the honor code.

Sam, a student in my class, reads this but does not care about what I say. He wants to get the paper done as quickly as possible, so he turns in a paper that ChatGPT generated for him using my assignment. Regardless of whether you think I am being overly strict, the rules are the rules and Sam knowingly broke them. He cheated, and by cheating he was dishonest.

Breaking the rules of an activity on purpose to gain an advantage, especially when you have voluntarily chosen to participate in that activity, is dishonest. Honest people would not do that.

Stealing. In the first volume of the *Hardy Boys*, Frank and Joe are on the lookout for a thief who stole jewels and securities from the safe in the Tower Mansion. The villain who did this was able to figure out the three-number code to the safe, take the valuables, and escape without leaving a trace. He stole, and in stealing he was dishonest.

Taking the property of others, and acting as if it belonged to you even though you know it does not, is dishonest. Honest people would not do that.

BSing.[1] An employee is working at a department store with a lot of unsold winter clothes. A customer comes up to the counter and asks,

> "Is it supposed to get colder the next few days?"

The employee has no idea; she forgot to check the weather forecast that morning. But she still says anyway,

> "It sure is, and we have plenty of winter clothes on sale at the moment!"

The employee is not lying in this case. She genuinely has no idea one way or the other. Instead, she just made up an answer that she thought would be beneficial to her. She gave a BS response, and in BSing she was dishonest.

Responding to others in ways that do not reflect what you think is true or false, but are just made up to suit your own purposes, is dishonest. Honest people would not do that.

Hypocrisy. The speaker has the crowd enraptured,

> "Eating animal products is terribly wrong. Animals deserve to have a long and healthy life, not to be confined to small pens wallowing in their own filth and injected with all kinds of hormones. We each have a moral obligation to become vegans!"

The crowd thunders in applause, and for the first time in your life you consider giving up the hamburgers you love so much. Sadly, though, later that night you spot the same speaker in the corner of McDonald's, clearly enjoying a Big Mac. He is being a hypocrite, and in doing so he is dishonest.

Telling people in public how they should behave, and then doing the exact opposite in private, is dishonest. Honest people would not do that.

Self-Deception. Deep down, Anna knows that her husband is cheating on her. She has found the text messages, the visits to the Ashley Madison website ("Life is short. Have an affair."), the hotel charges, and so forth. But she so wants to have the perfect marriage and to believe that her husband is faithful after all. So despite all the evidence suggesting otherwise, she gets herself to somehow believe in his faithfulness. She engages in self-deception, and in doing so she is dishonest (with herself).

Believing something because you want it to be true, despite knowing that it is not and having to ignore all the opposing evidence, is dishonest. Honest people would not do that.

Misleading, cheating, stealing, BSing, hypocrisy, and self-deception. Each of them is distinct from lying. Each of them falls under the scope of honesty. Each of them will show up in the chapters to come.

The list is even longer, in fact. We could add promising-breaking, fraud, and perjury. But the above is enough to correct the common assumption that honesty just has to do with truth-telling.

Here is an important implication of the above. Honesty and dishonesty cover a *vast amount of moral territory*. When we think about a lot of the moral mistakes we make in our lives, they turn out to have to do with honesty.

It is not just us. Every day the news is filled with stories of people doing morally bad things, and dishonesty usually finds its way into many of them. Just think of all the stories you have read about infidelity or fake news or plagiarism or financial mismanagement.

When we get to the final chapter on the significance of honesty, we will expand on all this more. But already it is coming into focus: honesty is an incredibly important virtue.

What Is Honesty?

"But wait, Miller—aren't you supposed to be a philosopher? Yes, you have told us that honesty is (surprisingly!) broad in scope. But you have not said anything yet about what honesty *is*. Aren't philosophers supposed to specialize in defining their terms?"

Yes and yes. But now we have a problem. For misleading, cheating, stealing, BSing, hypocrisy, and self-deception, along with lying, make up quite a list. Is there anything that they even share in common? How does dishonesty relate to all of this motley crew?

Or if we flip them around to their positive terms, like being forthright, complying with the rules, being respectful of property, caring about the truth, having integrity, and being authentic, along with being truthful, is there anything that they all share in common? How does honesty relate to all of these positive traits, as depicted in Figure 1.1?

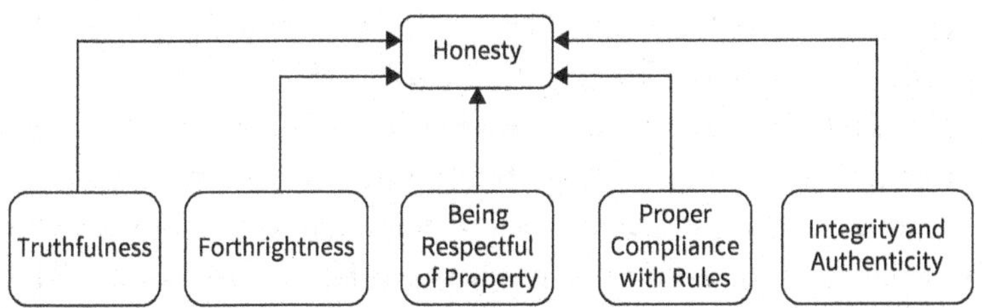

Figure 1.1 Relating honesty to other positive traits.[2]

To address these questions, maybe we should look to see what honesty researchers have said about them. Can they help us out? Alas, the answer is no. Looking back over the past 50 years of writings by philosophers working on the virtues, for instance, there is almost nothing out there to help us.[3]

Except for my proposal. Which makes it clearly the best one, if for no other reason than it is about the only one.[4] Here is the starting point for how I am thinking about honesty:

> An honest person does not intentionally distort the facts as she sees them.

Some examples will help.

Suppose one of my students claims that he could not turn in his homework because the dog ate it (for the record, I have never actually had any students try this one out on me!). He is lying to me, and thereby failing to be honest. How so? By intentionally distorting, or mispresenting, to me what actually happened. He knows that his dog was not involved at all because (a) he did not do his homework so the dog could not have eaten it, and (b) anyway he does not even have a dog.

The same is true of my ChatGPT cheating student from the last section. He intentionally distorted the facts as to his own contribution to the paper assignment. In other words, he was making it seem as if he had written the paper in its entirety, when in fact it was written by the artificial intelligence (AI).

The same holds with our Big Mac hypocrite. He presents himself as someone who is deeply opposed to eating meat, all the while intentionally mispresenting himself and what he really cares about. There he is, after all, sitting in McDonald's, having a Big Mac when he thought no one who knew him was looking.

The 'intentionally' is there for a reason. If you accidentally walk out of a store having completely forgotten to pay for something, you are not stealing. If you are playing a game and break one of the rules without even knowing it is a rule, you are not cheating. And so on.

The language of 'facts as she sees them' is also important. Indeed, it relates to another one of the surprising features of honesty. It turns out that honesty is not tied to the truth.

What? That sounds like heresy. Let me explain. There is the truth, objectively, which is the way reality in fact is. And then there are our own opinions or beliefs about what is true or false. Sometimes these come together. Sometimes they come apart.

For instance, I believe that the Earth is round. And the objective truth is that it is round. So my belief accurately captures the way the world is, the truth. Thousands of years ago, however, many people believed that the Earth was flat. Yet objectively it was still round. So in that case their opinions did not map on to the truth.

The same thing is going on with the example of the self-deceived wife. She has fooled herself into thinking that her husband is being faithful. As a matter of fact, he is not.

What does all this have to do with honesty? Surprisingly, honesty is concerned with our opinions and beliefs, *rather than* with the truth.

Again, go back to the flat Earth example. If someone had said, thousands of years ago, that the Earth is flat, she would not be dishonest. She is conveying the shape of the Earth *as she sees it*. In contrast, the self-deceived wife is distorting or misrepresenting the facts as she sees them (namely all the evidence that her husband is cheating), and so is failing to be honest.

This is why I say that honesty is not tied to the truth, in the sense of how reality actually is. It is tied to our *perceptions of* reality, or how we understand things to be. You can be wrong about reality, but honest in what you are saying or doing. You can be right about reality, but dishonest.

Now this approach to thinking about honesty has some startling implications. Here is one—people who communicate to you their crazy conspiracy theories can still be honest. For instance, suppose someone is a Holocaust denier or a follower of the 9/11 "Truth Movement," which thinks that the World Trade Center towers collapsed because of a prearranged controlled demolition. Let's imagine that the person really does believe these things; he is not just spouting them off for attention. Then when you ask him what he believes, and he says things like:

"The Holocaust never happened."
"6 million Jews weren't killed by the Nazis."
"The collapse of the Towers was an inside job."

According to my approach, he is being *honest* with you. He is conveying in his communication the facts *as he really does see them*. That is all that matters as far as honesty is concerned.

Don't get alarmed by what I am saying. There is still the objective truth that the Holocaust did happen, and 6 million Jews were indeed killed by the Nazis. None of that (ever) changes. Furthermore, it is unlikely that these individuals with their deranged views are blameless for holding them. Almost certainly they are worthy of scorn for thinking these things in the first place, and have character faults such as being too narrow-minded, or too gullible, or too biased.[5]

But in communicating what they believe, they are honest.[6]

The Heart Matters Too

Suppose I am hiking by myself when I come across a lost wallet. Inside is $100 in cash, along with the driver's license for the owner of the wallet. Without any hesitation, I pick up the wallet and bring it to the park ranger's office, where I turn it in, cash and all.

Surely this is an honest *action*. But am I being an honest *person*? The answer is—we do not know yet. For that, we need to know something about what motivated me to return the wallet.

Imagine this is the direction that the conversation with the park ranger goes, after I explain to him what happened:

> "Why did you turn this in? I can't believe you didn't just keep the cash," he says.

What if I give one of these answers?

> "Because I wanted to get a reward from the owner of the wallet."
> "Because I wanted to impress other people with how virtuous I am."
> "Because I did not want to feel guilty if I took the money."
> "Because I wanted to get rewards for myself in the afterlife."

What do you think about these answers? My reaction is simple. I do not think I get to count as being a virtuous person if one of these was really at work.

Virtues like honesty have to lead to good behavior, to be sure. But that behavior needs to arise from a good heart too. Action is but one piece to the puzzle of what makes someone virtuous. What then does a good heart look like in the case of honesty? The problem with the answers above to the park ranger is that they are all self-centered. The point of doing this honest action should not be how I can benefit from it.

To be virtuously honest, my motivation has to look beyond myself. Here are some other answers I could have given to the ranger instead for why I turned in the wallet:

"Because it was the right thing to do."
"Because it was what any honest person would do."
"Because we should always return things to their rightful owners."
"Because God told us to love our neighbors as ourselves."

These are all reasons of *duty* or *requirement*. I am doing this honest action because I should, because it is right, because it is required by God, and so forth. They are also impersonal reasons. If one of them was what led me to turn in the wallet, then I am trying to do the honest thing regardless of whether I benefit in the process or not.

How do these reasons strike you? They all seem to me to be *perfectly fine* reasons for doing the honest thing. If someone is telling the truth, or did not cheat you out of your money, or followed the school's honor code *because it was the right thing to do*, would you have any problem with that answer? I do not think so.

This is not the end of the story, though. For there are still other responses I could have given to the ranger, like these:

"Because I didn't want something bad to happen to the owner of the wallet."
"Because I was worried about what's going to happen to this person if he loses all this money."
"Because I respected the fact that it's his property, not mine."
"Because I cared about him and wanted what was best for him."

These are all reasons of *altruistic concern*. I am doing this action because I care in some way about what is best for this other person specifically. These reasons are also *personal* reasons, since they have to do with the owner of the wallet and not with doing what is right in general. Once again, if one of these altruistic reasons indeed led me to turn in the wallet, then I am being honest regardless of whether I benefit or not in the process.

How do these reasons sound? To me, they are also *perfectly fine* reasons for doing the honest thing. Using the same thought experiment again, suppose I did not leave out any important information about what happened at the bar last night, or I did not have an affair, or I played by the rules *because I cared about you*. Would you have any problem with that motivating reason? Certainly not, I would think.

So the emerging picture is something like what we see in Figure 1.2. This is a *pluralist* picture about what motivates an honest person. Lots and lots of motives count as being virtuously honest. There isn't a way I can see to narrow them down to just one motive. Nor do I see any reason why things have to be that simple anyway. Morality is rarely streamlined.

Loving motives (e.g., 'because I care about you')
Justice motives (e.g., 'because it would be unfair')
Friendship motives (e.g., 'because he is my friend')
Dutiful motives (e.g., 'because it was the right thing to do')
Honesty motives (e.g., 'because it would be honest')
(and potentially others as well)

Figure 1.2 Various motives for the virtue of honesty.

But there are limits to the pluralism. Once our heart becomes simply about trying to benefit ourselves, even if that leads us to act honestly, we are no longer acting from a place of virtue. We are acting from a place of self-interest.

Here is an extra wrinkle which complicates things a bit more. Many times in life we do not do something just from one motive. We have multiple reasons for why we do what we do. Returning to our park ranger case one last time, now suppose I said that I was turning in the wallet for these reasons:

> "Because it was the right thing to do, *and* because I did not want to feel guilty if I took the money."

How does that sound to you?

If we did not allow some cases like this to count as expressing an honest mindset, then that is setting the bar for honesty awfully high. In other words, demanding purity in our motives, free of all self-interest, is to demand something that is hard for us mere mortals to attain on a regular basis.

On the other hand, what if not feeling guilty was my *main motivation* for turning in the wallet, and doing the right thing was just a small additional motivating factor for me? Then I do not think that should count as living up to the standard of being an honest person. After all, if I could just get over my squeamishness about feeling guilty, then it is likely I would keep the money for myself. That is clearly not virtuous.

What we should say, I think, is that when we have mixed motives like this, the important thing is that the *stronger* of the two motives is the virtuous motive. That would be, in this case, the motive of doing the right thing. *Even if* the other, self-interested motive were to not be present in the first place, so long as the virtuous motive still carries the day and leads me to turn in the wallet, then that should be good enough for virtue.

We can now see that we need to refine our definition of honesty. Genuine honesty involves both:

> Honest Behavior: An honest person does not intentionally distort the facts as she sees them.
>
> Plus
>
> Honest Motivation: What motivates her is one of a variety of virtuously honest motives. In the case of mixed motives, the virtuous honest motive is the strongest one in the mix.

Are we done? Close, but not quite yet.

A Few More Pieces to the Honesty Puzzle

Okay, so now you hopefully are convinced that there is a lot more to honesty than it might have initially seemed. At this point, you might also be thinking that this is more than you bargained for, and that you are ready to move on. Enough is enough.

To call upon another important virtue, I'd like to ask for your patience just a little bit longer. For there are a few more pieces to honesty that are so important we cannot leave them out.

One has to do with how the thinking side of our mind matters to honesty, and not just the motivational side. This thinking side has to do with things like our moral beliefs and moral judgments. In an obvious way, it is hard to see how someone could be honest who believes things like:

I should cheat or steal whenever I can get away with it and help myself out.
There is nothing wrong with saying one thing and doing the other when no one is looking.
Lying is always the way to go when it will get me out of trouble.

The honest person is firmly opposed in their minds to all forms of dishonest behavior.

That so far is pretty obvious. There are other beliefs that matter too, though. We also need to recognize when is the right time to not distort the facts, and to whom, and to what degree.

Here is an example where things go rather badly:

> Thomas is riding the elevator with a co-worker whom he barely knows. To avoid an awkward silence, the co-worker asks Thomas how his day is going. Thomas proceeds to rattle off a long list of what he has done, including what he ate for breakfast and how many times he has visited the bathroom.[7]

There is a time and place to be honest, but this is not one of them. Thomas is failing to recognize what is the appropriate amount to share, and with whom. The thinking side of an honest person's mind would be able to pick up on these things.[8]

Two more really quick observations about honesty. One is that if you are honest, you better be *consistently* honest. Suppose I turn in the lost wallet to the park ranger. But I also cheat on my taxes, steal from my university, lie to my kids, and am radically self-deceived. Obviously, that is not going to cut it.

To be sure, you can be an honest person without being honest in *every* situation. You can slip up once in a while. But there has to be *some* consistency to your behavior across the different situations where honesty comes into play.

The same point applies, not just across situations, but also across time. Wouldn't it be weird to call me honest if I turn in the wallet this time, but the next 10 times I find a lost wallet I always keep the cash for myself? An honest person is reliable and consistent over time in their honesty.

So putting everything together, this is what we get:

> Honest Behavior: Across situations and across time, an honest person does not intentionally distort the facts as she sees them.
>
> Plus
>
> Honest Motivation: What motivates her is one of a variety of virtuously honest motives. In the case of mixed motives, the virtuously honest motive is the strongest one in the mix.
>
> Plus
>
> Honest Thoughts: An honest person is accurate in her thinking about the morality of lying, stealing, etc. She also is wise in exercising her honesty—when, where, how much, to whom, and so forth.

I could go on some more, as there is so much to say about honesty, but I promise I will stop here.[9]

Let's Get Vicious

Enough with all this virtue. Let's spice things up a bit with some vice. Just as things can go well in our moral lives, things can also go horribly wrong.

As was reported to have happened in the summer of 2023 to Carlee Russell, age 25 from Hoover, Alabama.[10] Carlee had just finished shopping at her local Target and was driving on the interstate when she called 911. According to the recording of the call, she was notifying the police that there was a toddler in a diaper and shirt wandering by himself along the side of the interstate. Carlee said she would protect the child until the police arrived, which only took a few minutes.

When they got to the location, there was no child and no Carlee, only her empty car. With Carlee mysteriously disappearing, a massive search was launched, and donations poured in to help with the effort. But it led nowhere.

Then, two days later, Carlee simply returned by foot to her own house and called 911 to let the police know she was back. During their interview with Carlee, she told them that she had been kidnapped by a red-haired man and a woman who kept her imprisoned in the back of a tractor-trailer truck. Yet, Carlee reported, she was thankfully able to escape and make her way back to her home.

There was just one little problem. Carlee was being completely dishonest. According to news reports, she made up the whole kidnapping story, as the police were able to quickly determine. Carlee ended up pleading guilty to two misdemeanors charges, thereby avoiding the possibility of serving up to a year in prison.

Carlee Russell, at least during this period of her life, was the polar opposite of an honest person. She joins a long list of people in recent years who have been given the name 'dishonest.' We can look to the political world (Vladimir Putin is an obvious example), the corporate world (such as the heads of Theranos, Enron, and WorldCom, according to reports), the sports world (Lance Armstrong, Barry Bonds, and Tiger Woods have all been accused of cheating in different ways), the financial world (Bernie Madoff, Elizabeth Holmes, and Sam Bankman-Fried were all found guilty of dishonest uses of funds), and the entertainment world (Kristen Stewart, Arnold Schwarzenegger, and David Letterman have all allegedly been unfaithful). What do all their reportedly dishonest actions have in common?

This is an easy question to answer. We already did the hard work in figuring out what honesty is. So now we can just invert the picture for dishonesty. For instance, take what we said about honest behavior, and flip it around to get:

> Dishonest Behavior: Across situations and across time, a dishonest person intentionally distorts the facts as she sees them.

That is what Madoff was allegedly doing with his Ponzi scheme, and what Armstrong later confessed to doing when he had claimed to be clean of performance-enhancing drugs.

Now there might need to be a bit more nuance to this picture of dishonest behavior. After all, it is not as if Madoff was cheating people whenever he got the chance, regardless of whether he would likely get caught or not. Rather, he was trying to be strategic in his cheating, balancing maximizing rewards for himself with minimizing the risk of getting caught.

Some dishonest people might be blatant about what they are doing, not caring whether others catch them or not. But more careful ones are better described like this:

> Careful Dishonest Behavior: Across situations and across time, a dishonest person intentionally distorts the facts as he sees them, provided he considers the risk/reward ratio to be sufficiently in his favor.

Few dishonest people are going to steal from a store when the police are watching, or lie in public when they know their statements are going to be immediately fact-checked.

As we will explore in the last chapter of this book, becoming increasingly dishonest is a dangerous road to go down. I will make my case there for why honesty is a far better path for us to be on. But to end here, it is surprising to find that dishonesty is not the only way we can be vicious in this area of our moral lives.

The Greek philosopher Aristotle famously held that for any virtue, there will be at least *two* opposing vices—a vice of 'excess' and a vice of 'deficiency.'[11] Take courage, for example. The vice we normally think of is cowardice. That is the vice of deficiency. But there is also rashness, say when an overly confident general orders his troops into battle against a superior opponent without any plan for victory.

Dishonesty is clearly the vice of deficiency with respect to honesty. What about the vice of excess? We actually saw a good illustration of this when Thomas shared way too much with his co-worker while riding the elevator. It wasn't that anything Thomas said was a lie or was misleading. By itself, each piece of information was communicated honestly. Rather it was the *amount* of information that got Thomas into trouble here. He was guilty of badly oversharing.

The vice of excess, then, is manifest when someone is honest about too much, or with too many people, or at the wrong time and place, or in a way that is cold and insensitive. It is not that they are out to intentionally distort or misrepresent the facts the way the dishonest person is. It is that they need to be wise in reining in their honesty.

To be an honest person is to walk a tightrope between two dangerous tendencies—being dishonest on the one hand, and lacking wisdom about how to be honest on the other. For most of us, though, it is dishonesty, the vice of deficiency, that we really have to watch out for. It is also where the honesty crises arise.

What's Next?

I was trying to be honest when I told you that honesty is both far more complicated and far more interesting than we might have thought. After all, we are not talking about one particular honest action, like turning in a lost wallet. We are talking about what it is to be an *honest person*, a person whose character has the virtue of honesty.

Along the way, we have seen that there are many ways to fall short of honesty, including lying, misleading, cheating, stealing, BSing, being a hypocrite, and deceiving oneself. As we will explore in the coming chapters, each of these failures of honesty is being encouraged and incentivized in new and powerful ways throughout our society.

But before we turn to the various honesty crises we will examine in detail in this book, let us first see that there is also some encouraging news coming from research these days on honesty.

Notes

1. My mother asked that I not use the complete word, even though it is now common in philosophy today. I try to listen to my mother.
2. This figure originally appeared in Miller 2021a: 22 and is reprinted with permission from Oxford University Press.
3. Thankfully, in part due to the Honesty Project that I led for five years at Wake Forest University, things are starting to change. For instance, we funded the research of the philosopher Sungwoo Um at Seoul National University, who has now proposed his own definition as a competitor to mine and tried to show how it is better. See Um 2023.
4. I first tried out my definition in Miller 2017a. I ended up developing it in many more papers, and eventually into an academic book called *Honesty: The Philosophy and Psychology of a Neglected Virtue* (Miller 2021a). Anyone who is looking for a lot more detail than is provided in this chapter is welcome to go check out that discussion.
5. I qualify these statements with "unlikely" and "almost" because there could be people who believed these things about the Holocaust or 9/11 because they received a very sheltered upbringing and were never presented with any other perspectives or sources of information. Then, while their beliefs are false, they might nevertheless be blameless for holding them.
6. We will return to these issues in more detail in Chapter 6 on politics and dishonesty.
7. I used this example first in Miller 2017a.
8. Further discussion of these issues would take us in the direction of the role of practical wisdom and its relationship to honesty. I get into all this in Miller 2021a: chapter 4.
9. For anyone who is interested in even more bells and whistles, check out Miller 2021a.
10. In what follows, I draw upon Wright 2023 and Franklin 2024.
11. See in particular Aristotle's *Nicomachean Ethics*, Book II.

2

Why the News Is Not All Bad

When we look in the coming chapters across various areas of life, including education, religion, politics, sex, and fame, the picture of honesty that we find may not be especially encouraging. While it might be our most cherished value, and while we might genuinely believe that things like lying, cheating, and stealing are wrong, honesty crises seem to be appearing all over the place. As a result, we can come away with a cynical outlook about other people (and maybe ourselves as well). Perhaps what we should accept is that most people today are dishonest and cannot be trusted.

In this chapter, I want to provide some balance. We will see that there is some encouraging news emerging from the research on honesty. It turns out that along with the obstacles to honesty still to come, there are bright spots to our characters as well.

Are Most People Liars?

Here is a question—how many lies have you told in the past 24 hours? Got the answer? I do not know what your answer is. But at least you can compare your answer to what other people have said.[1]

The classic study on lying frequency was conducted by the University of Virginia psychologist Bella DePaulo, who found that a group of community participants averaged 1 self-reported lie per day, while a group of student participants averaged 2 self-reported lies per day.[2] This result became the benchmark finding in the field of communication and helped lead to an assumption among many researchers that lying is commonplace.[3]

The Honesty Crisis. Christian B. Miller, Oxford University Press. © Oxford University Press 2026.
DOI: 10.1093/9780197840801.003.0002

But averages do not tell us about individuals. It could be that each individual in these groups tells about 1 to 2 lies per day. That is a genuine possibility. Here is another one, though—there are some people who lie a lot and others who lie rarely, and when you average them together you get 1 to 2 lies per day.

In recent years, additional empirical research has painted a fuller picture of our lying behavior. For instance, in an influential study published in 2010, the Michigan State University communication researcher Kim Serota and his colleagues gave a survey on lying to 1,000 Americans. He found the same average again (1.65 lies were told per day).[4] But the *distribution* of lying across this group was highly skewed. A whopping 59.9% said they did not lie at all during the past day. Of the participants who did lie, most of them told very few lies; 1,646 lies were reported in total from 1,000 people, but half of them were coming from just 5.3% of the participants.[5]

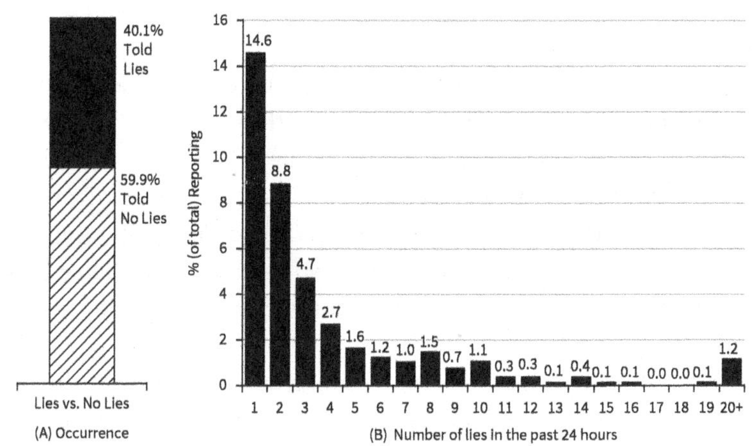

Figure 2.1 Number of lies reported in the past 24 hours.[6]

Figure 2.1 is a diagram from Serota's article to help visualize the data. It is important to stress that this pattern in the data is not idiosyncratic to Serota's research, but has been replicated several times.[7]

Perhaps then most people are rather honest, and most of the lying that goes on is confined to a few bad apples. This would be quite remarkable if it turns out to be true. Contrary to what you might have expected, lying would tend to be rare, except in the case of a small group of frequent liars.

But even in light of this more recent research, caution is still needed. After all, much of it involves administering a survey on one occasion. The researchers did not follow the same people *over time* to see how their lying varied from day to day and week to week. Hence, someone might have said only a few lies on one day, but a bunch the next. Or some might be considered prolific liars while just having a bad day.

Enter a new study by Serota and his team, published in 2022.[8] Their novel approach was to ask the same college students about their lying behavior *every day for an entire 3 months.* Usually the daily measure was this:

> In the past 24 h, how many times have you lied? Write in one number for your total lies. If you told no lies, write in "0."

What did they find?

A lot, and indeed far too much to report here. But these are some of the highlights. First, and consistent with what we have already seen, the overall mean was 2.03 lies per day. The lowest number of lies in a day was 0 (no surprise). The highest reported number was 200 (how is that even possible? Was this person lying about his or her number of lies?). In addition, only two participants said that they never lied once during the three months (really? Were they lying about their not lying?).

What was the benefit of tracking this group of people over time? Well, Serota and his colleagues were able to divide the participants into three groups:

Honest people: Those averaging 0–2 lies per day.
Intermediate liars: Those averaging 3–5 lies per day.
Prolific liars: Those averaging 6 or more lies per day.

How many participants in the study ended up in each of these groups? Once again, we see a big skew:[9]

% Honest people: 74.7% of participants were in this group.
% Intermediate liars: 19.6% of participants were in this group.
% Prolific liars: 5.7% of participants were in this group.

It would seem, then, that most people are not prolific liars, and a significant degree of truthful behavior is a consistent pattern in their lives over the span of several months.

Now here is a further question. Are those in the 'honest people' category telling 0–2 lies *every day*? Similarly, are people in the 'prolific liars' category telling 6+ lies *every day*? Again, averages can cover over variation. It is possible that people fluctuate wildly from day to day in their lying.

By tracking the same people over time, Serota can address this issue. The answer? Plenty of variation. For instance, even with the *prolific* liars, on 5% of their days they still told only 0–2 lies. So on those days they were quite honest. And on 25% of their days, they told 3–5 lies. They were intermediate during that time.[10]

The implication is that how much we lie fluctuates from day to day. A one-time measure of lying frequency can paint a very incomplete and potentially distorted picture about how truthful we tend to be in general. As Serota noted, "On any given day not all high-frequency liars are prolific, and those who are prolific do not always exhibit prolific lying. Observations of extensive lying on a single day only indicate a prolific liar about one time out of four."[11]

Serota and his colleagues take their findings to support some important conclusions, which they summarize in their own words as follows:[12]

(a) Lying is infrequent relative to honest communication.
(b) Most people are honest.
(c) The distribution of lying is positively skewed.
(d) Most lies are told by a few prolific liars.
(e) The telling of specific lies is situationally determined.

This is certainly a more encouraging picture of honesty than anything we will see later in the book.

Let me note a few cautions about their research, though, which Serota and company would likely agree with as well. First, it is noteworthy that the participants in this study are the usual college student population. They are also Americans.

Fortunately, in new research Serota surveyed people in China, Germany, Mexico, Israel, Kenya, Russia, and Brazil. What happened? There were similarly skewed distributions of lying behavior right across the board. For instance, in China the average rate was 1.92 lies in the past 24 hours, with 39% reporting no lies and only 5% reporting 6 or more lies.[13] So far so good, then, for the validity of their findings across cultures.

Another caution is that this is *self-report* data about lying behavior. Questions remain about how honest participants are about their own dishonest behavior. Plus, even if they are not trying to distort the facts, they may still suffer from faulty recall and miss some of their own lies.

Finally, even if the conclusions are more widely applicable and are accurate reflections of actual lying behavior, they do not let us draw any conclusions about how *honest* most people are. As we know, honesty is a virtue that pertains to much more behavior than just not telling lies. Also, this research does not tell us about underlying motivation to not lie. So what we get is only one piece of the much bigger honesty puzzle.

Nevertheless, results like these emerging from psychological research on lying are fascinating. Apparently, we can safely assume that strangers we are meeting for the first time are usually telling the truth. The challenge then becomes being able to pick out the rare prolific liar from the crowd.

Truth-Default Theory

In light of findings like those reported above, a new perspective on lying and truth-telling is beginning to emerge, and it strikes me as compelling. It is called truth-default theory and has been developed most extensively by the University of Oklahoma communication professor Timothy Levine.[14]

The starting point is what we have already suggested: "most communication by most people is honest most of the time."[15] When there is lying, it is not distributed evenly across a population. Instead, it is mostly done by a small group of frequent liars.

Of course, we all lie from time to time, even if it is to different extents. What is going on in those cases? Well, while it might be obvious to point out, when we lie it is for a reason or purpose. We are not just lying for lying's sake, but to help achieve one of our goals.

Now normally we can reach our goals just fine by telling the truth. There is no need to switch into a lying mindset. Truth-telling is the default. Nor do we even need to come up with a reason to tell the truth. We just do.

But sometimes telling the truth can seem incompatible with a goal we think is important. At that point the possibility of lying enters the picture. Of course, even then there is no *necessity* to lying. Some people might tell the truth anyway, even though in the process they cannot achieve one of their goals. Still, as Levine notes, "Deception becomes increasingly probable as the truth becomes a stronger impediment to desired outcomes."[16]

To help illustrate these points, suppose my friend is trying out a new birthday cake recipe for my big day. I take a bite of the cake and really enjoy it. It is great! She asks me what I think. Easy—I tell her that it is great. I did not have to think about whether to tell the truth or not. I did not need a reason to tell the truth. I just do. It comes naturally.

Think how strange it would be in that situation to effortlessly lie. Maybe a few people would do so anyway, such as pathological liars. But most of us do not work that way, thankfully. The default in this case is to just tell the truth.

Now there are ways of embellishing the story so that it could make sense why I *might* lie. Let us add the extra wrinkle that I have been harboring a lot of resentment and bitterness toward my friend (please note—this part is made up—honestly!). I really like the taste of the cake, but rotten person that I am, I tell her that it tastes terrible to crush her spirits and make her feel like she has ruined my birthday. Here in this case my goal is to be mean to her, and telling the truth would get in the way of attaining that goal. So, I shifted out of my default truth-telling mode and into a lying mode, which I used for spite.

Of course, the version of the story where I *liked* the cake probably was not the one you were expecting. What about if, instead, I took a bite and had a different reaction? The cake was not horrible, but it—um—was not my favorite, let us say. My friend asks me what I think. I could say the truth—"It's not my favorite." But I know she worked a long time on it, and I do not want to hurt her feelings. I worry that telling the truth will cause her needless pain, with little of value to show for it. So now I am torn between telling the truth and achieving one of my goals. In this case, as in so many other 'white lie' examples, achieving one of my goals might win out and lead me to lie.[17] How does this dress look on me? Do you like my new shoes? What do you think about my haircut? We have all been there.

Again, though, the main takeaway is that for most of us lies are the exception, not the rule. Truth-telling is the default option. Indeed, there is a *second* way in which the truth is the default in truth-default theory. It has to do with our trusting what other people tell us.

As Levine writes, "Most people believe most of what is said by most other people most of the time. That is, most people can be said to be truth-biased most of the time."[18] Here we are talking, not about being truthful in our *own* communication, but about assuming that other people are being truthful in *their communication to us*.

When I meet someone at a party and we start talking about what we do for work, my default assumption is that the other person is telling me the truth as she understands it. Same with when I ask a stranger for directions, or need help finding something in the store, or check in with my kids about their homework. Incidentally, because of our default trust in what other people tell us, it makes it easier for liars to fool us, and this explains why most liars are successful in pulling off most of their lies.[19]

Reflect on the last time you had an ordinary factual conversation with someone. It might have been just a few minutes ago. Did you debate whether to trust what that person was telling you? I bet you did not. More likely, the thought that the other person might be lying to you never crossed your mind.

Naturally we do not always trust what other people say. We can be shaken from our default mindset and shift into a skeptical mindset. Suppose the stranger at the party told me she works for Wake Forest University. I look her up in the directory later and find out that she left the school months ago. The next time I see her, I am suspicious and perhaps default into a lying outlook toward her. I doubt much of what she says, unless I can somehow reconcile what she told me with what I discovered on my own.

So there will be times when I am pretty suspicious of what my conversation partners are saying. But according to truth-default theory, that is because something happened, either during the conversation or earlier, to *trigger skepticism and doubts* about the truthfulness of the other person's communication.[20] At that point you shifted into more of a detached, evaluative mindset, assessing what was being said to you to see if it held water or not. You might conclude that it checks out after all. You might instead conclude that the other person is trying to deceive you. Or you might be on the fence for the time being, not sure what to think. The point is that you have been knocked off your default assumption of unreflective trust and have shifted into a different way of relating to this person.[21]

Summing up, truth-default theory is an important development that shows great promise in helping us to better understand our communication with each other. It predicts that we are doubly truthful by default—both in what we say to others and in how we receive their communications to us.

With one qualification, though—there are big liars out there too.[22]

Other Factors Impacting Lying

Thus far we have looked at some of the data on the *frequency* with which people tell (or do not tell) lies. But there are many other important aspects to lying which can be studied empirically.

For instance, does the type of person we are interacting with tend to make a difference? What if it is my wife or a close friend, versus a complete stranger? Initially, we might think that people are more inclined to lie to strangers than to friends and family. After all, I may never see the stranger again, so who cares if I fudge the truth? But being dishonest to those whom I care deeply about is a different matter.

Things are a bit more complicated, though. Earlier we saw the psychologist Bella DePaulo report that people tell between 1 and 2 lies per day as a general average. In addition, she also found that, indeed, lies tend to be told more often to strangers when they are 'everyday lies' like, "Told her her muffins were the best ever" and "Exaggerated how sorry I was to be late."[23] In one of her studies, people lied less than once per 10 social interactions with spouses and children.[24]

However, when it came to 'serious lies,' like having an affair or hiding an injury, the pattern flipped. Now 53% of serious lies were told to close partners in one of DePaulo's groups of participants. This number jumped all the way up to 72.7% when DePaulo focused just on college students.[25] I am tempted to speculate that these students might not have wanted Mom or Dad to know what they were up to on the weekends.

Perhaps in retrospect this finding is not that surprising. When interacting with people we care about, we might value preserving our relationships more than we value the truth. Whether we are *morally right* to do so is a different question which we will take up at the end of the book when we consider the ethics of white lies.

Here is another finding that is not all that surprising. Age makes a difference. Who do you think is more likely to tell you the truth—a teenager or a retiree? How about young kids, like my fourth-grader—where do they fall on the spectrum of lying?

A helpful study by Evelyne Debey from Ghent University in Belgium and her colleagues sheds light on this issue (it also has a great title—"From Junior to Senior Pinocchio"). They used the same measure of lying frequency that we have seen from Serota, namely how many lies you told in the past 24 hours. Nine hundred ninety-two participants were surveyed just once about their lying, and they were broken up into 7 age categories. The results are shown in the following table.[26]

	Average # of lies	% 0 lies	% 1–5 lies	% >5 lies
Early childhood (ages 6–8)	1.75	64	29	7
Mid-childhood (ages 9–12)	2.59	43	43	14
Adolescence (ages 13–17)	2.80	26	59	15
Young adulthood (ages 18–29)	1.94	37	52	11
Mid-adulthood (ages 30–44)	2.06	49	43	8
Older adulthood (ages 45–59)	1.82	51	39	10
Seniors (ages 60–77)	1.57	56	34	10
Total	2.19	46	43	11

Right off the bat we can see a familiar pattern again. There is a lot of variability in the frequency of lying, with many people not telling any lies at all; 51% of the lies were produced by just 9% of the participants.

What is most relevant here, though, is the change over time. We get an inverted U pattern—lying is low in early childhood, it peaks around adolescence, and then it declines toward the end of life.[27] Given my age, this makes me feel better about most of my friends and colleagues. On the other hand, I am starting to worry about my three children who are approaching their teenage years.

How about gender? Men lie more often than women, right? Is that what you would guess? Unfortunately, the findings are messy. It is safe to say that either there are no statistically significant gender differences or if there are, they are very slight.[28]

Perhaps more interesting is whether there are differences in *what* men and women lie about. Here we find an empirically supported trend. As two experts summarizing the literature note, "While men are more inclined than women to tell self-serving lies, women are more apt to tell altruistic lies aimed at making someone else feel better or aimed at strengthening a relationship."[29]

Finally, how about religion? To be honest this is the variable that interests me the most, as I have written about the impact of religious practices on our character.[30] So if we were to study just the major Western religions and their relationship to lying, what would you expect to find?

I would expect lower rates of lying among serious followers of their religion, as compared to those who are non-religious. After all, prohibitions against lying are found throughout the sacred texts of Judaism, Christianity, and Islam. One of the Ten Commandments is even, "You shall not give false testimony against your neighbor."[31] As Proverbs 12:22 says, "The LORD detests lying lips, but he delights in people who are trustworthy." And switching to the New Testament, Jesus describes the devil this way, "He was a murderer from the beginning, not holding to the truth, for there is no truth in him. When he lies, he speaks his native language, for he is a liar and the father of lies."[32] Note how the devil, the figure most opposed to God, is described using the language of dishonesty.

But what does the data show? Unfortunately, there is not much available to help us decide. There are a few published studies focused on religious believers, but when put together their findings do not always make for a nice consistent story. Consider the main results I could track down:

- One study in Israel found that deeply religious female Jewish students held stricter moral judgments about the wrongness of lying than secular students. In a situation where they could lie about what their die roll was to earn more money, they lied less.[33]
- Students at a university in Canada played an economic game with a partner where they could lie to get a bigger financial payoff for themselves. Students for whom religion was more important tended to lie a bit more.[34] But in another study, this time at a Catholic university in the United States, overall religiosity, frequency of prayer, and the importance of religion in daily life all increased the odds that a student would send an honest message in a similar situation.[35]
- A study found that undergraduate students at a school in the United States who tended to agree with items like "Lying is no big deal" and "What people don't know can't hurt them" also tended to be less religious. It was concluded that lying acceptability correlates negatively with religiosity.[36]

- Finally, a study examined counties in the United States that were more or less religious. It found that companies in more religious counties tended to be less likely to misrepresent their financial statements, to employ tax sheltering, and to withhold bad news in financial disclosures.[37]

As you can see, that is not much. Two patterns are suggested here. One is that serious followers of the major Western religions tend to think that lying is more morally unacceptable, as compared to those who are not religious. That is a claim about how seriously religious people *judge* lying. And secondly, religious belief seems to be linked (albeit at times weakly) to lower rates of actual lying in certain contexts. That is a claim about how religious people *behave*.

There are plenty of other factors which could potentially influence lying behavior, such as race, socioeconomic status, personality, and geographical location. Let us end, though, by considering in more detail just one factor that is especially timely and relevant to the rest of the book—and that completely fooled me.

What about Social Media?

Anyone who knows me, knows that I am a huge Notre Dame football fan. One of my favorite players of all time was Manti Te'o. If you remember Te'o, you can guess where this is going.[38]

It was the 2012 season, a season that would end with Notre Dame undefeated and playing in the national championship game against Alabama. Manti Te'o was a star linebacker on the team, who had a magnificent season for the Irish and ended up being a Heisman finalist, narrowly losing to Johnny Manziel.

Part of the compelling narrative of that season surrounded Te'o and a former Stanford student, Lennay Kekua, whom Manti was involved with for a year in a long distance relationship. They had never met in person, but communicated frequently online. Tragically (or so it appeared at the time), Lennay suffered from leukemia and passed away early in the football season, a few hours after Te'o's grandmother had also died. As one reporter characterized it,

> The story of how Te'o dealt with massive personal tragedy became front and center in his rise to national consciousness. In interviews with *Sports Illustrated* and on the Jim Rome radio show, Te'o described talking to [Lennay] by phone through the night as she dealt with the pain of chemotherapy treatments.[39]

In Te'o's own words from an October 4 press conference, "That has to be the hardest thing that I've had to do so far; to be able to operate, and to be able to try to continue with my daily routine, but knowing that I just lost two women that I truly loved."[40]

A catfishing scam is when someone creates a fake identity online in order to scam or deceive others. It is obviously dishonest, involving rampant lying. And tragically it is what happened to Manti Te'o.

For the person he was communicating with was, at the time, a guy named Ronaiah Tuiasosopo.[41] He was apparently a family friend, and used pictures of another woman he found online to help create the fake identity of Lennay Kekua. All this came to light at the end of that 2012 season. While tremendous support for Te'o poured in from some circles, there was also a "firestorm of controversy, speculation, jokes, insults, confusion and confrontation."[42] Here we see the terrible consequences that acts of dishonesty can have.

What happened to Manti Te'o was an extreme example of online dishonesty. But it raises questions about the impact of electronic communication on people's honest behavior. Note that all the research mentioned so far in this chapter has focused mainly on truthfulness and lying in face-to-face interactions. But what happens when we communicate with others using an electronic device of some kind, such as a phone or a computer? Will rates of dishonest behavior go up, down, or stay about the same?

Consider just the Internet. As the case of Manti Te'o illustrates, the anonymity that the Web can provide is notorious for facilitating deception. Even when people present their real identities online, as they often do on social media or online dating websites, we tend to wonder about the veracity of much of what they say.

When the psychologist Michelle Drouin asked participants in her research to estimate the percentage of people who were always honest on social media, the average answer was 2%. For online dating, it dropped to zero.[43]

Now here is something surprising. It turns out that this cynicism is mistaken. Despite the proliferation of blatantly false information in certain regions of the Internet, research suggests that the content on many online platforms is remarkably trustworthy. In some cases, it may even be *more* trustworthy than communication over the phone or face to face.

Consider online dating sites. In a 2008 study, the communication professor Catalina Toma and her colleagues found that about 80% of participants with online dating profiles lied about their height, weight, or age—but usually only to a very small extent (less than 1 inch off on height and 0.55 of a year on age, on average).[44] As she explained in a 2019 paper, online daters may tell small lies "to rectify shortcomings," but they seldom lie "indiscriminately simply because technology makes lying effortless."[45]

Something similar is true of the employment website LinkedIn. In a 2012 study by the communication researchers Jamie Guillory and Jeffrey Hancock, participants made either a traditional resume, a LinkedIn profile that was publicly viewable, or a LinkedIn profile that was viewable only by the researchers.[46] It turned out that the rates of lying were roughly equal in all three groups (about 3 lies, on average, per resume). LinkedIn resumes, however, were less deceptive when it came to the all-important matter of work experiences and responsibilities.

Studies of texting and Facebook use have also found surprisingly low levels of dishonesty. A 2014 study showed that when people reviewed their 30 most recent text messages, 23% reported no deceptive texts, and a vast majority of the remaining people reported that 10% or fewer of their texts were deceptive.[47] And a 2010 study found that the personality traits presented on a user's Facebook profile were very highly correlated with the user's actual personality traits.[48]

But what about the comparative question, i.e., is lying *more prevalent* on social media as compared to text, the phone, or email? Recent research by David Markowitz at Michigan State University speaks to this.[49] Based on survey data from 250 participants, Markowitz found something we are already familiar with: 1.08 lies were told per day, but once again with the distribution of lies skewed by some frequent liars.[50] The key finding is depicted in Figure 2.2, where social interactions had to last 10 minutes or more.

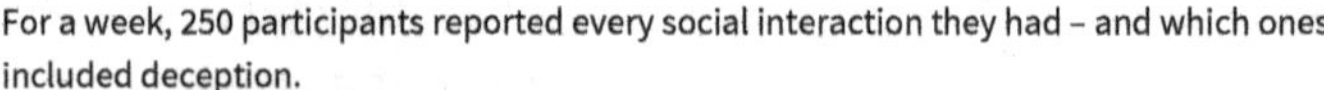

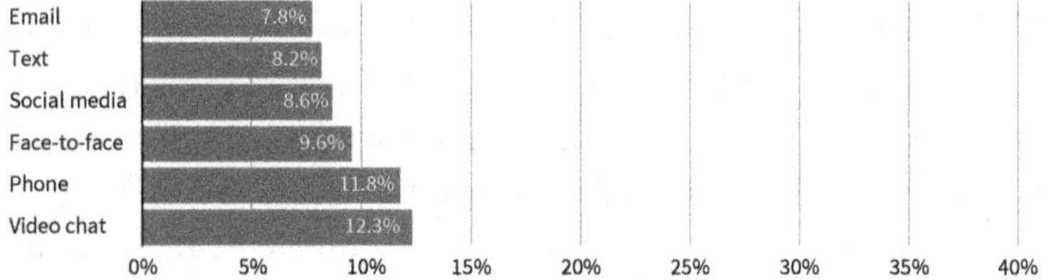

Figure 2.2 What percentage of social interactions involve a lie.[51]

Two things jump out at me from this figure. The first is that across the board the percentages are fairly low. Most interactions, regardless of how they were carried out, did not involve lies. Secondly, the differences in lying between the methods of communication were quite small. I would not have expected social media and face-to-face communication to differ by only a percentage point. Would you?

What might explain these low rates of dishonesty online? The easy answer is to say that most of us are honest people in general, and so this is just what you would expect to find. But if that were true, then when we turn to anonymous online settings, we should find lying to be low there too. It isn't.

A more likely explanation is that when you identify yourself online, your behavior becomes publicly exposed. With a traditional resume, for example, only a handful of people typically see it, and you might be tempted to slip in a falsehood or two. In contrast, hundreds of people will come across any dishonest statements in a LinkedIn profile, including past employers and current colleagues.

In such situations, lying online creates a heightened reputational risk. Most of us want to be thought of by others as honest people. That reputation matters for practical reasons—a significant lie on LinkedIn or a dating website could ruin a job opportunity or a first date—but most of us also care about how others view us, even apart from any tangible consequences.

An additional, more subtle factor is that most of us want to think of ourselves as honest. We will explore this desire in the chapter on student cheating, but the point is that it is hard to repeatedly distort the facts about ourselves online, and still view ourselves as honest people.

Whatever the correct explanation turns out to be, there is something deeply puzzling here. Why are our expectations about the trustworthiness of online communication so far off the mark from what the studies have found? Where did we go wrong?

Here is one proposal. When we interact with others in person, we tend to think we can detect deception fairly accurately on the basis of auditory and bodily cues (it turns out that we are very bad at this, as studies have shown, but that is a discussion for another time[52]). Because we often lose the ability to read those cues on the Internet, researchers have hypothesized that this makes us more suspicious of what people say online.[53]

The main conclusion for me as an ethicist, though, is that it is good news that deception online is not as widespread as we might expect. Yet there is a darker side to this story. If our reluctance to lie online is ultimately a function of preserving our image, then that truthfulness is motivated not by virtue but by self-interest. We are not caring about the truth for its own sake, or caring about having authentic relationships with others, or caring about treating people with dignity and respect. We are caring only about what will benefit us and keep our image intact.

Even when it comes to wanting to think of ourselves as honest, that is not the same thing as wanting to *be* an honest person. It is about being able to tell ourselves a certain flattering story, regardless of whether it is true. That is just another way of serving our self-interest.

As we have seen, an honest person does not only do honest things, like accurately representing herself on a dating website or on Facebook. She also does them for the right reasons, which are about something larger than herself.

So while there is surprisingly little deception on many online platforms, we may nonetheless be witnessing a failure of virtue, for there also does not appear to be much evidence of true honesty. Not that we expected there would be.

Final Thoughts

It is worth emphasizing that all the research summarized in this chapter is, I would say, rather preliminary. Further replication is needed, and cross-cultural studies using non-Western participants are scarce.

When it comes to honest behavior, however, the results so far are promising. Lying seems to happen rarely for many people in many contexts, even toward strangers and even via social media and texting. Where we need to be especially discerning, though, is in identifying (and avoiding) the small number of rampant liars out there. Unless, that is, we are one of them ourselves.

This is some of the encouraging news emerging from the research on honesty. But we know all too well that the story is not all positive. Honesty is under pressure in a number of areas of life, as recent developments have made dishonest behavior both easier to get away with and more tempting than before. Let's look at some of these honesty crises, starting with deepfakes.

Notes

1. Portions of this section are drawn from Miller 2022a, originally published on October 17, 2022, on Forbes.com and adapted with permission, and from Miller 2023, reprinted with permission from *The Conversation* under the Creative Commons—Attribution/No Derivatives license.
2. DePaulo et al. 1996.
3. For many quotes and references, see Levine 2020: chapter nine and Hart and Curtis 2023: 13–14.
4. Serota et al. 2010.
5. Ibid.
6. Ibid., 9, reprinted by permission of Oxford University Press.
7. See Levine 2020: chapter nine for a helpful overview.
8. Serota et al. 2022.
9. Ibid., 322.
10. Ibid.
11. Ibid., 329.
12. Ibid., 325.
13. Serota et al. 2024.
14. For a comprehensive and masterful presentation of the entire theory, see Levine 2019.
15. Ibid., 137.
16. Ibid., 154.
17. For an actual study along the lines of this example, see Levine 2019: 159–160.
18. Ibid., 176.
19. I owe this last point to Christian Hart.
20. Ibid., 185. Levine offers as examples of kinds of triggers: "(a) a projected motive for deception, (b) behavioral displays associated with dishonest demeanor, (c) a lack of coherence in message content, (d) a lack of correspondence between communication content and some knowledge of reality, or (e) information from a third party warning of potential deception" (Ibid., 193).
21. Ibid., 186.
22. For the label, 'big liars,' see the excellent book by Hart and Curtis 2023.
23. DePaulo and Kashy 1998.
24. Ibid., 72.
25. DePaulo et al. 2004: 160.
26. Debey et al. 2015: 64.
27. In another recent paper, the researchers did a meta-analysis of 558 studies related to honesty. Consistent with Debey's result, they found that honesty was lowest around the teenage years and then increased gradually with age. See Gerlach et al. 2019: 14. See also Hart and Curtis 2023: 21.

28. Indeed, when three researchers looked at the findings of 380 different published experiments that had to do with cheating and lying, they found just a 4% difference—42% of men versus 38% of women lied (Gerlach et al. 2019: 14). Not much to write home about, I would say.
29. Hart and Curtis 2023: 21.
30. See chapter 10 of Miller 2017b.
31. Exodus 20:16. All translations are from the New International Version.
32. John 8:44.
33. Shalvi and Leiser 2013.
34. Childs 2013.
35. Christie 2019.
36. Oliveira and Levine 2008.
37. Dyreng et al. 2012.
38. Material in this section draws from Miller 2021c, reprinted with permission from *The New York Times*.
39. Wolken and Myerberg 2013.
40. Ibid.
41. As of 2022, Tuiasosopo identifies as a woman and goes by the name 'Naya.' See Al-Khateeb 2022.
42. Wetzel 2022.
43. Drouin et al. 2016.
44. Toma et al. 2008.
45. Toma et al. 2019.
46. Guillory and Hancock 2012.
47. Smith et al. 2014.
48. Back et al. 2010.
49. Markowitz 2022. This study successfully replicates earlier findings by Hancock et al. 2004.
50. Markowitz 2022: 160.
51. The figure is a visual depiction of data from Markowitz 2022: 163. The figure first appeared in Miller 2023 and is reprinted with permission from *The Conversation* under the Creative Commons—Attribution/No Derivatives license.
52. See DePaulo et al. 2003 and especially the very thorough overviews of the research in Levine 2020 and Hart and Curtis 2023.
53. See Hancock and Guillory 2015 and Toma et al. 2018.

3
The Honesty Crisis Surrounding Deepfakes

> What a bunch of malarkey . . . it's important that you save your vote for the November election. Voting this Tuesday only enables the Republicans in their quest to elect Donald Trump again. Your vote makes a difference in November, not this Tuesday.[1]

This is what anywhere between 5,000 and 25,000 people in New Hampshire heard when they answered the phone during the 2024 US primary election. They were being encouraged to not show up and vote for then President Joe Biden.

Now that might not be so noteworthy if the voice on the call was Biden's rival, Donald Trump. But it wasn't. It was Joe Biden's own voice. Or so, at least, it would have sounded like to the listener.

In reality, this was a deepfake, a fake recording of a voice generated by an AI that was designed to sound just like Biden's voice. And it did.

Apparently, few people in this case were fooled by the deepfake. Why would Biden not want people to show up and vote for him in the primary, after all? But the story exploded nationally, and eventually a veteran Democratic political consultant admitted to being behind the whole operation. He had paid someone only $150 to make the audio file for him.[2] His reason? According to one report, he "claimed he planned the fake robocall from the start as an act of civil disobedience to call attention to the dangers of AI in politics. He compared himself to American Revolutionary heroes Paul Revere and Thomas Paine. He said more enforcement is necessary to stop people like him from doing what he did."[3]

The Honesty Crisis. Christian B. Miller, Oxford University Press. © Oxford University Press 2026.
DOI: 10.1093/9780197840801.003.0003

While I cannot approve of his methods, I do admire his goal. The dangers of deepfakes are significant, and we need more enforcement across the board to signal and in some cases prohibit their use. As we will see, creating and sharing deepfakes is typically dishonest, and they have sparked an honesty crisis with troubling implications for politics, education, pornography, and so much more.

Background

The Biden robocall is an example of an audio deepfake. Deepfakes are mostly known in popular consciousness today as video recordings, not audio ones. Indeed, they are often video recordings of a very specific kind, where the face of one person in an already existing video has been removed or swapped out, and replaced by the face of another person which is swapped in. Thus the faces of female pornographic actresses have been replaced with those of Scarlett Johansson or Taylor Swift, for instance, in hundreds of deepfake videos.

While common, there is nothing that says that deepfake videos *have* to involve face swapping. Other body parts, or even entire bodies, not to mention clothes, buildings, animals, or trees—everything is fair game in the world of deepfake videos.

Is that all there is to deepfakes? Is it just a matter of taking an audio or video recording, and manipulating the content in some way to make things happen which did not actually happen in the original recording?

No. After all, we have been able to do that kind of thing for decades, and in the process generated so-called 'cheapfakes' or 'shallowfakes.' We could slow down a recording of someone's voice to make the person sound less intelligent or coherent. That was done to a video of former House Speaker Nancy Pelosi, for instance, where she sounded drunk.[4] For still images, everyone knows about "Photoshopping," which we now use as a verb in ordinary conversation.

The new development associated with deepfakes is that they are generated by AI technology. An AI can be fed content about President Biden's voice or Scarlett Johansson's face, and then use that content to achieve whatever the user desires, such as a recording saying, "Your vote makes a difference in November, not this Tuesday."[5]

Early attempts to generate such deepfakes were notoriously poor in quality. A famous example involved what looked to be Ukrainian leader Volodymyr Zelensky at the start of the 2022 war with Russian, where he seemed to be ordering his troops to surrender.[6] But it did not fool many people. The verbal delivery was not smooth, and his face lacked emotion. There were differences in skin color between the face and neck, and his head was not even lined up with the rest of his body. The eye blinking was, well, weird.

Yet technological developments have exploded in this area in just a few years, and now hyper-realistic deepfakes are scientific fiction no more. While the message might have not been believable, the robocall sounded just like President Biden's voice. Pornographic deepfakes can easily fool someone into thinking that they are showing the real celebrity in her bedroom. Recordings can be made with someone appearing to speak a language that in fact they do not know at all—both the audio and the lip movements flawlessly give the impression of language mastery.

As the above examples already show, there are serious dangers lurking with the use of deepfake technology, and we will explore some of them below. But surprisingly, no one has explored how deepfakes strike at the heart of honesty. That is, until fellow Honesty Project team member Tobias Flattery and I started noticing how the work we were doing had important implications for better understanding and critiquing this new technology. In this chapter, we share what we have found.[7]

Observer Fakes

There are two different sorts of deepfakes, based upon what is happening in a recording. Sometimes the viewer or listener is just taking in the scene—observing whatever is happening in a video between, for instance, "Scarlett Johansson" and some random guy. Or listening to "John F. Kennedy" deliver the speech he would have given if he had not been assassinated. Let's call these "observer fakes."

In other deepfakes, though, the purpose is clearly to convey some kind of message *to the viewer or listener*. We are being told by "Biden" to not vote in the primary. "Zelensky" is sending a message to his troops to stand down. "Mayor Ernie Adams" is informing New York City residents about job opportunities while speaking Mandarin, Canton, and Spanish.[8] These "instruction fakes," as we might call them, are trying to get their audience to do something after they are finished with the recording.[9]

Which of these two kinds of deepfakes has been more common in recent years? You might think it is the instruction fakes. After all, we could imagine that creators of deepfakes mainly go through the trouble in order to get people to change their behavior—to manipulate us to vote differently, or to shop differently, or to donate differently, for example. But in fact, it is the *observer fakes* which vastly outnumber the instruction ones. Why? It all has to do with non-consensual deepfake pornography.

Deepfakes really came on the popular scene via Reddit, when a user with the handle "deepfakes" posted pornographic videos with celebrity faces replacing those of the original actresses. Soon thereafter, "FakeApp" appeared on Reddit too, which allowed anyone to participate in "face-swapping." Users did indeed, and the group grew to 100,000 people before it was shut down. Since then, such deepfakes have caught on like wildfire. According to an earlier study from 2019, 96% of all deepfake videos posted on the Internet are pornographic in nature.[10] By 2023 that percentage was up to 98%.[11] These fakes, sometimes labeled as "frankenporn," usually involve face swapping of a pornographic actress with the face of a female celebrity. And yes, such videos radically skew in the direction of females being the ones having their faces swapped in and out. How radically? One study found that 99% of facial appearances being inserted into porn videos were of women.[12]

So observer fakes rule the day, at least for now. Let's put instruction fakes to one side, and think more about these observer videos, with deepfake porn as our representative example. I do not want to call attention to any one particular deepfake pornographic video, and thereby boost something which is doing harm and is clearly morally wrong. So instead I will just describe a generic video, using Taylor Swift as the celebrity whose face is being swapped into an already existing pornographic movie.[13] Here then is my imaginary example, but of course there are plenty of actual videos already out there just like this:

> Scummy Sam has a pornographic video downloaded on his computer that was made by "XXX Videos." In the video, Brian and Lisa are doing the typical things that happen in porn videos. Using AI technology trained on images of Taylor Swift, Scummy Sam swaps out Lisa's face from the video and inserts Taylor Swift's face expressing the kinds of things you'd expect to see on someone's face in a pornographic video. Sam is an expert with this technology and there are no giveaways from his newly created video that anything fishy is going on. Satisfied with his work, Scummy Sam uploads the video to his social media accounts, without any disclosure that it is a fake. As with anything Swift-related, it is downloaded and shared millions of times.

Is there anything dishonest going on here? Of course there is. I do not need to point that out. What is noteworthy, though, is *all the ways in which there is dishonesty going on*. Dishonesty pervades every aspect of what Scummy Sam does.

Remember that dishonesty is a matter of intentionally misrepresenting or distorting the facts, as they appear to you. In sharing his deepfake video to social media, Scummy Sam is doing just that. To unpack this claim a bit more, let's start with *why* Scummy Sam shared his video. There could be lots of different reasons. Suppose it was to get people on social media to believe that he had a real video of Taylor Swift having sex with Brian. In that case, he is obviously intentionally distorting the facts. This resembles lying—he is communicating something he believes to be false, but hopes that his audience will come to accept it as true.

That is not the only reason why someone might share deepfake pornography, of course. Sometimes they might not care about whether their audience believes the videos are genuine or not. They just want more followers, or want to have people enjoy their videos, or want to make money off the downloads. Suppose Scummy Sam is instead motivated by one of these reasons. Then here, too, his sharing the video would be intentionally distorting the facts. The parallel now is to BSing, not lying. As we noted back in Chapter 1, the BSer is indifferent to the truth of his communication. Scummy Sam is indifferent to whether people are deceived or not. BSing, though, is also dishonest.

Regardless of what Scummy Sam's motive is, what is especially striking is how pervasive his distortion of the facts really is. Obviously in the example, he is intentionally distorting the facts with respect to Taylor Swift. But it does not stop there. He is also distorting the facts with respect to Brian, and Lisa, and even XXX Videos.

Starting with Taylor Swift, consider how:

> She never had sexual relations with Brian.
> She never was video recorded having sexual relations with Brian.
> She never consented to having sexual relations with Brian or consented to being video recorded with Brian.
> She never had these particular facial expressions before.
> That is not the rest of her body below her face.

In all these ways, Scummy Sam's video is depicting her in a dishonest way.

But let us not forget about Lisa, even though her face has been wiped from the video. Consider how:

> This is not her face.
> She was video recorded having sexual relations with Brian.
> She never consented to having her face edited or to having a recording of her body below her face be used in this manner.

These are additional ways in which dishonesty is going on in Sam's video.

Perhaps most surprising is that even Brian is treated dishonesty too, though nothing was done to the recording of him specifically. For consider:

> He had sexual relations with Lisa, not with Taylor Swift.
> He consented to having sexual relations with Lisa, not with Taylor Swift.
> He consented to being video recorded having sexual relations with Lisa, not with Taylor Swift.
> The enjoyment he is recorded experiencing was not due to Taylor Swift but to Lisa.

These are all instances of fact distortion too.

It does not even end there. Let us move on to my made-up company, XXX Videos. Even they are being treated dishonestly:

> XXX Videos did not make this new video, even though they are credited with it.
> XXX Videos did not hire, compensate, drug test, obtain consent from, and video record Taylor Swift making this video, even though that is implicitly what needed to go into making a pornographic video with her staring in it.

Alternatively, if Scummy Sam deletes any mention of XXX Videos and tries to pass his video off as entirely his own recording, then that introduces a whole slew of dishonesty worries about plagiarism. He would be taking the work of others and passing at least a large part of it off as his own.

So now we can begin to see how deepfake videos can be viewed through the lens of dishonesty, and just how much dishonest distortion can be going on in sharing even one short recording. Note that it is the *sharing* of the deepfake where the dishonesty resides, not the making of the video in the first place. Consider a variation of our example:

> As before, Scummy Sam used a pornography video from XXX Videos, but this time creates a flawless deepfake using Scarlett Johansson's

> face. Suppose he never had any intention of distributing this particular deepfake. He just enjoyed the process of creating the fake, and after he is done, he files it away on his hard drive, never to have it see the light of day again.

In this case, is Scummy Sam doing something dishonest simply by making the video but not distributing it?

I admit that there is something *wrong or bad* about what he is doing. Maybe he should not be looking at pornographic videos in the first place. Maybe it is disrespectful to Scarlett Johansson or to the original pornographic actress (or both!) for videos of their faces to be manipulated in these ways. Maybe it violates their autonomy or is something that they needed to consent to in the first place. That is all up for further debate.[14]

But would it be *dishonest*? That's the question. I am inclined to say no. Do we want to say that merely editing a picture with Photoshop is dishonest? Or that changing the length of a song that you listen to is dishonest? Or that writing a first draft of a book of historical fiction is dishonest? I do not think we want to say 'yes' to any of these. So too, I think we should be hesitant to call the private creation of a deepfake dishonest.

I seem to have gotten myself into a problem, though. "Miller," someone might say,

> If it is the distribution or sharing of deepfakes where the dishonesty lies, and not their mere production, then where is this alleged honesty crisis? After all, the whole point of diving into the topic of deepfakes in the first place was to highlight the presence of an honesty crisis, and to then look for ways to try to address it.

Yet I am not too concerned about this challenge. Clearly there *is* an honesty crisis here.

For one thing, since the technology is now so easy to use, and since there are so many ways to share audio and video files these days, it is hard to envision people typically just shoving their creations into their proverbial file-drawer. According to one study, "it now takes less than 25 minutes and costs as little as $0 to create a 60-second deepfake explicit video of anyone using just one clear face image."[15] In the coming years, technology will make things even easier here, not harder.

Second and more significantly, though, is what happens after a deepfake is initially shared publicly and seen by other people. Then there is the opportunity for others to share it again.

Let us imagine that Scummy Sam's deepfake is now out there on Twitter. Here comes user "Swiftie," who views the video. He recognizes it as a deepfake, and sees that Taylor Swift's face has been swapped into a regular pornographic video. But he re-tweets it anyway, in the hope that other people will think it is real. In doing so, he thereby disseminates the deepfake to thousands more people. Now in addition to Scummy Sam's dishonesty, we have Swiftie's dishonesty as well. What he is doing resembles lying.

That is one reason why Swiftie might re-tweet the deepfake. Alternatively, while recognizing that the video is a deepfake, Swiftie might instead share it anyway just for fun or to get more followers. That is dishonest as well. It resembles BSing.

Either way, the point is that there is not just the initial act of distributing a deepfake audio or video file. There is also the subsequent sharing of that fake by others. If they happen to not recognize that it is a fake, then of course their re-tweet or re-post would not be dishonest. But if they do spot the fake, then they are magnifying the amount of dishonesty involved even more.

So yes, there is an honesty crisis here. Of course, there has been image and sound manipulation for decades. Of course, Photoshopped fakes can be easily produced and shared too. But now we are talking about media which is often much more visually and auditorily powerful, having a larger impact and generating much more traffic.[16]

Compare Photoshopping a still image with what Scummy Sam can do.

Another Observer Deepfake

I might be accused of getting carried away by talking this much about deepfake pornography. But the attention is justified, given how these deepfakes swamp everything else. Still, when we move past pornography, do we really want to say that dishonesty and deepfakes are so closely intertwined?

I do. Let's consider another example of an observer deepfake that is pretty bland.

I alluded to the Kennedy deepfake already. In 2018, a text-to-voice company named CereProc released an audio reconstruction of the speech that John F. Kennedy would have given the day he was assassinated. Using 831 of Kennedy's actual speeches and breaking his voice up into 116,777 sound units, the company was able to produce a very realistic sounding version of the speech that lasted 21 minutes and was delivered in a voice just like Kennedy's.[17]

What CereProc did was extraordinary, and it went to great lengths to indicate that the recording was a reconstruction and did not capture the actual moment of Kennedy's speech. But we can imagine an example involving a fictional company called "History Videos" that instead does this:

> Using historical images of John F. Kennedy, the company History Videos trains an AI to generate a video of Kennedy at a podium delivering the speech he was traveling to deliver when he was assassinated in 1963. The AI does its job well, the audio sounds just like Kennedy's voice, and the video captures his appearance and mannerisms perfectly. History Videos distributes the video free of charge on its platforms, without a disclosure and alongside other, genuinely historical videos of moments in Kennedy's life.

Everyone keeps their clothes on in this example. But in sharing the deepfake, what History Videos does is dishonest.

Again, we get the same pattern. If it is trying to pass one over on the general public, then History Videos is being dishonest in a way that is akin to lying. If it does not care whether the public comes to see this video as genuine or not, then the company is being dishonest in a way that is akin to BSing.

What facts are being distorted in our fictional example when History Videos shares their Kennedy video? The answers seem pretty obvious:

Kennedy's voice never said these words.
Kennedy's body never delivered this speech.
Kennedy was never in this location.
Kennedy was not even alive at this point in time.
There were no audience members watching Kennedy deliver the speech.
The speech was never heard by anyone on that day.

No doubt there are more besides these.

We can imagine plenty of other observer deepfakes—suppose there is a recording of a politician taking a bribe (he did not), of a woman stealing from a store (she did not), of a husband cheating on his wife (he did not), or of a leader saying a racist word (she did not). Sharing any of them would be dishonest.

Instruction Deepfakes

So much for the observer deepfakes. What happens when we shift to the other kind, what I am calling "instruction" deepfakes? These are ones in which a speaker is (or should we say, "seems to be"?) delivering a message to viewers or listeners of a recording. The robocall in "Biden's" voice telling New Hampshire voters to stay home is one illustration. "Zelensky" instructing his troops in Ukraine to stand down is another.

Here is a new example. In 2019, an organization called Malaria No More UK used a deepfake with the soccer star David Beckham to try to increase awareness about malaria and bring about political change.[18] The video showed Beckham delivering his message about malaria by effortlessly switching from English to Spanish to Kinyarwanda and so forth for nine different languages.

Just to be clear, it was not that there were subtitles in the other languages, or that you could hear a translator's voice speaking on Beckham's behalf. No, this was meant to look like it was *Beckham* who was speaking in all these languages. But Beckham cannot speak nine languages. The English segment was real, but the other eight segments were generated using fake audio and mouth movements. They were all well done, and if you did not know any better, you might not have been able to tell which were fake.

Now far be it for me to fault the cause at all! This organization no doubt does great work. And there was likely little harm done by having the illusion of Beckham communicating in eight other languages. Still, it was dishonest. Malaria No More, in sharing the video without any disclosures or warnings, was intentionally misrepresenting the facts in several ways:

Beckham never said the words in the eight languages.
Beckham never was recorded saying anything in the eight languages.
Beckham did not know any of these eight languages.
That was not Beckham's real voice or facial expressions for that portion of the video.

This pattern should now be predictable of how deepfakes and dishonesty are related.

But wait, as an *instruction* deepfake there is more. For this video is intentionally designed to reach an audience. So, we also have misrepresentation in the following ways:

Beckham never addressed his audience in the eight languages.
Beckham never intended to be speaking to an audience in these languages to help combat malaria.
Malaria No More did not hire, pay, train, and support Beckham addressing their intended audience in these languages.

Malaria No More did not do anything to indicate that it was not Beckham addressing the audience in these eight languages.

So once we bring an intended audience into the picture, the ways in which a deepfake can be dishonest increase.

While unlikely, Malaria No More might have intended for their audience to really believe that Beckham was speaking these eight languages. That would be akin to lying. More likely, the organization was not concerned one way or the other about whether the audience really believed it. They just wanted to advance their message. That would be akin to BSing. The same points apply to people who watch the video, recognize that it is a deepfake, and yet share it anyway without a disclosure. That can be akin to lying or BSing too.

This example is pretty innocuous. Yes, there is dishonesty involved, but not many people are going to be fooled into thinking that Beckham can really speak all these languages. Plus, it is all for a good cause in trying to eradicate malaria. So it is worth highlighting one final example, this time of an instruction deepfake with malicious aims. The Zelensky fake would be a good illustration.[19] But let's take an example based on a shocking event that actually happened in 2018 in Hawaii.[20]

Early on a Saturday morning, the Hawaii Emergency Management Agency sent out this message to residents' cellphones:[21]

> **Emergency Alert**
> BALLISTIC MISSILE THREAT INBOUND TO HAWAII. SEEK IMMEDIATE SHELTER. THIS IS NOT A DRILL.

Unlike the robocall and Zelensky cases, this one was very authentic. According to a *New York Times* story,

> Within moments of the first announcement, people flocked to shelters, crowding highways in scenes of terror and helplessness. Emergency sirens wailed in parts of the state, adding to the panic.

> "I was running through all the scenarios in my head, but there was nowhere to go, nowhere to pull over to," said Mike Staskow, a retired military captain.
>
> Allyson Niven, who lives in Kailua-Kona, said her first instinct was to gather her family as she contemplated what she thought would be her final minutes alive.
>
> "We fully felt like we were about to die," she said. "I drove to try to get to my kids even though I knew I probably wouldn't make it, and I fully was visualizing what was happening while I was on the road. It was awful."[22]

It took 38 minutes until a follow-up text was sent to notify the public that the alert was an accident, and that everything was okay.

Now strictly speaking, the emergency alert was not a deepfake because it was not generated by AI technology, and we said at the beginning of the chapter that AI has to be part of the equation. But we can easily imagine a fictional version of something like this happening in the future. Suppose, for instance, that you receive a voicemail with what sounds like your mayor or governor saying in an extremely realistic way:

> EMERGENCY ALERT. BALLISTIC MISSILE THREAT INBOUND TO WINSTON-SALEM. SEEK IMMEDIATE SHELTER. THIS IS NOT A DRILL.

This could be accompanied by a text message from the same person with a link to a video recording giving further instructions.

Maybe these messages go out to thousands of people, like the Biden robocall and the Hawaii text message did. Or maybe they only go to your phone. Either way, some creep is out to mess with peoples' lives. In sending these texts and voicemails, the creep is doing something dishonest, intentionally distorting all kinds of facts.

There is the usual bunch of facts that are getting distorted:

> The mayor never said anything about an attack.
> The major was never recorded saying anything about an attack.
> There is no ballistic attack.
> This is not the major's actual voice and appearance.

Now add to them:

The major never addressed her audience about an attack.
The mayor never intended to be speaking to her audience about an attack.
The mayor's office did not film, train, and support the mayor addressing her audience.
The mayor's office did not do anything to indicate that it was not the mayor addressing her audience about an attack.

If the technology is believable, then all of this distortion and misrepresentation would likely lead to fear and panic.

This example clearly shows why instruction deepfakes can matter. Let's look in more detail at how the dishonesty of deepfakes can have bad effects both large and small.

Why Deepfake Dishonesty Matters

Not all deepfakes involve dishonesty. We already said that if you create a deepfake on your own and just leave it on your computer, there is no dishonesty involved.

That is not the normal case, though. People create deepfakes and want to share them, sometimes with malicious motives, sometimes with good ones.

When they do share a deepfake, that does not have to automatically be dishonest either. There could be a clear disclosure on the fake, indicating that the content has been manipulated or fabricated in some way. We will look more at disclosures in the next section.

Also, even without a disclosure, the context could make it clear that the recording is obviously a fake. It could be posted on a "deepfake website" or entered into a competition for the "most realistic deepfake." This would be akin to bluffing in poker or saying that you are Julius Caesar as an actor in a play. The norms and expectations of honesty have been suspended in these cases. These deepfakes are starting out in a place of transparency where there is no assumption of representational accuracy.

But alas, none of this is the norm either today as I write these words. Many deepfakes are being shared, they are not labeled as fakes, and they are not appearing just on "deepfake websites." In these cases, there is inevitable dishonesty. This causes problems. Lots of problems. I won't try to catalog all of them. But here are a few.[23]

Eroding Trust in Recordings. Perhaps the most obvious problem is that, due to their dishonesty, the proliferation of deepfakes can undermine our trust in audio and video recordings. Consider the next time voters in New Hampshire receive a political robocall with what sounds like a candidate's voice. They are going to be, quite understandably, suspicious. The same goes for when you see an actor appearing to speak a foreign language during a commercial or movie.[24]

There is more. We used to rely on recordings as the final word, such as in court cases or political matters. If a person was caught on tape doing X, Y, or Z, that was the end of it. But now with deepfakes, it is not. The accused can dishonestly plead—"deepfake!"—and crack open the door of reasonable doubt as to whether this source is reliable or not. Recordings can no longer be counted upon to serve as the final word they once were.[25]

Manipulating Trust in People. Instruction deepfakes try to take advantage of the trust that is already in place between the speaker in the recording and the audience. That is what the producer of the Zelensky deepfake was attempting to do with respect to Zelensky's soldiers. The same is true with Democratic voters and Biden, or the mayor and the citizens in my fictional example.

Some of the most perverse deepfakes play on relationships between parents and children or between couples. Because of their dishonesty, they can twist those relationships to their advantage. As the philosopher Tom Roberts notes, "There is a special kind of cruelty, I suggest, in invading or exploiting relationships like these by fabricating an act of speech and delivering it from one member of a partnership or group to another . . . it is *not my place* to treat this relationship as a resource for my ends . . . it is a violation of privacy and an invasion of intimacy for me to do so."[26]

Even if the recording is discovered to be fake, it is not guaranteed that the relationship will return to normal. Once associations are established in our minds, it is hard to rid ourselves of them, especially at the subconscious level.[27]

Increasing Misinformation. Dishonest deepfakes spread misinformation. Just recall the robocall, Zelensky's fake order, and deepfake porn videos. There are countless other examples. As the philosopher Don Fallis writes, "The main epistemic threat is that deepfakes can easily lead people to acquire false beliefs. That is, people might take deepfakes to be genuine videos and believe that what they depict actually occurred. And this epistemic cost could easily have dire practical consequences."[28]

This danger is obvious and real, and in a time where there is already so much misinformation being spread, we do not need more.

Violating Autonomy and Dignity. Taylor Swift did not consent to having her facial likeness used in deepfake porn videos. Neither did Zelensky or, in the case of his voice, Biden. To make it seem as if they did freely and voluntarily participate in these recordings, when they did not, is dishonest. It also violates their dignity and autonomy.

This is especially pronounced in the case of non-consensual deepfake pornography. As porn star Alia Janine explains: "It's really disturbing. It kind of shows how some men basically only see women as objects that they can manipulate and be forced to do anything they want . . . It just shows a complete lack of respect for the porn performers in the movie, and also the female actresses."[29]

Rights Violation. Closely related to these points is that non-consensual deepfakes violate what the philosopher Adrienne de Ruiter calls our right to digital self-representation.[30] Just as there are limits to what you can do with representations of me in print and verbally, so too there are limits to what you can do with digital representations of me. In dishonestly misrepresenting me as doing or saying certain things in deepfake recordings, you as the creator of the fake are crossing these limits. This is especially true when the fakes involve my face. As de Ruiter notes, "The immediate response of wanting to exclaim 'That's not me!' emphasizes the way in which one's face is intimately tied with one's sense of self. It is difficult to dissociate oneself from footage where digital representations of one's face are inserted in a realistic looking way because the face stands for one's sense of self to an extent that other body parts do not."[31]

Damaging Reputations. A dishonest depiction of someone in a deepfake video often harms their reputation. This is vividly illustrated by the wave of deepfake porn videos created by middle and high school boys, that swap in faces of girls in their schools, leading to deplorable harm to their reputations. Again, even if consciously everyone knows that the girls did not participate in these videos, negative stereotypes often become ingrained subconsciously. Those stereotypes could apply both to a particular girl and to women in general as objectified sexual objects.

Reputational harm is not the only kind that might result from a deepfake video, of course. There can be emotional harm for the victim of the fake, such as anxiety, depression, shame, anger, distress, humiliation, or embarrassment, even though the person was blameless. There can be irretrievable memorial harm, as a "fabricated recording could be used to destabilize or even overwrite first-personal, autobiographical memories."[32] Financial, relationship, and vocational harms could result too, such as lost scholarships, friendships, or job prospects.

To be clear, not all of these bad results will apply to every sharing of a dishonest deepfake. The re-creation by my imaginary "History Videos" company of John F. Kennedy delivering his planned speech the day he was assassinated does not damage his reputation. Nor does it violate his autonomy (since he is not alive anymore and so has no autonomy that can be violated). Pornographic deepfakes involving middle and high school girls, on the other hand, often have all of these bad effects, and can lead to tragic outcomes.

"Of course, Miller," someone might say to me, "I agree that some deepfakes are terribly harmful and clearly wrong, like high school porn ones. But, am I hearing you right—are you saying that *all* deepfakes that are shared dishonestly should be judged as morally wrong? Isn't that going way too far? Take the example of the Kennedy speech. Yes, there might be some unfortunate things about how the video was shared, such as the lack of a disclosure to let the audience know that it was not historically accurate. But did History Videos *really* do something wrong?"

I say in response to this challenge—I actually agree! There is a difference between saying that sharing a deepfake video is dishonest, and saying that sharing a deepfake is wrong. Most of us already accept this distinction for things that have nothing to do with deepfakes. To protect innocent lives, you might do something dishonest—lie, cheat, steal, break a promise, and so on. But it could still be the right thing to do.

The same can hold in the case of some deepfakes. With the Kennedy video, for instance, there is on the one hand:

> The increase in false beliefs and misinformation for those who think the video is historically authentic.

On the other hand, there is:

> The value of people learning about Kennedy's speech and increasing their awareness of his message and his life in general.

How to weigh these factors is tricky business that I am going to avoid here. The only point I want to insist on is that it may sometimes turn out that sharing a deepfake video is not wrong after all, even if it is dishonest.

Disclosures to the Rescue?

So producing and sharing a deepfake recording is often, but not always, dishonest. Furthermore, it is often, but not always, wrong to do. Given how much easier it is becoming every year for people to produce and share very realistic recordings, and given how impactful they can be in terms of reaching a wide audience, we have an honesty crisis on our hands. It is one that, I fear, is only going to get worse unless measures are taken to address it.

What can be done to mitigate this crisis? We should start at the institutional level. There needs to be legislation which requires digital watermarking or a disclosure on any deepfake which is being shared, with fines and even short jail time for repeated non-compliance or especially egregious cases. Images of individuals used without the person's consent in, say, deepfake pornography should open the creator of the video up to civil prosecution for damages, and even criminal charges.

In fact, there has been movement in this direction at both the state and federal levels in the United States. As of July 2025, 45 states had passed laws of some form against deepfake pornography, although only 18 had laws addressing both adult and children in explicit deepfake material.[33] There was initial progress made at the federal level with the DEEPFAKES Accountability Act (H.R. 3230), a bill which was introduced in the US House of Representatives in 2019, but alas never made it to a vote. A renewed effort was undertaken in 2023 with another DEEPFAKES Accountability Act, which required audio and video disclosures and would have instituted fines and even jail time for non-compliance or manipulation of a disclosure.[34] But it languished too.

Finally, with overwhelming bipartisan support Congress passed the Take It Down Act in 2025. This legislation bans the online publication of non-consensual intimate materials, including deepfakes, targeting revenge porn and boys posting manipulated pictures of girls to shame and humiliate them. It also requires platforms to remove such materials within 48 hours of being notified of its existence. This legislation is definitely a step in the right direction.[35]

Of course, there needs to be international cooperation as well. One good sign here is that the UK has penalized the sharing of non-consensual deepfake pornography with the Online Safety Act, passed in 2023, which allows for imprisonment in certain cases of up to two years. Yet it does not cover the creation of these fakes too. The Netherlands has taken this additional, needed step.[36]

Practically speaking, though, there are difficulties with tracking down the original creator of a deepfake for the purposes of meting out punishment. As law professors Bobby Chesney and Danielle Citron note,

> Civil liability cannot ameliorate harms caused by deep fakes if plaintiffs cannot tie them to their creators . . . the metadata relevant for ascertaining a deep fake's provenance might be insufficient to identify the person who generated it. It arises again when the creator or someone else posts a deep fake on social media . . . A careful distributor of a deep fake may take pains to be anonymous . . . In such cases a person or entity aggrieved by a deep fake may have no practical recourse against its creator, leaving only the possibility of seeking a remedy from the owner of platforms that enabled circulation of the content.[37]

So in addition, social media sites should continue to invest in deepfake detection, and at the very least flag anything that meets relevant standards. For instance, in 2023 Twitter adopted the admirable policy whereby: "You may not share synthetic, manipulated, or out-of-context media that may deceive or confuse people and lead to harm ('misleading media'). In addition, we may label posts containing misleading media to help people understand their authenticity and to provide additional context."[38]

Having said this, the use of disclosures needs to be handled with care. We are talking about recordings which, absent some kind of disclosure, would count as dishonest if they were produced and shared. So the disclosure is meant to be a warning to the potential viewer in order to negate the fake's dishonesty.

Note that, as I have already stressed, while it negates the fake's dishonesty, a disclosure does not automatically make any deepfake completely *okay*. For instance, in non-consensual deepfake pornography, even a "transparent" video clearly indicating that it is a fake could (and I say, would) be wrong, at the very least because the creator of the fake did not secure the consent of everyone involved. Dishonesty is one thing; wrongness is another. Disclosures are meant to just take care of the former.[39]

For the disclosure to be effective, though, it must be visible and impactful. But consider some of the challenges that lurk here. If we are talking about putting the warning on the place which houses the deepfake, like a CD disc case or a website page from which the recording can be downloaded, then that does not seem to go far enough. Many people will not pay attention to those warnings. Plus, the recording can be uploaded easily enough to other places, including other CDs and other websites without any warning messages.

It would be better if the disclosure were embedded in the actual recording, say at the beginning of a video or at the end. But obviously that has its limitations too, since many people skip over the opening and closing credits of an audio or video recording.

How about just flagging any deepfake material at the precise moment it is about to appear in a recording? That sounds good in theory, but my colleague Tobias Flattery has a nice example to show why sometimes even this is not ideal:

> [T]he 2016 film, *Rogue One: A Star Wars Story*, included a scene in which the already deceased actor Peter Cushing appeared to play a role, but which was accomplished instead using a stand-in actor and deepfake technology. No disclosures were given in the film at all, which no doubt led some viewers to assume that the actor was alive during the filming of Rogue One. If the filmmakers had added a visual notice appearing during that scene and disappearing afterward—e.g., "Dear Audience, please be aware that Peter Cushing did not actually appear in this scene. Guy Henry performed for this scene, which was then digitally altered so that Cushing's likeness appears instead of Henry's."—viewers would be less likely to assume that they were watching a performance by Cushing, and thus the filmmakers might have avoided a failure of honesty. But obviously this method of watching the film disclosure would detract from the experience.[40]

Hence while effective, this approach would be too heavy-handed and problematic in some cases.

Flattery discusses another clever approach—making the deepfake material refer to itself as fake! Here is his example of this idea:

> For instance, in 2018 the Flemish Socialist Party published a deepfake in which Donald Trump appears to call on Belgium to exit the Paris Climate Accords. At the end of the video, the deepfaked Trump says, "We all know climate change is fake, just like this video."[41]

This is the most straightforward and reliable approach of them all, since the very content of the video confesses to its being fake. But, alas, it does not follow that the audience will *believe* the confession of fakery. They might think that the rest of the video is real, and it is the *confession* which is a fake. Even if they do not think that, this approach is clearly not going to be adopted for many other deepfakes. Imagine the character in the Star Wars movie looking at the camera and confessing that he is a fake.

To be very clear, I am in no way objecting to the use of disclosures and warnings as an important way to address the threat of dishonest deepfakes. I am only highlighting how it is no simple matter to employ them effectively. What is needed is practical wisdom in thinking through the best approach on a case-by-case basis. Sometimes a disclosure at the beginning is enough. Sometimes more is needed. Sometimes less is best, say by just having the warning be on a website. This is a matter that cannot be decided with a simple rule.

So the approach recommended here is twofold. First there should be punitive measures designed to incentivize producers and distributors of deepfake material to have visible and effective disclosures alerting potential viewers to the inauthentic nature of the content. But on the assumption that some people will still try to create and share deepfakes without any disclosures, social media sites should, as much as possible, flag any deepfake recordings as a warning to unsuspecting viewers who might be duped into thinking the content is authentic.

To this we can add a third recommendation, which is to (continue to) ban non-consensual deepfake pornography. Manipulating someone's facial images and swapping them onto the head of a pornographic actress, without anyone consenting to their images being used in such a capacity, is morally wrong and should be legally wrong.

Since such a ban would apply to 98% of the deepfakes in existence today, it would have more of an impact than anything else.

Notes

1. Seitz-Wald and Memoli 2024.
2. Seitz-Wald 2024.
3. Ibid.
4. Reuters 2020.
5. This glosses over the details of how the technology actually works, details which won't be important for anything I say here. For those who want the details, see Mirsky and Lee 2020.
6. Available on YouTube at https://www.youtube.com/watch?v=X17yrEV5sl4&t=46s, accessed on July 15, 2025.
7. Various portions of the remainder of this chapter are drawn from Flattery and Miller 2024, with permission from Springer under the terms of the Creative Commons CC BY license (http://creativecommons.org/licenses/by/4.0/). Flattery is the one who deserves most of the credit for developing the framework for thinking about how dishonesty plays a role in deepfakes.
8. Fitzsimmons and Mays 2023.
9. This distinction mirrors Tom Roberts's distinction between 'open' and 'closed' recordings. His 2023 paper is one of the best recent reflections on the philosophy of deepfakes.
10. Chen 2019.
11. Security Hero 2023.
12. Ibid.
13. The choice of Taylor Swift as the example is not accidental, given the massive amount of attention deepfakes involving her have received. For instance, in one particular case, "the deepfakes of Swift on X amassed over 27 million views and more than 260,000 likes in 19 hours before the account that initially posted the images was suspended" (Morgan 2024).
14. For an interesting discussion here, comparing the morality of merely creating but not distributing pornographic videos to the morality of private sexual fantasies, see Öhman 2020.
15. Security Hero 2023.

16. For more on this point, see Rini 2020.
17. For excerpts, see https://digitaldozen.io/projects/jfk-unsilenced/, accessed on July 15, 2025.
18. Available at https://www.youtube.com/watch?v=QiiSAvKJIHo, accessed on July 15, 2025.
19. For discussion, see Roberts 2023.
20. For a similar use of this example, see Roberts 2023.
21. Nagourney et al. 2018.
22. Ibid.
23. For much more discussion, see Chesney and Citron 2019: 1771–1786, de Ruiter 2021, Kerner and Risse 2021, Rini and Cohen 2022, and Roberts 2023.
24. For extensive discussion of deepfakes and trust, see Laas 2023.
25. This theme is developed extensively by Rini 2020.
26. Roberts 2023, emphasis his.
27. For more on this point, see Harris 2021.
28. Fallis 2021: 625.
29. Quoted in Cole 2017. See also Rini and Cohen 2022.
30. De Ruiter 2021: 1325.
31. De Ruiter 2021: 1325.
32. Rini and Cohen 2022: 153.
33. Ballotpedia 2025.
34. The full text of the bill is available at https://drive.google.com/file/d/1vPoYKJAbPMzxGdl-7h5noI--2VCLrmzD/view, accessed on July 15, 2025.
35. To read the Take It Down Act, visit https://www.congress.gov/crs-product/LSB11314, accessed on July 15, 2025.
36. For reasons why this additional step is important, see McGlynn 2024.
37. Chesney and Citron 2019: 1792.
38. Available at https://help.twitter.com/en/rules-and-policies/manipulated-media, accessed on February 15, 2024. For helpful further discussion, see Chesney and Citron 2019: 1818.

    Still, it doesn't help if Google searches take users right to deepfake porn sites, and if Twitter is being supported by advertising dollars encouraging users to download apps which remove clothing from people's pictures. See McGlynn 2024.
39. For helpful discussion of these points, see Young 2021: chapter 11, de Ruiter 2021, and Story and Jenkins 2023.
40. Flattery and Miller 2024.
41. Ibid.

4

Online Infidelity and the Honesty Crisis in Relationships

In the last chapter, we saw that the main culprit for one honesty crisis was AI technology. There the dishonesty in question was sharing deepfake recordings. In this chapter, we turn to a different honesty crisis, where the focus is on infidelity. What is the culprit this time? It is the Internet. Let me first say something about infidelity by itself before we take a dive into the sordid world of Internet infidelity.

Understanding Infidelity

My wife and I have been in a monogamous marriage for over 16 years. Part of what we vowed to each other when we got married was that our relationship would be exclusive, both sexually and emotionally. We were not alone, of course. According to one study, between 94% and 99% of people report that they expect exclusivity from their relationship partner.[1] Another study reports that only 1% of survey participants thought that it was okay for people to engage in sexual behavior outside of a legal marriage.[2]

If I am unfaithful to my wife, then I will also be dishonest to her. Infidelity is a form of cheating, and cheating is a form of dishonesty. It involves intentionally distorting the facts, in this case about my following the relevant rules, standards, and expectations governing the exclusivity of our relationship. In cheating, my behavior would go against what these norms say I am allowed to do.

The Honesty Crisis. Christian B. Miller, Oxford University Press.
DOI: 10.1093/9780197840801.003.0004

Sexual infidelity extends much more broadly than two people touching each other in intimate ways. When it comes to the Internet in particular, here are some examples:

> Cybersex, online dating, chatroom flirting and sharing sexual fantasies, emailing nude pictures or videos of oneself, and trying to arrange an in-person sexual encounter with someone online.

Why do I say so confidently that these are examples of infidelity too?

One reason is that they meet any reasonable standard of what counts as cheating sexually with another person. But don't just take my word for it. When you ask folks in actual surveys what they think about these behaviors, they tend to agree with me. In one study, for instance, when rating various actions on a scale from 1 (*not at all unfaithful*) to 7 (*very unfaithful*), here were some of the results:[3]

Sending sexually explicit messages by text or email to someone	5.92
Masturbating with someone over webcam	5.84
Receiving sexually explicit messages by text or email from someone	5.47
Sending affectionate/flirtatious texts or emails to someone	5.23
Creating a profile on a dating website	5.19
Browsing an online dating website alone	4.79
Receiving affectionate/flirtatious texts or emails from someone	4.78

In another study, college students on their own came up with the following examples of unfaithful behaviors: cybersex or sexual chat (44.7% mentioned this), online dating (37.4% mentioned this), and online sexual interactions or flirting (37.4% mentioned this).[4]

To this evidence, it is also important to take very seriously the testimony of those who discover what their significant others have been doing online. Summarizing the research here, sex addiction researcher Jennifer Schneider writes,

> Partners overwhelmingly reported feeling that cyber affairs were as emotionally painful to them as live or offline affairs and that virtual affairs were just as much adultery or 'cheating' as live affairs; this was

> equally true of partners who had experience of their cybersex addicts having both types of affairs. Cybersex activities were considered particularly destructive in that (a) they took place right in the home and (b) were so time-consuming.[5]

Discovering what has been happening online elicits, "strong feelings of hurt, betrayal, rejection, abandonment, devastation, loneliness, shame, isolation, humiliation, jealousy, and anger, as well as a loss of self-esteem. Being lied to repeatedly was a major cause of distress."[6]

So there is every reason to think that the online behaviors mentioned above like cybersex and chatting about sexual fantasies fall under the heading of dishonesty—and specifically cheating—too. To this list I want to add another, very important example—viewing pornography online. The survey data backs me up to some extent here. In the same study cited above where 1 is (*not at all unfaithful*) and 7 is (*very unfaithful*), survey participants said that "viewing pornographic videos online alone" is an average of a 2.50. Not as high as the other online behaviors list above, but still indicative of some infidelity.[7]

Hold on, though, you might say. Watching a pornographic video while in an exclusive relationship is cheating? Dishonest? How can that be? All a husband (and yes, the consumers of online pornography are overwhelmingly male) might be doing, for instance, is viewing a video of some strangers doing some things. Is he really cheating on his wife? For now, I will leave that one as food for thought. We will come back to online pornography later in this chapter.

If I do genuinely cheat on my wife because of my online behavior, then I would be breaking our marriage vows. But of course I could cheat on someone if we were just dating or in a domestic partnership. Infidelity extends far beyond marriage. Indeed, it can even happen in polygamous relationships, if one party to the relationship strays outside of the boundaries.

When we think of infidelity, our minds tend to take us in a sexual direction. But that is not the only kind of infidelity there is. Another, very worrisome kind is having an *emotional affair*, where someone forms an inappropriate emotional connection with another person outside of the relationship. For instance, if I develop romantic feelings for another woman and communicate my love to her, then I would be committing emotional infidelity. This would apply, even if we never meet in person and even if nothing sexual ever happened between us online. My wife could rightly say that I am being unfaithful to her.

This aligns with how people tend to think about emotional attachments. For instance, of their own initiative, 39% of college students in one study listed behaviors associated with emotional affairs as examples of unfaithful activities when in an exclusive dating relationship.[8] In fact, some research suggests that people are *more distressed and upset* by the emotional online behavior of their significant other, than they are by that person's online sexual behavior.[9] Part of this surely involves how emotional connections online are bound up with intimacy. As researchers have noted,

> Electronic communication apparently allows at least some individually to subjectively feel less inhibited. Consequently, in the expression of their emotions, people are more likely to be open, honest, and forthright in revealing personal truths. As a result, the appearance of intimacy that might take months or years in an offline relationship may only take days or weeks online.[10]

In the case of sexual infidelity, the source of the sexual pleasure is often interchangeable and replaceable. In the case of emotional infidelity, there is more connection and attachment, so feelings of betrayal by the significant other can be deeper. But admittedly this is largely speculative.

The Internet and Infidelity

If there is anything discussed in this book that has been around forever, it is infidelity, both sexual and emotional. Wherever there are exclusive romantic relationships, there is also the threat of cheating. But the rise of the Internet has changed things for the worse here, as now we have another honesty crisis on our hands. An anonymous participant in a research study captured this sentiment well: "I have a deep mistrust of the Internet, and feel it massively facilitates infidelity."[11]

It should surprise no one that with the advent of the Internet, the frequency of infidelity has dramatically accelerated. As one anonymous cheater puts it straightforwardly:

> I don't know what's wrong with me but I just can't help fooling around with other women. During our 10 years together, [my wife] has never found anything that might imply me having [a relationship with] another woman . . . Nowadays, with the Internet and well advanced phones, it's even easier.[12]

For this person, he was already cheating on his wife before the Internet came along, and it just made things easier. For many others, though, the Internet is the onramp to their first experiences of infidelity.

What is it about the Internet that facilitates cheating? Well, think back to how things were for people in exclusive relationships in the United States just 50 years ago. If you wanted to have a sexual encounter with someone else while in a monogamous relationship, you had to discreetly venture out and find that person. Maybe it was a matter of hiring a prostitute or visiting a strip club outside of town. Or perhaps meeting someone at the hotel bar while on a business trip. Or you could buy a magazine or an explicit video at a seedy store.

Fast forward 50 years. Now, everything is right there on our phones, tablets, and home computers. With just the click of a few buttons, we can:

- Watch hours of completely unfiltered hardcore pornography for free.
- Hop into a chatroom and have anonymous sexual or emotionally laden conversations with anyone we want.

- Head over to the Ashley Madison website ("Life is Short. Have an Affair.") and try to arrange a rendezvous with another user.

If we do any of these things while in a monogamous relationship, we are being dishonest.

What is it about these electronic means of interaction that can make them so appealing? One of the key factors is the greater *ease of use* or *accessibility*. No more getting in your car, or talking with a store clerk. No more having to pay someone with money, or be spotted out in public. You can do whatever you want from the comforts of your home. Plus, there is no risk of pregnancy or catching a sexually transmitted disease.

And you can do all this *anonymously*. No one has to know who you are in the chatroom. As two researchers put it amusingly,

> Bad breath, dirty fingernails, or an irritating tendency to interrupt are irrelevant in e-mail and chat rooms. Lovers are not distracted by physical attributes, allowing them to listen with their inner selves—their souls.[13]

Similarly, no one in your life has to see you visiting the porn sites. Your online activities are pretty easy to hide.

Plus it is *cheap and affordable*. So long as you know where to look, the sources of sexual pleasure are basically free to use and bottomless in capacity. You could spend all your waking hours watching free pornographic movies on the internet and not see all of them before you die. You are just paying for your Internet service.

It gets better (or worse, as I tend to think). Opportunities for sexual or emotional interactions are *ever-present*. There is always someone there online, always someone to flirt with or fantasize with. The supply is 24/7.

Finally, I can *feel like I am in control*. I can talk with anyone I want. I can look at anything I want. I can try to arrange sexual interactions, whether online or in person, with whomever I want. And I can come and go as I please.

So the Internet seems to provide us with a reliable way to get sexual pleasure and emotional intimacy, a way which is easy to use, anonymous, cheap, ever-present, and agential. For many, this is too good to pass up. As a result, cheating—and thereby dishonesty—are greatly enhanced.[14]

All this is pretty straightforward. But what really struck me when I first started researching this topic is what happens in *just one instance* of Internet infidelity. A conversation in a chatroom, or a trip to the Ashley Madison website, can be bound up with so many ways of being dishonest. As a result, we damage the loyalty, trust, and commitment established between ourselves and our significant others in all kinds of ways that are rarely appreciated.

To better explore this idea and to appreciate more tangibly the honesty crisis we are facing with the Internet and infidelity, I want to look at three spaces in more detail: chatrooms, the Ashley Madison website, and online pornography.

Chatrooms and Infidelity

"Never before in history has a married person been able to bask in the familiarity of marriage and the thrilling dating world at the same time. Internet chat rooms have made this possible . . ."[15] So writes education professor Beatriz Lia Avila Mileham, in arguably the most influential study of Internet infidelity and chatrooms.

As a historical claim, what Mileham says here is probably false. But it is easy enough to appreciate what she is getting at. As she notes, "At a click of a button, thousands of potentially desirable individuals instantly become available. The medium offers an unparalleled opportunity to browse through names and profiles, start conversations, enter and exit interactions with no effort or second thought at all, and choose those that seem worthy of one's attention."[16] Welcome to the world of chatroom infidelity.

Imagine that someone named Vance has been married to Samantha for a long time. Now in his forties, he describes himself as happily married. But he has a habit of visiting Internet chatrooms with names like "Married and Flirting," where he carries out conversations with women anonymously. Typically, the conversations start off as flirtatious, and Vance takes some liberties in describing his body and his attractiveness. From there his discussions may evolve into sharing sexual fantasies and, at times, some form of cybersex.

Vance has been discreet about his behavior at home. Samantha does not suspect anything, at least not for the first few years. He has had plenty of opportunities to confess to Samantha what he is doing online, but he does not. Over time, though, Samantha starts to wonder about her husband's behavior. One morning she confronts Vance about why he is always visiting chatrooms in the middle of the night, and he makes up a story about how they are forums where he talks about work-related issues. Samantha trusts her husband and accepts his answer.

When they are out with friends, Vance extols the importance of being faithful in marriage, and he trusts Samantha's loyalty completely. He would be incredibly hurt if he ever found out that Samantha was having an affair, including engaging in cybersex online. The thought never crosses his mind that she would actually do this, though.

Vance's story is not unusual. Perhaps some people do not spend as much time in chatrooms as Vance, or they keep the discussions more at the level of emotional intimacy, or they prefer to exchange salacious pictures or videos rather than live streams. Regardless of the details, something in this general vicinity is all too familiar as a description of chatroom infidelity. And it is rife with dishonesty.

Now it is crucial to the example that Vance is in a relationship which is supposed to be grounded in an exclusive sexual commitment to Samantha. If Vance were single, or if he were married to Samantha but she fully supported his online behavior, then dishonesty would not factor into the discussion in the same ways.

But that is not Vance's actual story. In that story, he is living a lie. Or, more precisely, he is living out at least *seven* ways of being dishonest. Some are obvious, and some are more subtle.

Take the flirting, the sharing of sexual fantasies, and the cybersex. I think those are rather obviously dishonest. Vance is enjoying sexual relations with other women. His goal is to experience sexual pleasure, not with his wife to whom he has made a commitment to follow exclusive sexual norms and practices, but with someone outside of their bond. By cheating on Samantha, he is being dishonest.[17]

Now Vance might deny this. Indeed, many chatroom users like Vance deny that they are cheating on their significant others because there is no *physical* contact going on. One study found that fully 83% of chatroom users surveyed went with this line of thinking to justify why they were not cheating.[18] Here is how a couple of participants in the study explained it:

> It is all fantasy (at least for me). In my head, cheating means touching another human. It is all in your HEAD. You can create 'friendships' here and those lead to a more intimate conversation . . . It's not a big deal, it's not cheating. (42-year-old male)

> Online? Cheating? No, not at all. We're physical beings, mere communication is not cheating. Cheating in my mind requires physical contact. (49-year-old male)

Many others say the same thing.[19]

But this is just rationalization. These chatroom users are coming up with BS reasoning to assuage their own consciences. I mean 'BS' here in the way it was introduced in Chapter 1. Their justifications are not concerned with the truth, but rather with what will make them feel better. After all, they would hardly be okay with their wives or girlfriends sharing nude videos of themselves with men they meet online, even though nothing "physical" ever happens there either. So this rationalization is another source of dishonesty. They are being dishonest with themselves.

Even those who *do admit* that they are cheating on their significant others often come up with BS rationalizations to justify their behavior to themselves and minimize its severity. Hence one person admits:

> Yes, in the world of morality, I think it is cheating, but I also believe that it can give you an outlet to relieve certain sexual tensions that you would

> never be able to relieve in any other way. I have a very loving and stable relationship with my spouse, but I need something else, an outlet, something. I mean that, if you were going to have an affair, the Internet is the best way to go. (50-year-old male)[20]

Another such rationalization is that it 'helps the marriage' by making the cheater more sexually excited. But again, these are BS rationalizations, and so dishonest.

Vance embellishes his physique and how in-shape he is to women he meets in the chatrooms. Like so many of us online, he fabricates an alternative identity that accentuates his positive features and hides his negative ones.[21] This is obviously dishonest as well—he is lying to these women.

Then there is the disguise and concealment, not in the chatroom, but in real life. Vance is pretending like he is doing work, when he is actually having a steamy chat. The hiding from Samantha in another room so she won't catch him. The wiping of his computer's memory. And on and on. These are all examples of dishonesty by deception.

Plus, it is not as if Vance never has a chance to tell Samantha what was going on. They talk every day, and he is very open about plenty of other subjects. Just not this one. So he is deliberately dishonest in this way too—he is lying by omission.

Of course, Vance does not have to tell Samantha everything that is going on in his life. If he fails to mention a small itch, a trip to the bathroom, a hangnail—so what? Not all omissions of personal information count as dishonest. But not sharing that one is having sexual encounters with other people, encounters that strike at the very core of your marriage or partnership, is a different story. That is lying by omission.

As time went on, we see that Samantha gets suspicious. She asked Vance directly about what he was doing on the computer. The answer he came up with about using the chatroom for work, was a lie. This is clearly dishonest—it is lying by commission.

Then there is Vance's hypocrisy. When around others, he praises faithfulness to one's significant other. But in his private life he turns his back on faithfulness. So too, he would be aghast if he ever found out that Samantha was having cybersex online with strangers. He would condemn her actions, while never bringing that condemnation down upon himself. Hypocrisy is dishonest too.[22]

Finally, there is what happens to any sexual activities between Vance and Samantha. They become dishonest too, because Samantha has been deceived about the nature of their activities. She thinks her sexual interactions with Vance are exclusive, and Vance tries to keep her thinking that way, even though they are not. Yet as the philosopher Natasha McKeever notes, "if they are in a sexually exclusive relationship, when they consent to have sex with each other, they do so on the understanding that the sex they have is exclusive. Sex can be a different experience when it is exclusive . . . you [did] not consent to non-exclusive sex, which might, for you, come along with a variety of different and unpleasant emotions, such as anxiety or insecurity."[23]

So in the sad story of Vance and Samantha, we see no less than seven different examples of dishonesty at work. What Vance has done is take a perfectly trusting and loyal relationship, and corrupt it.[24]

One final note about these chatrooms. Vance's story has been centered around sexual infidelity. But chatrooms can foster emotional infidelity too. As one user said,

> I have a lot of chats, start off real great then they disappear. I got one that I am talking with for a year and a half and I never met her. We chat on the phone, talk just about everything, she is married too. We talk about life, things that happen to her and her husband and vice versa, things we like in the opposite sex and so on. Vacations, how fun it was, [our] jobs, and hypocrites. (33-year-old male)[25]

Emotional infidelity can follow the same ebbs and flows of dishonesty: cheating, BSing, deception, lying by omission, lying by commission, and hypocrisy. Just because there is nothing sexual going on does not mean that there is not an honesty crisis here as well.

Ashley Madison and Adultery Sites

The expressed goal of the Ashley Madison website is to help bring people together who are looking to cheat. With the slogan, "Life is Short. Have an Affair," it became an Internet sensation.

Not surprisingly, perhaps, Ashley Madison's history is wrapped up with dishonesty. Founded in 2002, it "billed itself as the premier destination for adulterers—no judgment, no risks, no strings attached other than the payments required to secure enough 'credits' to talk to other users."[26] And the marketing strategy seemed to work. By 2015, it reported 37 million users.

In July of that year, though, a hacker named "the Impact Team" successfully accessed Ashley Madison's databases and released private data on 30 million users, exposing a number of celebrities, religious leaders, teachers, and all the rest. In doing so, the hacker revealed the dishonest behavior of these users. The Impact Team also exposed Ashley Madison's apparent dishonesty too. As Evan Back, the former vice president of sales for the company would later reveal, "The promise of security, anonymity and safety was just something we said. It wasn't something we did . . . It was like gambling."[27] Despite this massive security breach, Ashley Madison is still up and running today, with one report indicating that memberships surpassed 70 million in 2020 during the height of the pandemic.[28]

Why would people go to a website like this to seek out an affair in the first place? A recent study by the psychologist Dylan Selterman from John Hopkins University sheds some light on this question.[29] In one of the groups of website users Selterman surveyed, he found that the average age of users was 51 years, with a huge skew male (684 out of 810 participants) and straight (738), and with 52% either engaged, married, or in domestic partnerships.[30] Additional questions covered everything from their current relationship, views about sex and love, self-esteem, interactions (including sexual) with other people on Ashley Madison, motives for having an affair, and feelings after having an affair (if they were successful).

Three results really jump out. One has to do with how people described their current relationship. They tended to report being in love with their partner, and to a high degree—about a 4 on a 5-point scale. On the other hand, sexual satisfaction was below 2.5, and about half of users said they were not sexually active with their significant other.[31]

Why then were people going to a place like Ashley Madison to seek out an affair? The usual reasons we might expect would be a lack of love in their relationship, anger at their partner, or a feeling of neglect. But when asked about those specific reasons, participants did not score them very highly at all. Instead, it turned out that "sexual dissatisfaction was the most strongly endorsed motive for wanting an affair. Other commonly endorsed reasons included low commitment, autonomy (i.e., wanting freedom and independence) and a desire for a variety of sexual partners."[32]

Now many of the users surveyed had not been able to have an affair with someone yet on Ashley Madison. But for those who had succeeded, what were their feelings afterwards? Here the results were, quite frankly, alarming. Emotional satisfaction was above a 4 out of 5, and sexual satisfaction was above 4.5. On the flip side, regret was rated very low—less than a 2 out of 5. In other words, these users tended to get what they wanted and not feel bad about it afterwards.[33]

I suspect that a large part of what explains why regret was so low after having an affair is that these were already habitual cheaters. Indeed, Selterman noted that 64% of the participants in one of his groups reported having an affair *before* they used Ashley Madison.[34] Over time I imagine they got used to what they were doing, and so were not bothered as much. It would be interesting to compare regret levels between Ashley Madison users for whom this was their first affair, and those who reported prior affairs.

Regardless, as an ethicist it is hard for me not to find these results discouraging. Reasons like sexual dissatisfaction and wanting a variety of partners seem like especially bad reasons. Not to mention that after having broken personal bonds of commitment, loyalty, and honesty, these users experienced satisfaction and not regret. This reveals something badly askew with their moral compass.

But here I want to keep our focus on the topic of dishonesty. Some of the dishonesty involved is obvious, and it repeats the same ground as chatrooms. Carrying out sexually charged conversations or forming emotional connections with a stranger on Ashley Madison is dishonest. If it leads to making arrangements to try to meet in person, that is dishonest too. So is hiding this behavior from your significant other, or outright lying about what you are doing if confronted. And again, rationalizing it is BSing, and judging others negatively for using the website is hypocritical.

A new wrinkle, though, is the fact that you have to register and pay money for the services provided by Ashley Madison. I want to suggest that, even if you never end up spending much time on the site or meeting anyone special, *the mere act of registering* for Ashley Madison itself is dishonest (assuming, of course, that you do not have your significant other's blessing to use it).

Why would this add yet another dimension of dishonesty? Because the very nature of the site is to facilitate infidelity. Unlike chatrooms, there is no ambiguity about what Ashley Madison is for. And we are not talking about just visiting the site out of curiosity—this is a matter of paying money and registering. What are you registering for? "Life is short. Have an affair."

Someone who is trying to follow the standards of exclusivity (both sexual and emotional) that ground his relationship with his significant other would not register for such a site. To do so is to intentionally distort the facts as to what he should be doing in this relationship.

And this brings me to perhaps the deepest form of dishonesty we find here. As Selterman notes, "Participants sought affairs despite strong feelings of love for their primary partners/spouses . . . they endorse values that would ostensibly prohibit infidelity, while also engaging in infidelity themselves."[35] Of course not all people who use websites like Ashley Madison are still in love with their significant others. But apparently many people are.

To be in love with my wife is to be concerned with what is good for her *selflessly, for her own sake.* I may benefit; I may not benefit. But that is not the point. The point is that my loving focus is on her good, not my own. But to register for and then use a website whose purpose is to facilitate adulterous sexual and/or emotional relationships with strangers does not promote the good of my wife. It directly contradicts the promotion of her good.

This is hypocrisy. It is a hypocrisy that is far worse than just telling people that adultery is wrong, while using the Ashley Madison website. No, this is a hypocrisy where someone genuinely loves and also genuinely betrays the same person.

Internet Pornography and Dishonesty

Internet chat rooms get lots of traffic. We said that Ashley Madison reportedly surpassed 70 million users during the pandemic. But nothing can come close to touching the popularity of Internet pornography.

The statistics are mindboggling. According to one estimate, adult websites in the United States had a market size of $1.2 billion in 2024.[36] An earlier report from 2012 claimed there were roughly 25 million pornographic websites at the time, making up 12% of the internet.[37] In November of 2024, the leading pornography site was averaging 5.25 billion visits each month.[38]

Our focus is not on the overall morality of pornography, or whether it is right or wrong, good or bad. That is a big topic, worthy of a book in its own right. Rather we are just looking at what happens to the honesty of someone who is in a committed and sexually exclusive relationship with another person and who seeks out Internet pornography.

Online pornography could seem far removed from concerns about dishonesty. There might be some serious moral issues with both making and consuming pornography. But does any of that involve *dishonesty*?

Furthermore, if there *were* dishonesty lurking here, then it seems like we might be making a lot of trouble for ourselves. For then, wouldn't we have to say the same thing about being dishonest when we have private sexual fantasies in our minds about other people like celebrities or passing infatuations. How is that any different, really, from watching things play out in an X-rated video?

Do you really want to say that? What I mean is, do you really want to say someone would be engaging in dishonest behavior—cheating on their significant other—simply by having such fantasies in their minds? That is going to be highly controversial.

And yet, I *do* think viewing pornography online is rife with dishonesty. Let me briefly mention some of the reasons we have seen already. If you hide your pornographic viewing from your significant other, that is lying by omission. If you lie when asked directly by her about what you are watching online, that is lying by commission. If you say how opposed you are to pornography, but watch it anyway, that is hypocrisy. And if you make up some excuses or rationalizations about why it is really not a problem for your relationship with your spouse that you spend hours getting sexually stimulated by these videos, then that is BS.

As in the case of other forms of online infidelity, regularly viewing pornography can introduce dishonesty into the couples' bedroom as well. As one woman described her experience after discovering her partner's online pornography use:

> I am no longer a sexual *person* or partner to him, but a sexual *object*. He is not really with *me*, not really making love to *me* . . . He seems to be thinking about something or someone else—likely those porn women . . . He is just using me as a warm body.[39]

Pornography can introduce deception even into the couple's sexual activities.

Finally, studies have found that regularly viewing pornography is a pathway for some to engage in cheating behavior in person. The link is there between pornography and both in-person infidelity as well as cyber-infidelity.[40] So viewing this stuff can have downstream effects which are dishonest, too.

All this strikes me as pretty straightforward. The interesting question, though, is about *the very act of viewing* a pornographic picture or video. Independently of what happens later (the rationalization, the coverup, the hypocrisy, the cheating, and so forth), is the searching, locating, and watching of these materials *itself* a form of dishonesty?

I want to say, yes. The point is pretty simple. You are seeking out sexual pleasure from someone other than your significant other with whom you have formed a bond based, in part, on sexual exclusivity. The only sexual interaction is supposed to happen with this one person. But this expectation is not met when you deliberately search for and consume a pornographic video online. Now the aim is to experience sexual pleasure from watching someone else. Now there is a sexual interaction happening with a third party.[41]

This is to cheat on your significant other. Why? Because it intentionally violates some of the standards and commitments which tie the two of you together in the first place. And that is dishonest.[42]

What then should we say about a private sexual fantasy that we have just in our minds, but never act on with another person in real life? Is that dishonest too? Of course, there are some big differences between doing that and the case of, say, viewing a pornographic video online. The content of the video is outside of your control, and so is its length. With our sexual fantasies, we can dictate how long they last and what happens in them.

But these are not differences that, so far as I can tell, get us off the hook of dishonesty. If anything, they might make things worse. For as the author of the fantasy, we can take it in whatever direction we like. We can make it just be about our significant other. Yet if we purposively choose to craft the fantasy around our imaginary sexual interactions with someone else, and we become sexually stimulated in the process—well—it is hard for me to see how that would not be violating a commitment to sexual exclusivity.

So here is the big picture. The Internet has dramatically escalated the availability and amount of pornography that is easily attainable for people to view. Hundreds of millions of people have taken advantage of the opportunity to do so. Among them are many people in sexually exclusive relationships. In doing so they are cheating on their significant others. They are, in other words, being dishonest.

Is There Any Hope?

What can be done to resist these online sources of sexual temptation in monogamous relationships? Some strategies are familiar and well-documented. For instance, based on a survey of therapists who are professionally treating Internet infidelity, one study found seven "essential elements" to proper treatment.[43] The elements are commonsensical, and are not specific to Internet use per se. Here they are, along with specific illustrations:[44]

Develop physical boundaries: Less accessible location, restriction on pages, monitoring software, presence of partner while using computer.

Developing psychological boundaries: Review relationship contract, review definition of infidelity.

Manage accountability, trust, and feelings: Validate and normalize, hearing the betrayed partner, acknowledge the sexual and/or emotional nature of the relationship, discuss the actual events and their impact on each person.

Increase client awareness around etiology of the Internet relationship: Explore motivations, explore potential relationship needs, work on boundaries, insight-oriented questioning.

Assessment of the couple's context and readiness for change: Ask about negotiation skills, previous positive relationship experiences, previous history of infidelity throughout the generations, evaluation of relationship expectations, identify goals for both individuals and the couple, assess commitment.

Assess the presence of unique circumstances: Determine whether it is an addiction, evaluate whether there are physical issues contributing to the problem, evaluate expectations of gender and if or how they play into the relationship, circular questions, take problem out of context, clarify presence of third person.

Work toward forgiveness: Communications, assess willingness to move toward forgiveness, psychoeducation around forgiveness as a decision.

People often want new and bold strategies for dealing with behavioral problems. These are mostly familiar and reasonable. But that does not mean that they are not worth taking very seriously and developing further.[45]

Another strategy besides those listed above focuses on the power of social norms, in this case norms of infidelity which can become contagious. Increased exposure to adulterous behavior has been found to increase interest in alternative partners, decrease commitment to one's significant other, and increase effort to interact in the future with an attractive third party.[46] The alternative strategy, then, is to avoid environments which normalize adulterous behavior, combined with the increased presence of moral reminders of one's commitment and loyalty to one's significant other.

But the strategy I want to focus on here is different from any of these, although it is also very commonsensical. It involves reminding ourselves to adopt the perspective of those we love.

Suppose I am tempted to seek out a stranger in a chatroom for an intimate conversation, or to do a quick Google search for pornography. The strategy to help resist this temptation starts by trying to see things from my wife's perspective. I imagine what her reaction would be if she were to suddenly discover me looking at porn. Then I take on her feelings. If it is any kind of negative emotion—anger, disappointment, resentment, jealousy, disgust, hatred, or the like—then I too will be distressed. Because of my attachment to her, her imagined distress becomes my distress. Thus, knowing both what she would think and how she would feel about my potential behavior would serve as a psychological roadblock for me from going down this path of internet infidelity.

In a word, this is just *empathy*. Empathy involves taking someone's perspective (trying to see the world through her eyes) and emotion-sharing (feeling what she is feeling, as a result of understanding what she is going through).[47] Normally we feel empathy for other people when they are going through some hardship. Here, though, we would be using our capacities for empathy—to think and feel with how someone else we care about *would* react to an imaginary scenario that *could* become real.

New research has given a boost to this strategy. For instance, Gurit Birnbaum from Reichman University in Israel and her colleagues ran three studies examining the relationship between perspective-taking and attraction toward a third party.[48] Here we will look at just the first two studies. Study 1 recruited 130 Israeli participants who were in a monogamous relationship for more than 4 months. They were divided up into a control group and a perspective-taking group; this second group imagined, "what they might be thinking, feeling, and experiencing if they were their partners, looking at the world through their partners' eyes and walking in their partners' shoes, as they go through the various activities they experience during a typical day in their lives."[49]

Did perspective-taking make any difference to being attracted to someone outside of their relationship? Birnbaum and her team went on to show each participant 20 pictures in rapid succession, with 10 of them being of attractive individuals of the same gender as their partner, and 10 pictures of unattractive individuals. For each picture, the participant had to press a yes or no button for "whether they would consider this person to be a potential partner."[50]

The results? Control participants said yes to 6.51 alternative partners, while those in the perspective-taking group said yes to 5.58 alternative partners, a statistically significant decrease.[51] Birnbaum takes this result to suggest that perspective-taking "leads to prioritizing the goal of relationship maintenance relative to the temptation of straying and thus helps inhibit interest in attractive others."[52] Still, one might wonder how much weight to put on this one finding. After all, looking at a bunch of pictures seems somewhat tame compared to actually interacting with attractive others.

Fortunately, this was not the only study that Birnbaum ran. In Study 2, 147 new Israeli participants, also in monogamous relationships, were divided up into the same control and perspective-taking groups. But at the end of the study, instead of evaluating photos, they talked with an interviewer over text. During the interview, participants saw a profile picture of this interviewer which depicted him or her as an attractive member of the same gender as their own partner. After the text chat, they had to answer a few questions about their interest in this interviewer and their commitment to their partner.

The results this time? Compared to controls, the perspective-takers reported *significantly lower sexual interest in their interviewer* (on a five-point scale, an average of 1.33 versus 1.58 for the controls). They also reported *significantly greater commitment to their existing relationship* (a 4.86 out of 5, versus 4.68 for the controls).[53]

So suppose there is indeed a link between perspective-taking and decreased attraction to strangers. What would explain it? We cannot say from this study, but my hunch is that perspective-taking reliably increases empathic concern for a person, and is accompanied by a greater sense of closeness.

We should not get too excited about this research just yet, though. It needs to be replicated in different cultures and with larger numbers of participants. As Birnbaum herself notes, it also does not speak to whether perspective-taking has a long-term effect, nor do the studies measure actual infidelity (which after all might be hard to do!).

Finally, even if future studies on these topics are promising, we should not expect perspective-taking to do too much. It might diminish people's cheating desires, but it will fall short of eliminating them altogether. It is not a cure-all when it comes to preventing infidelity. There are no cure-alls, alas.

Still, I see it as a big help. When I try to imagine what my wife would feel if she were to see me ever using Ashley Madison or talking about sexual fantasies with someone in a chatroom (not that I ever have!), a lot of powerful responses come to mind—anger, resentment, envy, betrayal, sadness, and disappointment, just for starters.

"But wait, Miller," you might say to me,

> "I thought you were supposed to be promoting honesty as a *virtue*. How virtuous would it really be to not go to these places online, solely because you fear your significant other's harsh reactions? Doesn't that

> make it all about *you*—about your not wanting to be punished and blamed and yelled at, etc., by this person if she ever found out what you were doing online?"

I agree that this does not sound like the best reason for not engaging in these dishonest activities.

There is another way to see what is going on, however. It is not that you fear what might happen to you, but rather you fear *what might happen to your loved one.* You know that her finding out about the Internet infidelity would lead to a lot of pain and negative emotions for her. Because you love her, you do not want her to experience these things. So you do not go down this cheating path.

That is a much better, more virtuous mindset to adopt. Note that the focus of concern is now on the other person—what would protect and preserve her feelings—rather than on what blowback there might be on you. This is an altruistic and selfless attitude, which is entirely compatible with virtue. Hence by adopting the perspective of our loved ones, we can resist temptation to engage in online infidelity, and we can resist it for the right reasons.

So Birnbaum's results help to remind us once again of the great moral value of trying to get out of our own narrow perspective and see the world through someone else's eyes. Doing so just might save our relationship.

Notes

1. Reported in Thompson and O'Sullivan 2016: 1.
2. Reported in Hackathorn and Ashdown 2021: 170.
3. Thompson and O'Sullivan 2016: 4.
4. Henline et al. 2007: 117. There is actually a lot of research on what people think is infidelity online and what is not. If you are interested, check out the papers cited here as well as Cravens and Whiting 2016 and Vossler and Moller 2020.
5. Schneider 2003: 353.
6. Ibid. See also Hertlein and Webster 2008.
7. Henline et al. 2007: 117. See also Docan-Morgan and Docan 2007.
8. Henline et al. 2007: 117.
9. Ibid., 120.

10. Young et al. 2000: 60.
11. From Vossler and Moller 2020.
12. Anonymous 2005, quoted in Hertlein and Piercy 2006: 366.
13. Maheu and Subotnik 2001: 27.
14. For more discussion of these and other aspects of the Internet which seem to encourage infidelity, see Cooper 2002, Hertlein and Piercy 2006, and Vossler 2016.
15. Mileham 2007: 28–29.
16. Ibid., 25.
17. For an excellent philosophical discussion of the relationship between sexual activities, sexual interactions, and sexual infidelity, see McQueen 2021.
18. Mileham 2007: 20.
19. Ibid., 20–23. In another study, a woman says this about her partner's chatroom use: "His reasoning is that's it's ok as he is never going to meet these people . . . that it's just fantasy. However it affected his real relationship as he never has time to spend as a couple, and I'm constantly worried about him actually meeting up one day with someone online. He believes it is not being unfaithful as it's online and I believe it is" (Vossler and Moller 2020: 72).
20. Mileham 2007: 23.
21. For more on creating alternative identities and Internet infidelity, see Vossler and Moller 2020: 72–73.
22. For data about the extent to which people exhibit hypocrisy by judging behavior as more indicative of infidelity if it is done by their partner than it if it done by themselves, see Docan-Morgan and Docan 2007 and Thompson and O'Sullivan 2016.
23. McKeever 2020: 522.
24. Now admittedly not all real-world cases will have all of this dishonesty to them. For instance, some chatroom users do admit (at least to themselves) that they are cheating on their spouses outright, without any rationalization. Or sometimes they may not embellish their appearance or mannerisms. Or sometimes they do not arouse suspicion at home, and so avoid lies of commission. When it comes to the outright cheating, the lies of omission, and the hypocrisy, though, that's a different story—those are almost always going to be present.
25. Mileham 2007: 18.
26. Horton 2024.
27. Ibid.
28. ruby Life 2020.
29. Selterman et al. 2023.
30. Ibid., 2564.
31. Ibid., 2566.
32. Ibid., 2568.
33. Ibid.

34. Ibid., 2567.
35. Ibid., 2571.
36. IBISWorld 2025.
37. Cited in Ahmed et al. 2016.
38. Cited in Statista 2024.
39. Quoted in Manning 2006: 143, emphasis in original.
40. Ferron et al. 2017.
41. Admittedly, if sexual interactions require sexual activities between two or more parties participating together, then merely looking at a static pornographic photograph or watching a video on Pornhub will not count as a sexual interaction. That seems right to me, and that is a difference from our earlier cases of chatroom exchanges and Ashley Madison exchanges, which clearly meet the standards of sexual interactions. This difference might go some way toward explaining why viewing pornography is more controversial as a form of infidelity than those other behaviors are.

    Having said this, I don't think that having a sexual *interaction* with another person is necessary for there to be infidelity (here I part ways with McQueen 2021). What *is* necessary is sexual activity aimed at getting sexual pleasure for yourself from some person or depiction of a person other than your significant other, combined with background norms and standards which forbid such sexual activity. And these *are* present in the case of a husband, for instance, watching a video on Pornhub. He is engaged in an activity whose goal is sexual pleasure for himself via a video depiction of other people engaged in sexual behavior. Yet he does this, despite having committed to his wife being the only person who is meant to be the source of sexual pleasure in his life.
42. For a review of some of the opposing views to what I say here, and for very helpful discussion of pornography and infidelity, see McQueen 2021: 460–464.
43. Hertlein and Piercy 2012.
44. What follows reproduces Table 1 from Hertlein and Piercy 2012: 261, with permission to reprint from John Wiley & Sons.
45. For an overview of a number of strategies, see Hertlein and Piercy 2006, although they note that "The gap with these treatments in their application to Internet infidelity is the lack of empirical evidence supporting the utility in clinical work" (170).
46. Birnbaum, Zholtack et al. 2022.
47. I unpack this in great detail in Miller 2013: chapter 5.
48. Birnbaum, Bachar et al. 2022.
49. Ibid., 3.
50. Ibid., 4.
51. Ibid.
52. Ibid.
53. Ibid., 5.

5

AI, Academic Cheating, and the Honesty Crisis in Education

My friend who is also a philosophy professor posted this in the fall of 2023 on Facebook:

> The academic misconduct office website is now on my browser's favorites because it's one of my most-visited sites. Thanks, ChatGPT!
>
> How much cheating did you find?
>
> At this point I'm pushing 200 cases.

Here is what another philosophy friend said: "I'm currently managing a tenfold increase in suspected academic integrity violations this semester—all due to ChatGPT."[1] We have an honesty crisis. Teachers are drowning in AI-based academic cheating.

This honesty crisis strikes close to home for me as a professor. It should also strike close to home for every middle school, high school, and college teacher today.

Of course, teachers have always been worried about student cheating, and rightly so. Studies from the early 2000s found that average cheating rates of students in college were as high as 60%, 70%, and even 86%.[2] Things got even worse with COVID-19 and the turn to remote learning. It is hard to not give exams in some academic disciplines like the sciences. But with students taking their tests at home, we were asking a great deal if we expected them to resist looking for help in places where they were not supposed to, such as their notes, their friends, or the Internet.

The Honesty Crisis. Christian B. Miller, Oxford University Press. © Oxford University Press 2026.
DOI: 10.1093/9780197840801.003.0005

COVID-19 subsided and we returned to in-person teaching and assessments. Then along came the greatest challenge to academic honesty ever invented: AI.

AI cheating fits the characterization of an honesty crisis perfectly. It is not that producing fraudulently written academic papers is new. It is that it is so much easier to do today. By giving an AI the class assignment, it can immediately generate a paper that is at least of decent quality. If a few easy steps are taken, the paper will be essentially undetectable to plagiarism checking software and to many teachers themselves. Studies have found that, despite what they might think about their own abilities, professors are not in fact reliable in telling whether a paper is AI-generated or not.[3]

What we have are actually two honesty crises in a row—one with COVID-19, and the other with AI. We will explore both of them in some detail. First, though, let's return to the good old days before the spring of 2020, when academic cheating was present, but at least it was pretty predictable. We will look at what tended to motivate students to cheat back then, and what countermeasures seemed to show some success in combatting cheating. From there we can better examine how things evolved (or devolved) with COVID-19, and what challenges (and resources) exist for professors in the era of AI today.

A disclaimer up front. If you are a teacher reading this in the hopes of finding a new solution to AI student cheating, let me calibrate expectations. Unlike some of the other honesty crises discussed in this book, this is one where I have little hope that we can reign it in. I will offer some tips and advice, but no promising solutions. Indeed, I do not think anyone has a promising solution to offer at this time.

The Psychology of Student Cheating

Prior to COVID-19, I was always on guard against two kinds of cheating by my students. One was unauthorized help during an in-class exam. Think of things like looking at someone else's answers, or using crib notes, or checking a cell phone in the bathroom. The other kind of cheating I was on guard against was plagiarism. In fact, the course I had the most trouble with was my Ethics course. Yes, the irony was stark.

Even though we did not have AI yet, my students still had Google. So plenty of material on the Internet was at their fingertips. I did not want them to consult that material when writing their papers, and shuddered at the thought of their cutting and pasting or even just reworking Internet material into their papers. My reaction was similar to many other professors. I wanted their work to be a reflection of *their own thinking and original ideas*, not what they could track down on the Internet and pass off as their contribution.

Now admittedly this was just my experience guarding against cheating. There are plenty of other forms that student cheating can take. For instance, in massive lecture hall courses, there is always the possibility that someone else might take an exam for a student. Or there is the rough equivalent for papers, which is buying a paper from an online company (we will come back to this when we get to the era of COVID-19). There is also data fabrication in the social and natural sciences, or faking a reason for not turning in work on time, or even sabotaging the research of a fellow classmate.[4]

There is cheating behavior, and there is what explains that behavior. In recent decades, important research has been done by psychologists which sheds light on what leads students to cheat. To explore this, let us start with one of my favorite ways of studying cheating, which is to bring people into the lab to take a test and get paid for how they perform.[5]

Researchers have come up with many clever variations of this approach. Here is one I especially like, by Lisa Shu at the London Business School.[6] The study had different groups of college students each taking the same 20 problem test. Unlike in my classes, there is a monetary incentive to perform well on the test—you will get $0.50 per correct answer. In the first group, the students take the test and then turn it in to be graded. They get paid based upon their performance. There is no opportunity to cheat. Another group does the same thing, but first they read an honor code ("I understand that this study falls under the [name of university] honor system."). A third group reads and also signs the honor code before taking the test. The following table shows how the three groups performed:[7]

No opportunity to cheat	Actual performance
No honor code	7.79 answers correct
Read honor code	7.39 answers correct
Signed honor code	7.38 answers correct

No surprise that there is not a difference between the three groups. The results do, though, helpfully give us our baseline to see how hard the test was.

Much more interesting results were found when three other groups of students are given an opportunity to cheat. They take the test, but they get to grade it themselves, destroy all their materials, and then just verbally report how they did. So while there is nothing that says that they had to cheat, the door to cheating is wide open. If they inflate their performance, they know they will get paid more and not get caught. We can call this the "recycling group" since they actually recycled their materials.

Here too, one group had no honor code, another read the honor code, and a third read and signed the honor code. The results are shown in the following table:[8]

Opportunity to cheat	Reported performance	Actual performance
No honor code	13.09 answers correct	7.61 answers correct
Read honor code	10.05 answers correct	7.23 answers correct
Signed honor code	7.91 answers correct	7.45 answers correct

Note the big difference when there was an opportunity to cheat: 7.79 versus 13.09 problems answered correctly! Or perhaps I should say, "correctly." For as we can see from their actual performance, on average they are dishonestly inflating how they did.

Also striking is the difference between 13.09 without an honor code, and 7.91 with a signed honor code. The latter is roughly the same as their actual performance; 13 out of 23 students overreported in the first group, whereas only 1 out of 22 overreported in the second.[9]

Now it is hard to come up with an explanation for why students cheat based on this one study. But fortunately, we can combine it with a host of other results to paint what is now a leading picture of what goes on when students cheat. The picture has three main elements, starting with:

> *The Cheating Desire*: Many students want to cheat in school if they think it will improve their performance on a writing assignment, exam, or other academic assessment, and they think they can get away with it and not get caught.

Naturally if the student thinks the chance of getting caught is too high, that will dampen this desire. The student might not be willing to risk failing the assessment or the course, or be suspended from school. There is also the matter of shame in the eyes of the professor, parents, and sometimes other students. Plus, cheating might simply not be worth it, even if the student knows he would likely not get caught.

But when the stars align and cheating is seen as both beneficial and anonymous, then that ramps up motivation to cheat. We see this in Shu's study—look at the difference in "performance" from the control condition to the recycling condition.

There is more to the picture than this, though. After all, if students are so willing to cheat, then how do we make sense of what happened with the honor code? Those students could have signed the honor code, and then turned around and cheated with abandon. Hence, we get a second element of the picture:

> *The Wrongness Belief*. Many students genuinely believe that cheating in school is wrong, at least in most cases.

In Shu's study, what signing the honor code does is remind the students of the wrongness of cheating, which they knew all along but which they may not have paid conscious attention to. Once that belief is made salient, though, it can work against cheating, even if cheating would be undetectable and beneficial.

Of course, this one study does not show that many students believe cheating in school is wrong. That is backed up by plenty of other data.[10] As one of the leading researchers on academic cheating notes, "There is surprising consensus among students about the morality and personal acceptability of cheating behaviors. Students at both the secondary and post-secondary levels endorse the statement that cheating is, at some level, wrong."[11]

I am struck by how significant this is. For—thank goodness!—it is *not* the case that students are typically ignorant of whether cheating is right or wrong. And—thank goodness again!—it is *not* the case that students have typically concluded somehow that cheating is okay or good. Those are the two main alternatives. Rather, just as you would expect an honest person to believe, students tend to agree that cheating in school is something that should not be done.[12]

That is the second element of the picture. But note that a puzzling feature of the results from Shu's study remains. In the recycling condition with no honor code, the participants averaged 13 out of 20 problems answered "correctly." None went all the way. Yet if they were willing to cheat already, why not go for it and just say that they got 20 problems correct to maximize their payout? Why, in other words, be half-hearted in their cheating?

The third element of the picture offers an answer:

> *The Honesty Desires*: Many students want to be able to think of themselves as honest people, and want to be thought of as honest by other people too.

Technically these are two different desires, as you could care about seeing yourself as honest but not about what other people think about your character, or vice versa. Indeed, it is not clear which of these two desires might have done most of the work in the Shu study.[13] Regardless, the point of the third element is that we care about what others think of our character, and we also care about being able to think of ourselves as good—and in this case, honest—people.[14]

When we put all these pieces together, what we do *not* see is a picture of a student who is honest. After all, an honest person would not have the *Cheating Desire* and let it motivate her to cheat in various contexts like the recycling condition. But we also do not get a picture of a student who is *dishonest* either. A dishonest person would not have the *Wrongness Belief*, which prevents him from cheating even when he can get away with it.

Rather what teachers should expect, it seems to me, is that students will tend to be a mixed bag when it comes to cheating. In some cases, they will be motivated to cheat by their *Cheating Desire*, and they will follow through on that. In other cases, they will be prevented from cheating by their *Wrongness Belief*, perhaps together with the *Honesty Desires*.

With this picture in place, we can better predict when students might be motivated to cheat even though they think it is wrong to do so. That would be very helpful to know as we ultimately think about ways to try to curb academic cheating.

One type of situation is when students do not think that what they are doing even counts as cheating in the first place. Maybe they are just ignorant of that fact. Or maybe they have rationalized to themselves that, say, their helping a friend with her homework would not really count as cheating if it is for a good reason. The upshot is that the student cheats, but if caught and accused, would deny it. Call this the *Ignorant Cheater*.[15]

Another type of situation is when students recognize that their behavior would clearly count as cheating and is wrong, but the perceived rewards are just too great, and outweigh the influence of the *Honesty Desires* and the *Wrongness Belief*. So the students go ahead with cheating. Call this the *Self-Interested Cheater*.

Yet another type of situation is where a student tries to have it both ways. He recognizes that, say, behaving this way during the test is indeed both cheating and wrong, and perhaps also in conflict with wanting to think of himself as an honest person. At the same time, he might think that he can get away with the cheating and benefit himself in the process. So he cheats *just a bit*, but not enough to have it really threaten his self-image of honesty. He might even rationalize what he is doing to himself by saying that just a bit of cheating probably isn't *that* big a deal. This, indeed, is what seems to be going on in the recycling condition, with the students fudging how they did on the test, but not being willing to lie aggressively and say they got all 20 problems correct. Call this the *Marginal Cheater*.

Finally, there is the situation where the student just does not cheat in the first place. Perhaps she does not even consider it; cheating simply holds no appeal for her in this case. Or perhaps cheating has some appeal, but that is outweighed by her conviction that cheating is wrong, her desire to think of herself as an honest person, her not wanting to get caught and punished, the benefits from cheating being modest, the importance to her of appearing honest to others such as her teacher, or some combination of the above. Call this the *Honesty Situation*.

Let us see how this all plays out more specifically in the classroom context by looking at the factors that encourage students to cheat, and how they make perfect sense given what we have just seen about the psychology of academic cheating.[16] Then we will flip things around and see what can be used to discourage student cheating.

What Encouraged Student Cheating in the Good Old Days

Anyone who has spent enough time in the classroom can probably predict the main factors which are linked with student cheating. They are pretty intuitive, but are also backed up with research evidence and make a lot of sense given the psychological picture above. I want to highlight four of them.[17]

Peer Cheating. Many researchers claim that the *number one factor* influencing whether students cheat is what they observe their peers doing. If other students are seen cheating, then the likelihood of a given student cheating goes way up.[18]

This is not surprising. Think back to when you were in school. If I saw my fellow students cheating and getting away with it, I might doubt whether it was really that big of a deal to cheat. I might also wonder whether my school really cared about honesty. If it did, the school would have done something to crack down on all the cheating.

But it gets worse. If I had seen my fellow students cheating and getting away with it, then I would also know that my chances of not getting caught are probably pretty good too. And still worse again, I would have known that they were probably going to get very good grades. I did not want to fall behind them academically.

Lack of Clarity About Plagiarism and Other Cheating. Another significant factor which can boost cheating, especially on written work, relates to the idea of the Ignorant Cheater. It is when there is insufficient clarity as to what is permissible and what is off-limits in academic work.[19] For instance, a student might plagiarize material from the Internet, and when confronted by the teacher, she could honestly say that she did not know any better. There was nothing in the syllabus or paper assignment which told her that this was off-limits.

One thing I find students really struggle with is citing their sources, even when they are completely rewriting material from those sources. Without an acknowledgment of their intellectual indebtedness to the original author, this is plagiarism, as we will see in the next section. Yet without sufficient guidance from the teacher, many students do not know any better.

Performance Mindset. If a professor puts a heavy emphasis on graded performance, then a student's main focus can become demonstrating her ability on exams and papers. Everything else about the course, including learning, is instrumentalized as a means to performing well. If cheating will help her perform better, then that can fuel her motivation to cheat so long as the risk of getting caught is low.[20]

Disinterest, Detachment, and Demandingness. A student might not be interested in the material that is being covered. This sometimes happens in required courses not in the student's major, for instance, and she might check out and just go through the motions. Sadly, for many decades philosophy used to be this very course at Wake Forest, where I teach, although we have managed to reverse this unfortunate trend. Thank goodness.

Alternatively, the material might be interesting enough, but not the professor. The professor might have checked out, not giving a damn about the students and just going through the motions himself. Students can easily pick up on this and be turned off from the class as a result. Or instead, the professor might be trying hard but end up undermining student trust and relationships by being unfair.

Then there is the perceived difficulty. The concepts in lecture might be too challenging, the readings impenetrable, the exams impossible, the teacher's standards unrealistic. This might be true just for a particular student, or for everyone in the class. All these bear on a student's perception of her own self-efficacy, and the research suggests that, "[w]hen students do not feel academically capable, they are more likely to cheat."[21]

Obviously if the student does not care about the material, the professor does not care about her, or she is struggling badly with the difficulty of the course, then why not try to make life easier by cutting some corners academically?[22]

For each of the four factors we have outlined here, we can also see what steps might be taken to try to push back against them. But first, because it is central to student cheating during both COVID-19 and our current AI era, it is worth spending a moment on one of the most pervasive forms of academic dishonesty, namely plagiarism.

An Interlude on Plagiarism

What is plagiarism? It is the presentation of someone else's work—including their words, their ideas, or their images—as if it were your own work without suitable acknowledgment.[23] Cutting and pasting text is the most obvious example. Here, for instance, is some of the text that the former president of South Carolina used in his commencement speech:

> A few last words to the graduates. Know that life is not fair, and if you're like me, you'll fail often. But if you take some risks, step up when times are toughest, face down the cowardly bullies and lift up the downtrodden, and never, never give up—if you do those things, the next generation and the generations to follow will live in a world far better than the one we have today. And what started here, today, will indeed change the world for the better.

This is word-for-word identical to what is found in a 2014 speech by retired Admiral William H. McRaven.[24] Because there is no acknowledgement, this is a clear case of plagiarism.

Altering some of the wording from a source while still conveying its main ideas also counts as plagiarism. Indeed, even if *all of the words* were different, but they are being used to communicate someone else's ideas without acknowledgment, that is plagiarism. The author is presenting someone else's work as if it were his own, without giving credit where it is due.

Strikingly, on the proposed definition if there is not suitable acknowledgement, it does not matter if the original author even *consented* to her words or ideas being used by another person. For instance, I might wholly support another philosopher, Simon, expanding upon my theory of mixed character traits, which I have developed over the years in a number of books and articles.[25] But if Simon takes my theory and runs with it in print, while never acknowledging that I am the one who came up with it in the first place, then that is plagiarizing from me. It is intellectual misrepresentation.

Note something crucially important about this way of thinking about plagiarism. It does not mention anything about *intent* on the part of the plagiarizer. As Harvard University nicely clarifies in their plagiarism policy, "Taking credit for anyone else's work is stealing, and it is unacceptable in all academic situations, whether you do it intentionally or by accident."[26]

Of course, many cases of plagiarism are intentional. The example of Simon is one such case. When one of my former Ethics students cut and pasted material from the Internet into his paper the night before it was due, that was not an accident on his part. He knew what he was doing.

Still, there can be cases of plagiarism which are more accidental. For instance, a student might paraphrase a source in her notes, fully intending to acknowledge it with a footnote when making final revisions. But then weeks later when the paper is due, she forgets that she got it from another source and so leaves out the citation. Nevertheless, someone else's work is being presented as her own without giving it proper credit.[27]

Now intent often matters a great deal when it comes to *praise and blame*. This is why students—and professors too—so often say in their defense when they are accused of plagiarism: "I didn't mean to do it—it was an accident!" They try to get off the responsibility hook for any significant discipline by convincing others that they were not doing anything wrong on purpose.

But even if the missing acknowledgement was not intentional and so blame might not be warranted, that does not by itself settle whether there was plagiarism. My friend and fellow philosopher Philip Reed makes the helpful analogy to driving over the speed limit. You are still speeding if you are going 60 mph in a 45-mph zone, *even if* you were not aware that you are. If the officer pulls you over, you might try to argue yourself out of a ticket—maybe you were rushing your loved one to the emergency room, for instance. But if you really were going 60 mph, it would be odd to try to convince the officer that you were not *speeding* in the first place.

Whether it was intentional or not, plagiarism is clearly a bad thing. One important reason is that it does not give credit to the original source. That person's work is being disrespected and their accomplishments are not suitably appreciated.

Another reason is that it generates mistaken assumptions on the part of the reader of the plagiarized material. The reader is assuming that the author is the one who came up with the material in front of her eyes. In the example, the reader naturally assumes that Simon developed mixed trait theory. She is giving credit where it is not due.

Finally, it is bad to inflate one's own accomplishments undeservedly. To the extent that presenting mixed trait theory as his discovery is a boost for Simon in some way—increasing sales of his book, enhancing his reputation in the field, fostering more invitations to do prestigious stuff—then these are ill-gotten gains. Rewards are bestowed on Simon for something he did not do, namely come up with the theory.[28]

Plagiarism is bad, and when it is done intentionally it is also *dishonest*. It is intentionally distorting the facts, in this case about being the source or creator of the work in question. An honest person would be transparent and forthcoming about when something is her own contribution and when it is drawing upon the work of others. A plagiarizer hides his sources from the eyes of his readers. That is dishonest.[29]

Working Against Student Cheating in the Good Old Days

So much for plagiarism, then. We will return to it many times both here and when discussing sermon plagiarism in the chapter on religion. We had been looking at factors which contribute to student cheating in the days prior to COVID-19. Now we can turn the tables and see what measures have shown some success in promoting *honesty* in students. For each of the four factors earlier, we will see that there is an opposing way to try to, if not eliminate cheating entirely, at least reign it in somewhat.[30] First, though, we should mention an obvious approach.

Threat of Punishment. If you want to reduce student cheating, what is the easiest thing to try? Just increase the stakes. Make it really costly to be caught cheating. Change the punishment from failure of the paper or test, to failure of the entire class. Or perhaps even more, make it suspension from the school. Ensure the punishment is well-publicized so that all the students know what to expect. Perhaps even make the guidelines come down from the administration, so that there is uniformity across classes and teachers.[31]

What should we make of this? I think we do need there to be some punitive consequences for academic dishonesty. Schools should send a strong message about where they stand. At the same time, many researchers have made the case that threats of punishment should not be the only, or even the primary, means of defense here.[32]

To what others have already said, I will add one more point. Even if a student is deterred from cheating by the prospect of punishment, that is not the same thing as actually promoting honesty in her character. Sure, it is better to not cheat than to cheat. I would take that any day. But to promote *virtue*, we saw that a person's heart needs to be in the right place as well. Fear of punishment is merely a self-interested reason for not cheating. It is not a virtuous one. So ideally we should want students to not cheat, and to do so for the right reasons.

Culture Building. The biggest influence on student cheating is what their peers are doing. So the appropriate counterbalance, it seems, is to build a culture of honesty and integrity in a school.[33]

A centerpiece of such culture building is often an honor code. As one researcher defines it, "An honor code is a community code of conduct guided by ethical principles defining the expectations for students to act with honesty and integrity and acknowledging the shared responsibility of all members."[34]

In my experience, such codes are pretty familiar in the United States, but not nearly as much in other places around the world. So some examples might help. Here, for instance, is the honor code that students at my school have to affirm:

> Wake Forest University is an academic community that subscribes to an honor system. By accepting membership in this community, each student assumes the obligation to be trustworthy in all pursuits. I pledge that I have not given or received information concerning this exam.

As another example, at the Air Force Academy cadets follow the Honor Code Oath:

> We will not lie, steal, or cheat, nor tolerate among us anyone who does. Furthermore, I resolve to do my duty and to live honorably (so help me God).[35]

Each school with a code has its own unique wording.[36]

As you can see just from these two examples, there is quite a bit of range in how to develop these codes. One component of an honor code has to do with the student's own behavior when it comes to honesty and integrity. In some cases there is another component, as with the Air Force Academy Oath, that concerns observing others taking part in academic dishonesty ("nor tolerate among us anyone who does").

As you might imagine, there is lots of controversy about this last part. Students often do not like it. To 'rat out' their friends and fellow classmates is asking an awful lot of them, and many are not willing to go there. Whether their feelings are justified or not, they are certainly understandable. Let's leave this component of an honor code aside.[37]

Is there any evidence that honor codes actually make a difference? There is a lot. We already saw the recycling study where cheating on an exam basically disappeared when students had first signed their university's honor code. I do not want to put too much weight on just that one result until the study is replicated. Given the broader replication crisis in psychology, and the fact that many studies of cheating in particular have not replicated, we should tread cautiously.

Fortunately, more recently there has been another study like Shu's. This time the students had to complete as many problems on a logic test as they could in five minutes, with the reward being $1 on a Starbucks gift card per right answer, with a max of $10. One group first committed to following their university's honor code before they began, while another group was not presented with the honor code. All participants graded their own exams without any supervision. As an extra wrinkle, in some cases there were two actors who encouraged cheating when grading the logic test, in other cases they were silent, and in still other cases these actors discouraged cheating. The results are shown in the following table:

	Percentage who cheated
No honor code, actors silent	20
Honor code, actors silent	9
No honor code, actors encouraged cheating	34
Honor code, actors encouraged cheating	23
No honor code, actors discouraged cheating	19
Honor code, actors discouraged cheating	3

Similar to Shu's results, we see a big drop-off in cheating in all three variations of the study where an honor code was used.[38]

In addition to these experimental studies, there is lots of data from students completing surveys about their cheating.[39] For instance, two of the leading researchers on honor codes, Donald McCabe from Rutgers Business School and Linda Treviño from Penn State's Smeal College of Business, found that 9% of college students said they helped another student on a test at schools with an honor code, but this number jumped to 28% at schools without an honor code. Some other differences are shown in the following table:

	With honor code	Without honor code
Plagiarism	7%	18%
Unauthorized crib notes	9%	21%
Unpermitted collaborations	21%	39%

Other studies have found similar trends.[40]

Why might honor codes make a difference? We do not know for sure, and there are probably multiple reasons. One is that they help to educate students. Schools are able to clarify what the boundaries are for permissible student behavior, and also get ahead of their attempts to rationalize any future cheating behavior.[41] Also relevant to the influence of peer cheating, studies have found that students at honor code schools see lower rates of cheating going on and take it to be less acceptable to cheat.[42]

But perhaps the central contribution honor codes can make is to serve as moral reminders. Recall we said earlier that:

> *The Wrongness Belief.* Many students genuinely believe that cheating in school is wrong, at least in most cases.

Just because they might believe this, does not mean it is something that is actively on their minds or impacting their behavior. What an honor code can do is activate a student's moral beliefs and values, which in turn can motivate her to not cheat. It can also call to mind the *Honesty Desires* and the importance to her of being able to think of herself as an honest person. When we are reminded that cheating is wrong and that we care about being honest people, it is much harder to then turn around and blatantly cheat. Finally, added on top of all this is the reminder that the student has already committed to uphold the standards of the honor code at their university, and so is expected by her community to live up to those expectations.[43]

Not surprisingly, there are better and worse ways of implementing an honor code. For some schools, it is clear that their code is just window dressing. They use it as a marketing strategy for prospective students and their parents, but it amounts to little more than virtue signaling. For others, though, it is part and parcel of their larger culture of honor and integrity.[44]

At Davidson College, for instance, first-year students take part in a ceremony during their orientation to sign their Honor Pledge, and at Vanderbilt University they go one step further by posting the signatures in the student center for the ensuing years. Haverford College involves students in modifying and re-affirming their code every academic year. When I was an undergraduate at Princeton University, we had to write out the honor code at the end of all of our written work, and then sign our name. At Wake Forest, when I give in-class exams, they have the honor code already typed on their answer books. Yet we recite it out loud together, and then my students sign it before beginning the test. They thereby publicly affirm the code in front of me and their peers. But I also publicly affirm it as well. It is not just top-down. I am committing myself and my honor too.

A good way to implement an honor code so that it is not just a façade, then, is to make sure that there are constant reminders of the code (and all that is bound up with it, including honesty, integrity, and respect) throughout the student's years at the school, starting with the very first week of orientation. Those reminders need to come from the administration, but also and perhaps more importantly from the teachers and even other fellow students who all collectively pledge their honor to uphold the value of honesty.[45]

It is crucial in such a culture that there not be hypocrisy and double standards. Students need to see that their teachers and administrators are abiding by the honor code as well. That is one thing that some students at Harvard said upset them the most about the situation surrounding Claudine Gay, the former President. For a while it looked as if she was not going to be held accountable for what seemed to be multiple instances of plagiarism. But if Harvard students had been found to do the same things, they would likely have been punished. To let Gay off the hook would have undermined whatever culture of honesty there might have been at Harvard.[46]

Clarify the Boundaries of Plagiarism and Other Cheating. Another component to building a culture of academic honesty is the importance of the teacher being very clear about what is and what is not going to count as permissible behavior when it comes to academic honesty.

Take the use of sources in writing assignments. As we saw earlier, any use of someone else's words, ideas, images, or the like needs to be acknowledged, even if it is paraphrased or rewritten by the student. This might be a high bar for students to meet. But it is the right one. By stressing the importance of respecting other peoples' work and giving credit where it is due, the teacher communicates in the process the wrongness of plagiarism and the importance of academic honesty.

Now of course not all professors will follow this approach. Some might not care as much as I do about student citations if the actual text is completely rewritten from the original source. This isn't wise, in my view, but whatever the approach is, the key point for now is to repeatedly make it clear to the students what the standards are for permissible and impermissible usage of material. That way there can't be any reasonable "I didn't realize it" defenses if a student transgresses those boundaries. And indeed, studies have found that "[s]tudents with more knowledge self-report less cheating."[47]

Mastery Mindset. Here is another tangible thing that educators have promoted for a long time to curb motivation to cheat. Earlier we talked about how a performance mindset is linked to cheating. In contrast, a mastery mindset has been linked to honesty.

With such a mindset, the ultimate focus of the student is on understanding and knowledge. As the education scholar James Lang writes, students,

> should be motivated, instead, by their interest and fascination with the subject matter or the challenge of the assessments, or by the perceived utility of the subject matter for their lives or futures, or by some other factor that drives them to learn the material more deeply from their own internal motives.[48]

Teachers who are effective at fostering such a mindset also tend to have few high-stakes grading assignments which count for a big percentage of the final grade. Instead, they develop different kinds of opportunities to let students show they understand the material, and have few opportunities for students to make comparisons between themselves. As many researchers have noted, a master mindset is linked to reduced cheating. So you can get the best of both worlds—reduced cheating and increased learning.[49]

Trust, Caring, and Respect. Finally, there is the counter to the indifference to honesty caused by having a professor who is detached and disinterested, or material that leaves students cold. The remedy is easy to identify, but hard to bring about.

It starts with caring about the material you are teaching. As Lang notes, "students are both less likely to cheat and more likely to learn when they see the course material as intrinsically fascinating, useful, or beautiful."[50] Also important is caring about the students themselves. By that I mean, caring about them as individuals worthy of respect. This is especially apt as students are experiencing an educational environment which increasingly instrumentalizes them, and where the classroom experience can seem very transactional.[51]

Some illustrations of what this care and concern might look like include meeting individually with students outside of office hours, being willing to do an independent study or supervise a student research project, going on peripatetic walks or having meals on campus or even at one's home, showing respect for the student's contributions both inside and outside of class, and being generally available in times of need (with appropriate boundaries in place, of course, in order to respect one's other professional commitments, personal responsibilities, privacy, and so forth).[52]

What relevance does this have for honesty? If a student respects her professor, and feels as if the professor values and cares for her as a person in her class, then cheating takes on a different tone. Now it is something that can damage or destroy a valued relationship. There is an emotional price to pay for cheating. This isn't to say that students wouldn't ever cheat anymore, but just that the stakes have gone up considerably in terms of what would be sacrificed in the process.

Of course this might all sound good for the teacher with small classes. Then it is much easier to get to know your students and develop personal connections with them. It is another story altogether if you are staring at 200+ anonymous faces twice a week in a huge lecture hall. Then the professor can still demonstrate that she cares about the material and about her students collectively. But there is no getting around the practical impossibility of developing a relationship with her students individually.

To sum up, no strategy for reducing cheating has been found to be flawless, and no strategy should be carried out in isolation. All of the ones above have shown some promise over the years, and there is good support for implementing them when feasible, with the ultimate goal in mind of building a culture of honesty and integrity in our schools.

At least, this was true until COVID-19 came along.

The Honesty Crisis with COVID-19

On March 11, 2020, I sent this email to my students in my philosophy course on "Virtue and Character":

> Greetings,
>
> By now I'm sure you have seen the news about classes being canceled followed by online instruction. I don't have any more details at this point than you do, but please know that I will work very hard to come up with a good plan for the rest of the semester. I will be in touch again next week with a lot more details, including clarification about how to do the readings and what online platform we will be using.
>
> Stay well, everyone, and more soon,
>
> Christian Miller

At the time, I had no idea what we were in for.

For the rest of 2020, like so many of my other colleagues, I taught on Zoom. In my classes, things actually worked fairly smoothly. Because I have always used handouts when I teach, we were able to continue to go through them on Zoom, while having robust and engaging discussions.

But in the back of my mind, I wondered about what would happen to student honesty. While I did not put it in these terms, the possibility of an honesty crisis loomed.

At the time, I was not worrying very much about an increase in dishonesty on essays and papers. I assumed that students would still be working on them at their computers like they always did, except now it would be back home instead of in their dorm room or the library. Not a big deal.

Yet with remote learning came the erosion of attachments and relationships between teachers and students. Attendance was often down, some teachers grew accustomed to looking at black boxes when students had their cameras off, and there were few informal opportunities to get to know students on a more personal level. As we already saw earlier, with increased distance and detachment comes a greater likelihood of cheating.

Unbeknownst to me, it was at this time that contract cheating really took off, which involves having a third party complete some form of graded academic work for a student, often for money. If the student is not physically present in the class (or even at the school), the teacher does not know what she looks like, and she is not (as) engaged by the material when learning remotely, why not make things easier and have someone else write the paper for a small fee?

The Internet made this very manageable. There were websites like EssayShark.com, which boasts that, "We can write any paper on any subject within the tightest deadline."[53] Paper projects could be auctioned off to third-party writers, and during the pandemic there were thousands of contract-cheating websites.

Kenya was one of the most popular hubs for contract cheaters who were willing to take on this work. There were plenty of good deals to be had by students. One study found that the going rate for a 2,000-word paper was only $11.46.[54] Yet a worker like "Collins" could make $900 to $1,200 a month writing papers, and during COVID he could count on 50 to 70 assignments per month.[55]

Contract cheating with monetary payments has been around for decades, but many studies had found a consistently low rate of participation by students, hovering around 2.5% to 3.5%.[56] That figure shot up during COVID.[57]

Again, though, papers were the least of my worries during COVID and remote learning. What were we going to do about exams? Were we really going to trust students to not look on the Internet or ask their other classmates for the answers while taking unproctored exams by themselves in their bedrooms at home?

I certainly was not. In my introduction to philosophy course, I normally give three in-class essay exams. But it would be disastrous, I thought, if I made them take-home exams. So instead I switched to all papers for this course.

I had the luxury of this flexibility with my assessments. But not all professors did. In many subjects, such as the sciences, economics, or psychology, you often do not write papers. Exams are a crucial form of assessment.

Now it is true that a professor could have had an exam proctored during remote learning. How? By paying for a remote proctoring service, where the student might be video recorded during the exam, with any suspicious web browsing or eye movements reported. In considering this at the time, I thought it might be effective to some extent, but it also struck me as crude and heavy-handed, relying on active surveillance which creates an overt atmosphere of distrust. Naturally enough, there were also privacy concerns, as well as some anecdotal evidence that remote proctoring technology encoded racial biases.[58]

Alternatively, a teacher could apply the strategies against cheating that we saw from the good old days. The teacher could try to establish personal relationships with students over Zoom. She could still be clear about her expectations for student honesty, still try to focus on mastery of the material versus mere performance, and still stress the importance of abiding by the school's honor code.

The difficulty was that, while these strategies were available even with remote learning, their impact was going to be diluted. When the professor resides in a box on a screen which students see only a couple times a week, it is hard to get to know that person or think that she really cares about them. When the Internet, text-messaging, and paper mills are so tempting, easy to access, and undetectable in their usage, it is hard to be motivated as much by an honesty pledge. And when the student is not actually present at the school and suspects that many other students are probably cheating in their bedrooms at home, it is hard to feel the force of a culture of honesty and integrity.

So, predictably, we saw student cheating soar during the remote learning period of COVID.[59] Looking at data from 19 studies, one team of researchers found that for online exams cheating increased from 29.9% to 54.7% during COVID.[60] Another study found that after COVID began, 74.8% of students reported cheating on some graded assignment, and 46% reported cheating for the first time.[61]

We had an honesty crisis on our hands. Cheating was much more tempting and easier to accomplish than it had been in the past.

This crisis lasted for about a year, and then it came to an end. Not because we discovered any new strategies aimed at addressing cheating. It was because we brought students back to the (physical) classroom. This was deemed safe enough to do, given vaccines, masks, distancing, and the like. And frankly, many schools had to do this—they needed the dollars from room and board.

Of course it was hardly business as usual. I would go an entire semester, for instance, without seeing a student's face. There were cases where, when we dropped masks, I would not recognize my previous students when our paths crossed. But at least in-person exams could resume, and the old ways of addressing cheating could be ramped up again.

So the COVID-19 honesty crisis dissipated, and I stopped worrying as much about student cheating for a little while. Then everything changed again.

The Current Honesty Crisis with AI

"It's just about crushed me. I fell in love with teaching, and I have loved my time in the classroom, but with ChatGPT, everything feels pointless." So reports an English teacher after witnessing six months of AI-based student cheating. He continues: "It has been so completely demoralizing. I have gone from *loving* my job in September of last year to deciding to completely leave it behind by April."[62]

November 30, 2022 was when AI, and specifically ChatGPT, went mainstream. It did not take long for a series of articles to come out about professors like this one who were deeply concerned about what AI was doing to student honesty. The titles tell you all you need to know:

"The First Year of AI College Ends in Ruin."[63]
"AI Bot ChatGPT Stuns Academics with Essay Writing Skills and Usability."[64]
"Professor Catches Student Cheating with ChatGPT: 'I Feel Abject Terror.'"[65]
"GPT-4 Can Already Pass Freshman Year at Harvard."[66]

As anyone who has played around with one of the newfangled AIs knows, this fear is justified. There are all kinds of things you can have an AI do, such as:

Write your entire essay.
Supply the main argument of your paper.
Supply problems with your own argument, and how to address those problems.
Organize and structure your paper.
Correct the grammar in your paper.
Rewrite an AI-produced paper so that it doesn't read like an AI-produced paper.
Locate sources and materials for you to read on the topic.

Now some of these uses seem perfectly legitimate. Asking for help tracking down sources for a paper is not obviously objectionable if the professor wants outside research to be done.

But, alas, most of these other uses constitute plagiarism, *if* the student does not cite what the origin of the material is, which in this case is just the AI itself. When the student turns in a paper written by AI without suitable acknowledgment, that is plagiarism. When the student uses her own words, but the main ideas are supplied by AI, that is plagiarism. Same thing with the objections, problems, and responses being supplied by AI.

Now you might say, how can this be plagiarism since an AI is not a person? It is not as if the student is taking material from another human being and in the process disrespecting them by not giving them credit for their work.

This is not the place to get into bigger issues about agency, personhood, and AI. Those matters are hotly contested at the moment among philosophers, computer scientists, and other AI researchers. Suffice it to say this at least—when the student submits work done by an AI without sufficient acknowledgment, then it was not *the student* who came up with the ideas or writing. It was *another source* which did the work for him, and then the student is simply passing off that work as his own. This is highly objectionable.

As I write, it is 2025, not 2022. The AI platforms have only gotten more sophisticated. Their outputs are less artificial and less easily detectable. They are fast, and many of them are free. Students know about them and are using them all the time. Indeed, a year after ChatGPT 3.0 was released, 75% of students who use AI writing tools say they would continue to use them *even if* their professor prohibited their use.[67] In one survey in the UK, more than half of undergraduates reported using AI for classwork that would be graded.[68]

And they are often not using AI in a flatfooted way, just telling it to write an entire essay and then turning it in for a grade. In a provocative article, Owen Kichizo Terry notes that instead, "it's very easy to use AI to do the lion's share of the thinking while submitting work that looks like your own." How? As he says, "have the AI walk you through the writing process step by step. You tell the algorithm what your topic is and ask for a central claim, then have it give you an outline to argue this claim. Depending on the topic, you might even be able to have it write each paragraph the outline calls for, one by one, then rewrite them yourself to make them flow better."[69]

And remember contract cheating? There is little need for that anymore. Why pay someone when you can get the same work done in a matter of seconds for free? Hence business for freelance writers in Kenya like Collins is way down. In 2023, his earnings and the number of writing assignments he took on were basically cut in half from the previous year. Quite rightly, he "now fears that the rise of AI could significantly reduce students' reliance on freelancers like him in the long term, affecting their income. Meanwhile, he depends on ChatGPT to generate . . . content."[70] Even the contract cheaters are using AI!

We are in the midst of another, far worse honesty crisis with student cheating.

What Can Be Done Now?

That is the crisis. Is there anything practical that can be done to help address it? Technology is changing so quickly in this area, and it is risky to offer any suggestions which might already be out of date by the time this book appears in print. Having said this, I will plow ahead anyway. Here are three broad approaches that teachers can take in responding to the threat of AI-induced plagiarism.[71]

Surrender. Teachers might simply surrender to AI rather than trying to fight against it. In doing so, they would stop assigning take-home work and instead make all assessments tied to the classroom in some way.[72] For instance, rather than writing a paper at home, a student might have to write a short essay during a class period. Or instead of paper assignments, there might be more of an emphasis on in-class written exams and quizzes.[73]

Yet another approach under the heading of surrender that has received some support is switching from papers to oral exams. If done in person, they are hard to cheat on, and can effectively reveal how well the student understands the material. At the same time, they are time-consuming and also unrealistic for large classes.[74]

For some disciplines in academia, surrender might work well enough. While traditional paper assignments can be a nice exercise, the same learning goals could be achieved with other forms of assessment like written or oral exams.

As a philosopher, however, there is nothing that compares to an assignment which asks students to think long and hard about a particular issue, develop their arguments, raise important challenges from critics, defend their position against those challenges, and arrive at a definitive conclusion. And I know that mine is not the only field where professors rely, for good reason, on out-of-class written assignments as their primary mode of assessment. To give up on them because of the AI honesty crisis would be a huge loss.[75]

Complete Acceptance. The opposite extreme is to welcome AI with arms wide open. Students would either be encouraged, or at least they would not be actively discouraged, from using AI on any paper assignments that they want to. They would know that there would be no disciplinary consequences for their using AI.[76]

Perhaps it would depend on the course and the professor, but for the most part, the strategy of complete acceptance strikes me as, well, completely unacceptable. For it would allow AI to write an entire paper and the student to turn that paper in, perhaps earning a good grade. That is unacceptable.

A variant of this strategy would require the student to disclose which parts of the paper were AI-generated and which were not. If they do not, there could be academic discipline. If they do, then there is no discipline.[77] But this hardly seems any better, since it would still allow for an entire AI-generated paper to be submitted for a grade.

Maybe the thing to do is to prohibit *that* amount of AI assistance, but allow the student to do everything else, provided she discloses where AI helped and did not help. Sorry, I am still not buying it. What would we be saying as teachers if we allowed AI to, say, come up with all the ideas in the paper, even though the student put them in his own words? Who would we be rewarding with an 'A' on such a paper? The AI gets an 'A' for the good ideas, and the student gets an 'A' for the good writing? Is this the kind of education that parents or the student herself should bother paying money for? Would her degree have any significance to it anymore? The answers are clearly no, in my opinion.[78]

So maybe we should restrict the use of AI even more, so that students are prohibited from using it to provide any substantive ideas at all. But then we have basically given up on accepting the use of AI, except perhaps for more mechanical tasks like grammar and suggesting references. This is no longer the acceptance approach, but rather the third and final one still to come.

As Owen Kichizo Terry has noted, "When we want students to learn how to think—something I'm sure all educators consider a top priority—assignments become essentially useless once AI gets involved."[79]

Muddling Along. Surrendering to AI and completely accepting AI both have their challenges. For the first few years after students started using AI, the most popular approach was just to continue muddling along with at-home work, while trying to push back against the possibility of AI-based plagiarism.

A more punitive approach to muddling along emphasizes detection and consequences. So long as AI-based cheating is reliably detectable, then fear of punishment can deter students from relying too heavily on AI with their paper assignments.

The obvious problem here is that such cheating is not reliably detectable. The detection software we have now is not 100% accurate, and as a result there will be false negatives (missed AI cheating) and, even worse, false positives (alleged AI cheating that wasn't). Without 100% accuracy, it is hard to see how students can be convicted of academic dishonesty by their school's honor committees.

Now apparently there could be reliable detection. Indeed, according to a report in the *Wall Street Journal*, "OpenAI has developed a tool that can reliably detect ChatGPT-generated writing but has declined to release it, the *Journal* found. An internal survey found that nearly 30% of users would use ChatGPT less if OpenAI rolled out the feature."[80] What is the likelihood that a company is going to risk losing that many users?

Plus, none of this helps when it comes to using AI to supply the main ideas of the paper, and perhaps an outline too. There isn't detection software which is going to be able to spot that. To make matters worse, there are paraphrasing and masking algorithms which will rewrite a paper so that it does not sound AI-generated.

Some professors do not rely on detection software, and just trust their own skills of detection. They claim to be able to recognize the artificial, stilted writing of an AI. Plus there will be times when the content of the paper does not match the content of the course, which immediately looks suspicious.

This is seriously flawed as an approach too. It will let a lot of AI-based cheating slip past. As we already noted, studies have found that professors are no better than chance at being able to detect AI-generated content.[81] As the years go by and AIs get more and more sophisticated, things will only get worse.

Even if a teacher is rightly suspicious, what can she really do about it? She can meet individually with the student, voice her suspicion, and hope to get a confession. That sometimes works. But any halfway clever student who did in fact use AI in a prohibited way would just dig in his heals at that point and deny that he did. What can the professor do then? There is no conclusive evidence, and taking it to the honor committee for a trial will just result in wasting a lot of people's time.

None of this, by the way, should be taken to suggest that there should not be punishment for AI-based plagiarism. Nor am I implying that teachers should not try to catch it when it happens. The point is that detection will only take you so far.[82]

Alongside detection should be prevention. Ideally there would be nothing to detect since AI-based plagiarism would be prevented from occurring in the first place. Since that is completely unrealistic, instead the goal should be to keep rates of such plagiarism as low as possible.

Here we could return to all the strategies we saw earlier that were used in the good old days to try to mitigate cheating. Back then, there was still the danger of outside sources being used to supply material for a paper without suitable acknowledgement, such as consulting articles on the Internet. Now the outside source happens to be much faster and more helpful than a Google search ever was.

So there would be a renewed emphasis on building a culture of honor, complete with a robust honor code. Mastery rather than performance would be the goal. The professor would still aim to build relationships with individual students. And, crucially, every paper assignment would be maximally clear about both (i) what the boundaries are for unacceptable use of AI, and (ii) what the punishment will be for transgressing those boundaries.

It is hard to object to any of this. If those strategies worked in the good old days, it seems to me that they will still be helpful today. The worry, though, is that they are not enough. What teachers are working against is so much easier and tempting to use than what was available to students in the past. An AI can, in a matter of seconds, do the thinking needed for the student to get at least a decent grade on the paper, with little concern about detection. Indeed, a student at Harvard asked seven professors and teaching assistants to grade an essay for a major assignment in the student's respective classes, essays which they would not know in advance whether they were AI-generated or not. The AI papers all got As and Bs.[83]

Are honor codes and relatable professors really going to be enough to counteract the temptation to offload the work onto AI? It is at this point that I have to confess a feeling of hopelessness. Certainly, for large, more impersonal classes of, say, 40+ students, assigning any graded work to be completed at home just invites AI-use in completing the work, no matter what steps are taken to discourage such use. Even if a given student might have some personal qualms about going down this path, she also will know that if she does not, she will be at a disadvantage relative to her peers in the class. But even in smaller classes, such as more advanced courses for majors or even graduate seminars, I am doubtful that much can be done to stem the tide.

To be sure, some clever strategies have been developed to try. For instance, students can be required to submit their papers as Google Docs, so that the professor can look over the history of edits that were made to the paper. If a segment of text was suddenly pasted into the document, that suggests it came from an outside source, which could lead to follow-up conversations with the student about what happened. But many students will not be this brazen, and will add material from AI into a Google Doc more slowly and carefully.

Another strategy is to tailor the paper assignment extremely specifically to the course material. Perhaps the student's paper needs to engage with material from the daily handouts, or it needs to combine material from multiple course readings. If AI is used to do these tasks, it might be easy to catch by the professor, provided its outputs do not fit with what was actually covered in class. Nevertheless, in this case, the handouts can be uploaded to an AI, which can also integrate material across course readings. It is a mistake to underestimate the newest AI's capabilities.

The philosopher Casey Landers, among others, has supported using in-class writing assignments as a check on at-home writing: "Students turn in small writing assignments that they have written in class without any use of technology . . . If a student turns in a final paper with a different writing style or quality at the end of the semester, this may be strong evidence that the work is not authentically their own."[84] I know a number of academics are using this approach. I worry, though, why an AI can't make the writing style resemble the in-class writing. And even if there are grounds for suspicion about the final paper, nothing can be done if the student is firm in claiming it was their own work.

Finally, not as an alternative to any of the above but as a potential addition, multiple low-stakes papers which are short and on engaging topics could disincentivize students from relying on AI. Such assignments have been recommended long before AI came along, in particular because they fit well with a mastery mindset rather than a performance one.[85] They can be tailored closely to course material, and in virtue of being short and easy to complete, there is less concern of cutting corners for students with little time or stamina or motivation for larger projects. This indeed might help, but even if they are short and low stakes, when you believe that your peers are getting help from AI and it would only take a few seconds for you to as well, the temptation will still be strong to do so.

No doubt there are other promising strategies out there, and clever new ones will be developed going forward. So, I hope my pessimism is ill-founded in the long run. But for now the path of surrender may be the best one to take.

We began this chapter with a philosopher reporting that she is pushing 200 cases of AI-based cheating in her class. She, like most teachers today, has had to confront this new honesty crisis in education. Yet I fear that unlike with COVID-19, this one is not going away anytime soon.

Notes

1. Davis 2023.
2. See Klein et al. 2007, McCabe et al. 2006, and Rokovski and Levy 2007, respectively.
3. See, for example, Kreps et al. 2022 and Scarfe et al. 2024.

4. For similar examples, see Tatum and Schwartz 2017.
5. For a review of a lot of these studies, see Miller 2021a: 214–222.
6. Shu et al. 2011.
7. Ibid., 341.
8. Ibid.
9. Ibid., 342.
10. See, for example, Rettinger 2017: 104, Stephens 2017, and Waltzer and Dahl 2022, 2023.
11. Rettinger 2017: 104.
12. Granted, they may make some exceptions to this. For instance, a student might say that helping a friend with her homework, even when that is prohibited by the professor, is okay if the friend is going through a personal emergency.
13. It could have been that the students were worried that if they answered with "20 problems," that would arouse suspicion. Or it could have been that they did not think anyone else would become suspicious, but they just had a hard time thinking of themselves as honest people if they lied this badly. Or maybe it was a bit of both. For a study trying to separate the impact of these two desires in the context of cheating, see Yaniv et al. 2019.
14. For a few among many researchers who appeal to one or both of these desires, see Mazar et al. 2008, Young et al. 2012, Bryan et al. 2013, and Gerlach et al. 2019.
15. A recent study found that about half of students who had actually cheated said that they did not think what they were doing actually counted as cheating at the time. For a group of engineering students, this percentage rose all the way to 79% (Waltzer and Dahl 2023: 140, 143).
16. I should stress that these four options are certainly not the only way that the psychology of student cheating can work. For instance, we already mentioned in an earlier footnote that sometimes a student will think that cheating is wrong in general, but not in a particular instance when it would involve helping a friend going through a really tough time. Plus, there are individual difference—not all students will think cheating is wrong in the first place.
17. For a comprehensive presentation of these and many other factors, see Goldman et al. 2022.
18. For relevant research, see Lang 2013: 50–53 as well as Tatum and Schwartz 2017: 131 and Tatum 2022: 37.
19. For discussion and relevant research, see Tatum and Schwartz 2017, Stephens 2017, Tatum 2022, and Waltzer and Dahl 2022, 2023.
20. For further discussion and studies, see Anderman and Koenka 2017, Miller et al. 2017, and Anderman et al. 2022.
21. Anderman et al. 2022: 77. For much more on self-efficacy and cheating, see Lang 2013: 47–50, chapter 7, Onu et al. 2021, and Anderman et al. 2022.
22. This is what research has confirmed does in fact happen. In one study, for instance, dislike of the professor was the third leading reason given by students

for cheating (Tatum 2022: 39). In another, roughly 25% of students admitted they would cheat with an unfair professor (Graham et al. 1994). For more studies and additional discussion of these various factors, see Rettinger 2017, Anderman and Koenka 2017, Stephens 2017, and Tatum 2022.

23. My thinking about plagiarism in this section has been helped by Reed 2024. For a similar definition, see Waltzer and Dahl 2023: 131.
24. Morales 2021.
25. Miller 2013, 2014.
26. https://usingsources.fas.harvard.edu/what-constitutes-plagiarism-0, accessed on July 15, 2025.
27. Reed 2024 makes a similar point.
28. These three reasons are also developed by Reed 2024.
29. None of the above is meant to deny that *figuring out* whether plagiarism has been committed (whether intentionally or not) can sometimes be a difficult matter. This point is emphasized by Lang 2015.
30. For an overview of these strategies and others, see Goldman et al. 2022.
31. Tatum 2022: 40. For some research which suggests that harsher penalties for cheating might actually make the situation worse, see Lang 2013: 207.
32. See, for example, Lang 2013: chapter 10 and Tatum and Schwartz 2017: 132.
33. For discussion, see Stephens 2017 and Miller et al. 2017.
34. Tatum 2022: 33.
35. Available at https://www.usafa.edu/about/honor/, accessed on July 15, 2025.
36. For the range of different formulations of honor codes, see Tatum 2022.
37. For more concerns and data about this component, see Lang 2013: 169–170.
38. Malesky et al. 2022. For yet another study, this time involving honor codes and cheating on homework assignments in a real course, see Bing et al. 2012.
39. The remainder of this paragraph is adapted from Miller 2017b: 132, with permission from Oxford University Press.
40. For the data reported in the text, see McCabe et al. 2001: 224. For additional studies, see McCabe and Treviño 1993, McCabe et al 2001, and Thorkildsen et al. 2007.
41. See Tatum and Schwartz 2017: 132, Miller et al. 2017: 126, and Tatum 2022: 36.
42. Tatum and Schwartz 2017: 132 and Tatum 2022: 37.
43. For more discussion, see Stephens 2017 and Tatum 2022.
44. As Tatum notes, "Attending a school with an honor code is associated with reduced cheating, but only when the honor code is embedded in the culture of the school . . . This means that the mere existence of an honor code will not necessarily reduce academic misconduct" (Tatum 2022: 34).
45. See also Lang 2013: 172.
46. For much more on honor codes and cheating, see Lang 2013: chapter 8.
47. Tatum 2022: 36. See also Tatum and Schwartz 2017: 130–131, Miller et al. 2017: 126, and Waltzer and Dahl 2022: 110–113.

48. Lang 2013: 40.
49. For much more on mastery mindsets and their relationship to reduced cheating, see Lang 2013. See also Anderman and Koenka 2017, Miller et al. 2017, and Anderman et al. 2022.
50. Lang 2013: 152. See also Anderman et al. 2022: 80.
51. Some of the material here and in the next paragraph borrows from Miller et al. forthcoming, with permission from *Faith and Philosophy*.
52. Due to limitations of space, I do not talk about how to improve self-efficacy here, which is a huge topic. For a good starting place, see Lang 2013: 47–50, chapter 7 and Anderman et al. 2022.
53. https://essayshark.company/, accessed on July 15, 2025.
54. Lancaster 2022: 50.
55. Siele 2023.
56. For an overview of past studies, see Curtis 2022.
57. Hobbs 2021. Similarly, there is evidence that plagiarism increased as well. See, for example, Eshet 2023.
58. This paragraph draws on Miller 2020, with permission from *The New York Times*. For a review and citations to relevant research, see Susnjak 2022.
59. For citations and relevant discussion, see Bilen and Matros 2021, Susnjak 2022, and Curtis 2022: 33–34. For a popular level overview, see Dey 2021.

    There is over 15 years of research comparing in-person versus online assessments, prior to COVID. For two reviews of the existing research finding higher academic dishonesty online, see Garg and Goel 2022 and Noorbehbahani et al. 2022. For an interesting study which did not find increased online cheating by comparing in-class exam performance during the first half of the spring of 2020 with take-home exam performance in the second half, see Chan and Ahn 2023.
60. Newton and Essex 2023.
61. Jenkins et al. 2023.
62. Bogost 2023, emphasis in original.
63. Ibid.
64. Hern 2022.
65. Mitchell 2022.
66. Bodnick 2023.
67. Tyton Partners 2023.
68. Adams 2024.
69. Terry 2023.
70. Siele 2023.
71. And of course we can just ask an AI for help too! That is what was done in an article by Cotton et al. (2024), the first six pages of which were completely generated by ChatGPT.
72. This is recommended by Terry 2023.

73. See Landers forthcoming: 8–9.
74. For a nice story on AI cheating and oral exams, see Belkin 2023. See also Landers forthcoming: 9.
75. For other philosophers expressing the same sentiment, see Davis 2023 and remarks by Darren Hick in Horowitch 2023.
76. For helpful discussion of this strategy and its many problems, see Landers forthcoming: 10–11.
77. This approach is suggested by Muir 2023.
78. As Tricia Bertram Gallant, one of the leading scholars of student honesty notes, "If a degree no longer designates legitimate academic achievement it will cease to hold value . . . . 'We're at the real risk of becoming diploma mills' " (Belkin 2023).
79. Terry 2023. See also Wallbank 2023.
80. Barnum and Seetharaman 2025.
81. Kreps et al. 2022 and Scarfe et al. 2024.
82. For related discussion, see Landers forthcoming.
83. Bodnick 2023.
84. Landers forthcoming: 7.
85. See Landers forthcoming: 12–14.

6

Fake News and the Honesty Crisis in Politics

The most obvious place to look in America for an honesty crisis today is politics. Or so I bet you are thinking. Dishonesty abounds among our elected representatives in America, or so it can seem.

But remember that for there to be an *honesty crisis*, there needs to be an increased level of dishonesty both because it is more tempting than it was before and because it is easier to not get caught than it was before. Has there *really* been an honesty crisis in politics in the last, say, 20 years? Are politicians actually lying, misleading, BSing, and cheating a lot more than they were in, say, the 1970s or the 1980s?

I do not know. I am not sure that anyone does.

Fortunately, for the purpose of this chapter we do not need to know. Because I do not want to focus here on politicians anyway. Why not? Because that makes it too easy for us to detach ourselves in a discussion of dishonesty and just think about what is going on with *those people over there* in city hall or the state capital or Washington, DC.

Instead, I want to keep the focus squarely on *us*. Does dishonesty abound among you and I, ordinary citizens that we are, when it comes to political matters? And for there to be an *honesty crisis*, have the temptations and opportunities to be dishonest in this area of our lives increased in recent decades?

The answer, I think, is surprising.

The Honesty Crisis. Christian B. Miller, Oxford University Press. © Oxford University Press 2026.
DOI: 10.1093/9780197840801.003.0006

Our Political Honesty Crisis

Now wait, you might say. What could be more obvious than that we are in the midst of an honesty crisis today? After all, a sizable percentage of the American people thinks that the 2020 US election was invalid, and that Donald Trump should have been the rightful winner. In 2023, 69% of Republicans were doubtful about the legitimacy of the 2020 results, and 39% claimed that there is solid evidence to back up their skepticism.[1] To them, President Biden and his supporters were being dishonest in claiming that he had won. And of course it goes in the other direction—many think that Trump and his supporters were dishonest themselves in claiming the election was stolen. Surely at least one of the sides here is being dishonest, right?

Or take climate change. A sizable percentage of the American population is not moved by what, for the other side, is seemingly overwhelming evidence for climate change. Surely the deniers are being dishonest, right? Or maybe it is the other way around? Perhaps believers in climate change are being dishonest, and it is the skeptics who are the honest ones.

Or take the many political debates that have swirled around COVID-19, such as the origin of the virus. One side has claimed that the virus arose naturally, while the other side holds that it leaked from a lab in Wuhan, China. In 2024, a House of Representatives Select Subcommittee on the Coronavirus Pandemic released a 520-page report that sided with the lab-leak hypothesis. But it was criticized by Democrats on the panel who released their counter-report.[2] Millions of Americans are divided on this issue.

With political divides like these, it is common to condemn the other side as 'dishonest.' They are a bunch of liars. Or BSers. Or deceivers. Do not trust anything they say.

Sometimes these labels are perfectly appropriate. I do not mean to deny this. But here is the surprising part. Sometimes we think a group of people holds downright indefensible views, and yet whatever their faults are, dishonesty is not one of them. Let me illustrate with two extreme cases, and then return to election denial.[3]

As an initial example, consider the handful of people today who seem to sincerely hold that the Earth is flat. There is even a Flat Earth Society which has convoluted explanations to try to take care of the scientific evidence against them.[4] Are members of a group like this being less than honest when they are espousing their beliefs? Let's consider an imaginary case of Samantha:

> *Samantha and the Flat Earth.* As a member of the Flat Earth Society, Samantha sincerely believes that the Earth is flat. One day she is asked by a friend about the shape of the Earth, and she responds forthrightly that she believes the Earth is flat. In saying this, she has no intention to deceive her friend at all.

What is your reaction to this case? Mine is that there is no failure of honesty on Samantha's part when she responds to her friend's question. Communicating this badly mistaken belief is compatible with honesty.

Now suppose we change the case as follows:

> *Samantha and the Flat Earth Part Two*: One day Samantha is asked by a friend about the shape of the Earth, and to keep her own beliefs a secret, Samantha tries to deceive her friend and replies that the Earth is round. She succeeds and her friend now assumes that Samantha believes the Earth is round.

Here it seems clear to me that, even though her statement is now true, Samantha is being dishonest.[5]

Hence as a reminder of what we said in the first chapter, being wrong is compatible with being honest. It is possible in cases like Samantha's for someone who makes true scientific claims to be far less honest in her communicating, than someone who has radically mistaken scientific beliefs.

To be sure, this is *not* to let Samantha off the hook. She may be suffering from other serious character flaws, such as failures of open-mindedness, curiosity, understanding, and wisdom. But dishonesty is not one of them, at least in the first case when she tells her friend that the Earth is flat.

The same conclusion holds in the case of extremist religious views. It is possible for there to be genuine believers of such views who are not being dishonest in their communication with others. Consider another imaginary case:

> *The Cult*. James has been raised in a cult to believe that the world is ending in ten days, and because of his very sheltered upbringing, he is blameless for thinking this. Suppose he tells people he knows that the world is going to end in ten days.

Here too I say that James, even despite his untenable views, is not being dishonest in talking to these people. But if he had replied and said the world is ending in one day, when he thinks it will not be ending for ten more days, he would thereby be falling short of honesty.

A pattern is starting to emerge here, which should remind you of what we said about honesty in Chapter 1. Honest behavior, the kind of behavior that stems from the virtue of honesty, is behavior that does not intentionally distort the facts as the person sees them. If you misrepresent the facts on purpose, that impugns your honesty. If you just get the facts wrong but genuinely represent them in your communication to others as you see them, then that by itself does not impugn your honesty.

Now let's return to the election denial example we have already seen, but this time use a historically vague description of the case:

> *Committed Supporter*. Ron is a committed supporter of a presidential candidate in the US election. He has attended rallies and donated to his campaign. After the last election, Ron comes to sincerely believe that the results in states like Michigan and Wisconsin were fraudulent, and that his candidate actually won the election. When asked about the election, he says, "My candidate really won by a wide margin, but the election was stolen from him."

Now this example might make you think of events surrounding Donald Trump and the 2020 election. But note that some supporters of Kamala Harris have alleged that there was election fraud in Michigan and Wisconsin in the 2024 presidential election. So this example is intentionally vague to fit candidates on both side of the aisle and not let feelings about Trump or Harris distract from the points which follow.

What should we say about Ron in this example? I think we can say that Ron is acting honestly. We can say this, *even if* we also suppose that there is no good evidence to support his claim that the election was rigged. Again, that does not automatically get Ron off the hook. His not being dishonest in what he says is compatible with Ron also having other character flaws in this area of his life.

"But wait a minute, Miller," someone might say. "What about the *leaders* who were responsible for coming up with the mistaken views in the first place?"

I agree that here things are different. These leaders could be lying, by communicating what they believe to be false, with the intention to deceive their audience. Or they could be BSing by lacking a concern for the truth in the first place. The BSer is making things up to suit his wants and desires, regardless of whether they are true. Or, in some cases, the leaders could be honest themselves, if they sincerely believe what it is they are expressing.

If lying or BSing is going on by certain leaders, then we would have a clear failure of honesty. But that failure does not have to transfer down to their followers, even if the lie or the BS itself does.[6] To illustrate, suppose that Ron's candidate was BSing about the results of the election. Then he would have produced a piece of BS about the election results being fraudulent which was transmitted, by him and other leaders of his group, to his followers. Many of his followers in turn came to believe that the piece of BS was true.

But just because these followers stepped into a pile of BS, so to speak, does not have to make *them* BSers as well. You can be an honest person and come to believe other people's BS, because you trust them to be telling you the truth, without realizing that you are actually being fed BS instead. The dishonesty here tracks the original making and communicating of the BS. It does not have to also track the stepping into it as well.

Of course, if you recognize that you are being BSed to, and come to believe the information anyway because you do not care where it is coming from, then that is a different story. If you turn around and feed it to others without being transparent about what you are doing, then you are being a dishonest conveyor of BS yourself.

The same observations here apply to lying as well. Suppose the leader of the Flat Earth Society actually believes that the Earth is round, but communicates that it is flat to other people in his organization. His lies are thereby transmitted to members of the Society, but that does not make those people liars. You can be an honest person and sincerely believe other people's lies, without recognizing that they are lies.

So the upshot is that we should be very cautious about how we label members of groups we do not agree with by calling them 'dishonest' and wielding accusations of lying and BSing. Indeed, it could be that *we* are the ones who are BSing ourselves if we do not have any good reason for thinking that they are lying or BSing. We are just making up stuff about what they are doing, without having solid evidence to back up our claims. After all, determining whether someone else is lying as opposed to BSing or even genuinely believing something is often very hard to do. Humility is needed here and should be our default course of action.[7]

Bizarre as it might seem, sometimes when we accuse others of being dishonest, it can turn out that we are less honest than they are, even when they are the ones who are mistaken.

Going a Bit Deeper

I can imagine someone getting agitated at this point and declaring:

> "Miller, your discussion is much too simplistic! Sure, in your example there might have been a lot of supporters of the failed presidential candidate like Ron who, when you ask them, will be honest in telling you

> about their beliefs. I am happy to agree that they are being perfectly honest in communicating to you that they think the election was stolen. But *that's* not where their dishonesty resides. Their dishonesty is in how they ever came to think such a thing in the first place. In order to believe the election was stolen, they had to ignore tons of evidence to the contrary and deceive themselves so they could somehow believe what they wanted to believe was true (even if it was not). Surely self-deception like *that* is a dishonest thing to do."

This person is onto something here. Without a doubt there is a type of voter whose reasoning takes this form. And if so, then it is dishonest.

Let us take this challenge seriously and go a little slower. Start with an example that does not have to do with politics:[8]

> *The Affair*. Suppose Andrew had always assumed that his wife was being faithful. But one day a friend reports that he observed Andrew's wife meeting a man at a seedy motel room. Andrew also notices that his wife starts being absent from the house for hours at a time. Her clothes start smelling like men's cologne, and there are texts on her phone to schedule future visits to the motel. Nevertheless, Andrew comes to form the belief that his wife is still being faithful to him.

With just these details before us, it is fairly clear that Andrew is suffering from self-deception about his wife's faithfulness. It is also fairly clear that he is not being honest with himself.

Why is he not being honest? By not forming his beliefs in a way that is properly responsive to the evidence that is available to him, Andrew is intentionally distorting the facts as he sees them. He wants to believe his wife is faithful, and so that leads him to misrepresent the evidence. This is a case of *intellectual* dishonesty.

Note that Andrew's friend might ask him a few weeks later if Andrew still thinks that his wife is being honest, and Andrew could (honestly!) reply with "Yes." After all, he does genuinely believe this. The dishonesty is not in his telling others what he believes. The dishonesty is found in his believing it in the first place.

The application to Ron's support for the presidential candidate should be straightforward. Ron could genuinely believe and report to others his belief that the election was stolen. No dishonesty need be present there. But given that Ron wanted to believe that his candidate had won, he was prepared to ignore contrary evidence that he was seeing in the news in order to get himself to believe what he wanted to believe.

This is self-deception, an endlessly complex and fascinating phenomenon that has inspired researchers for decades. There is no one way that self-deception works. For instance, someone could engage in any of the following:[9]

> *Negative Misinterpretation*. Ron's wanting to believe that his candidate genuinely won the election may lead him to misinterpret data as not counting (or not counting as strongly) against a rigged election when it really does count against a rigged election. If he didn't have this desire, he would easily recognize that the data counts (or counts more strongly) against a rigged election.
>
> *Positive Misinterpretation*. Ron's wanting to believe that his candidate genuinely won the election may lead him to interpret data as evidence supporting a rigged election when it does not support a rigged election. If he didn't have this desire, he would easily recognize that the data does not support a rigged election.
>
> *Selective Focusing/Attending*. Ron's wanting to believe that his candidate genuinely won the election may lead him to fail to focus attention on evidence that counts against a rigged election and to focus instead on evidence suggestive of a rigged election.
>
> *Selective Evidence-Gathering*. Ron's wanting to believe that his candidate genuinely won the election may lead him both to overlook easily obtainable evidence for a fair election and to find evidence for a rigged election that is much less accessible.

These different ways to deceive oneself about the election could be at work in different supporters of this candidate (or in the same supporter!). People who are self-deceived do not have to be dishonest with themselves in the same way.

So, the challenge raised at the start of this section has a point. If lots of supporters deceived themselves in any of these ways about this election, then there would be rampant dishonesty after all.

But consider another type of supporter for this same failed presidential candidate. For these folks, when you ask about whether they thought the election was fair, they say "It was stolen." Yet in saying this, they are being *dishonest*. More specifically, they are lying, since they secretly do not believe at all that it was stolen.

Why say it was stolen, then? Because of in-group pressures. Embedded in their political culture, they know that this is what you are *supposed* to say. So, they intentionally distort the facts about their own beliefs to keep up appearances. They reap the benefits of social conformity and preserve their reputation in the process. This is clearly dishonest.

Now we have two possibilities where dishonesty has emerged, albeit in different ways:

> A supporter saying the election was stolen and genuinely believing that it was stolen, because he formed the belief via self-deception. The self-deception is the source of the dishonesty.

> A supporter saying the election was stolen but lying in the process because he does not genuinely believe this. The lying is the source of the dishonesty.

We should not leave things here, though. For there is a *third possibility* which, I suspect, could better capture the psychology of some people who would deny an election, and which does not involve dishonesty *either* in the formation of the belief in a stolen election or in their reporting that they believe it was stolen. How could that be?

According to this third possibility, some of the failed candidate's supporters formed a belief in a stolen election, and did so on the basis of what they took to be *genuine evidence* coming from sources which they trusted. They did not have to deceive themselves, since from their perspective the preponderance of evidence favored thinking that the election was stolen.

For instance, online articles or television programming coming from sympathetic sources might have been enough to convince them that their candidate had really won. They trusted these sources, and so believed accordingly. Or it may have been that these supporters formed their belief simply on the basis of testimony from the candidate himself and other leaders in his party. The leaders told people that the election was stolen, and so that is what their supporters came to believe. End of story.

If so, is any of this dishonest? Not as far as I can see. It is not dishonest to trust the testimony of a political leader you align yourself with. There could be flaws and mistakes on display in choosing to align oneself with a Trump or Biden or Bush or Obama or Clinton or Reagan—take your pick. But *once* you are aligned with that person, then taking what the leader says as an important basis for forming beliefs about the political world does not seem dishonest to me. The same applies to news sources as well, whether it is FOX News on one end of the spectrum or MSNBC on the other. It might be problematic to trust certain sources in the first place, but given that one does trust them, it is not dishonest to form beliefs on the basis of what they are reporting.

With this said, we now have three possible ways for thinking about what might be going on in our election example:

> A supporter saying the election was stolen and genuinely believing that it was stolen, because he formed the belief via self-deception. The self-deception is the source of dishonesty.

> A supporter saying the election was stolen but lying in the process because he does not genuinely believe this. The lying is the source of dishonesty.

> A supporter saying the election was stolen and genuinely believing that it was stolen, because he formed the belief on the basis of sources of evidence which he trusted. None of this needs to be a source of dishonesty.

Remember, our election example was fictional. But the points here generalize broadly to debates about actual elections, or climate change, or COVID-19. It was helpful after all to be alerted to the first type of person who might participate in those debates. The second type is psychologically possible, but I suspect is also uncommon. What I want to suggest is that the third type exists too, and while it is just speculation on my part, it likely reflects a significant number of people. Of the three, it is the one that does not involve dishonesty.[10]

It is worth asking our question again. Where is an honesty crisis in contemporary politics? I have been suggesting that dishonesty might be *less* common than you might think. Have I lost the script?

Fake News

Not yet. It is just taking a bit to get to the main plot line. At this point, let's consider fake news.

If we look back to the central examples used at the start of this chapter—2020 election denial, climate change, and COVID-19—these are three topics where you regularly see people making accusations of fake news. But as a label, 'fake news' really took hold in the 2016 election when then Republican candidate Donald Trump used it to criticize the media. Interestingly, that year on Facebook the 20 leading fake election stories had more uptake, in the form of shares and reactions, than did the 20 leading real stories. Indeed, in the three months before the election in 2016, "156 misleading news stories got just under 38 million shares on Facebook."[11] No surprise then that the concept of fake news started to gain a lot of traction.

How would you define this concept? According to perhaps the most widely cited definition, fake news is "fabricated information that mimics news media content in form but not in organizational process or intent."[12] More simply, I would define 'fake news' as any news story that is fabricated and yet is being presented as if it were coming from a reputable or reliable news source. That news source itself might be highly reliable in general, or it might be notoriously unreliable. That by itself does not matter. Similarly, the news source could be hyper-partisan or it could be avowedly neutral. That also by itself does not matter. What matters is the nature of the story—how it was put together and how it was packaged.

As an example, what has been called the "most well-known 'fake news' story of 2016" had this headline:

> Pope Francis Shocks World, Endorses Donald Trump for President.

It was mainly found on a hyper-partisan website, "Ending the Fed," and received a great deal of engagement on Facebook.[13] But even if it had appeared on a more neutral website, that would not have changed its counting as fake news.

It is crucial that fake news be—in fact—fake. The central claim of the story has to be false. The Pope Francis headline certainly meets this criterion for fake news. But if somehow the 2020 election really were stolen, then it cannot count as fake news to have a story appearing claiming that it was stolen.

It might seem obvious that fake news has to be false news. But consider this example from the Cambridge psychologist Sander van der Linden. In the midst of COVID in 2021, the *Chicago Tribute* published a story with the headline: "A Healthy Doctor Died Two Weeks After Getting a COVID-19 Vaccine." Now technically speaking this headline is true. But it is also dishonest because it is misleading—it seems to be trying to get the reader to draw the implication that it was *because of the vaccine* that the doctor died. Yet there was no evidence for *that* conclusion. Nevertheless, this story went viral, with over 50 million views on Facebook.[14]

Should we say that this is a case of 'fake news'? Well, people have different definitions of the expression, and it has only been around for a few years. I am not sure it makes sense to insist on there being only one right way to define it. So I will just declare that, again, fake news has to be fake. The key is that the content of the piece of news (or even just the headline) has to be false itself, regardless of what implications people might draw from it. So I will not be including true but misleading stories under the heading of fake news, and hence will not be equating fake news with dishonest news.

There is more to say here. After all, just calling any piece of information 'fake news' which is false, no matter where it came from, is too broad. I could make up a bunch of bogus stuff and post it on Facebook or a personal blog. That does not make it fake news. False information in general goes by the heading of 'misinformation.' Fake news is a specific *type* of misinformation that *also* has to be presented as if it were coming from a legitimate news source, even though its content is fabricated or not truthful. My posting something on Facebook does not make it appear to come from a legitimate news source.

Now does the news source for a piece of fake news have to be *aware* that it is fake when it publishes or distributes that story? Or can they be blamelessly ignorant in making a mistake, but still have one of their stories count as fake news anyway? As a simple example, consider:

> *MLK Bust*. In early 2017, as Donald Trump was at the very beginning of his first term, TIME White House correspondent Zeke Miller reported that the bust of Martin Luther King Jr. had been taken out of the Oval Office. In fact, it was still there, and Miller had just not seen it. He issued a correction later that day and apologized profusely for what he claims was an innocent mistake.[15]

Was Miller's initial report fake news?

Again, I will just stipulate and say that cases like this do not get to count as fake news. Innocent mistakes are one thing. Deliberate fabrications or distortions are another, and they are what count in my mind as fake news. At the same time, it may be that the fabrication was just done by a lone journalist, without the knowledge of the rest of the staff at the news outlet. So long as there was someone involved in the deliberate fabrication, that is enough, even if the rest of the group was blamelessly ignorant.

Finally, and crucially, fake news is an objective matter. In other words, a news story could be fake news and very effective at fooling people. So effective, in fact, that it could have major implications for election outcomes, public health, or the results of wars. Fake news does not always wear its fakeness on its sleeve.

Given that fake news is not automatically recognized to be fake news, someone could be perfectly honest in coming to believe it. That is no doubt what happened to some people in 2016 when they initially saw the headline about Pope Francis endorsing Donald Trump. Much more disturbing was the impact of an alleged news article on Facebook and elsewhere with the headline: "Pizzagate: How 4Chan Uncovered the Sick World of Washington's Occult Elite." The allegation was that a D.C. pizza restaurant was a cover for a child abuse operation led by Hillary Clinton, and #pizzagate because a viral conspiracy theory.[16] Yet however awful these fake news stories might be, I do not think that when people trusted them and formed their beliefs on the basis of them, that automatically detracted from their honesty at the time.

Those are some thoughts on what fake news is. With this background in place, we can get closer to finding the source of an honesty crisis in politics.

Fake News and Sharing Misinformation

Let us return to the discussion of the failed political candidate. Suppose the election was not stolen, but news reports in some outlets suggested that it was. This had the effect of impacting the beliefs of the candidate's supporters and led some of them to think it was stolen. As we said earlier, by itself this need not be a failure of honesty on their part.

Things would be different if they had *recognized* that the reports coming from their trusted new sources were fake news, but nevertheless believed the election was stolen anyway because that aligned with their partisan desires (they wanted their candidate to win, after all, and did not want to confront the prospect of defeat at the hands of the opponent). This corresponds to the first type of supporter we saw earlier, the one we described as self-deceived.

Research on the psychology of fake news suggests that partisan desires definitely do play a role in whether someone believes a piece of fake news or not. If the news content happens to align with our political views, then we are more likely to believe it. If not, then we are less likely to believe it.

Other factors have also been found to play a role in influencing belief in fake news stories. For instance, the mere fact that the story is being repeated more than once makes a difference—this is the 'illusory truth effect' at work in the case of fake news and social media, and holds even for outlandishly fake stories and stories that have been fact-checked as false.[17] The source of the news matters too, as well as the extent to which the user engages in analytical thinking,[18] and how emotionally charged the particular story is (say by evoking in readers moral outrage).[19]

Let's stick with political alignment for a moment more. Despite impacting belief in fake news, political alignment appears to not make a *huge* difference to what we believe. Instead, perceived accuracy tends to be much more impactful. As two of the leading researchers on fake news, Gordon Pennycook at the University of Regina and David Rand at MIT, note, "the effect of political concordance is typically much smaller than that of the actual veracity of the news. In other words, true but politically discordant news is typically believed much more than false but politically concordant news—politics does not trump truth."[20]

To illustrate, consider an imaginary headline like this one for a fake news story:

> Pope Francis publicly endorses Kamala Harris for President in the 2024 U.S. election.

While this headline might be welcome news to some Democrats, they are also not likely going to believe that it is accurate. Since perceived accuracy is more important for many of us than political alignment—and this applies to Democrats and Republicans alike—few are likely to form the belief that Francis endorsed Harris. This, anyway, is what a body of research on political psychology and fake news tells us.[21]

More good news for honesty, I want to say. We at least tend on average to care more about the accuracy of our informational sources than about whether the information aligns with our political views, and that is what you would expect of an honest person. So too when people are more reflective and deliberative, they are much less likely to believe information from fake news stories.[22]

But now, consider this research finding from Pennycook and his collaborators. Participants in a study published in 2021 were given the following headline:

> Over 500 "Migrant Caravaners" Arrested With Suicide Vests.

Pennycook reports finding that:

> This was rated as accurate by 15.7% of Republicans in our study, but 51.1% of Republicans said they would consider sharing it.[23]

This is a stunning disconnect.

Presumably few Republicans in the study were going to believe that there were 500 people arrested with suicide vests. Even though the story might fit into an anti-immigration narrative many Republicans endorse, the seeming implausibility of such a story (hence the low accuracy) makes it really hard to believe. *And yet* the majority of these participants said they would consider sharing it. Admittedly, that is not the same as deciding they *would* share it, which is also not the same as *actually* sharing it on their social media accounts. Still, if you don't think it is accurate, then why would you even consider sharing this story?

Now we have the makings of an honesty crisis.

What is going on here? Ordinarily we might think that if you share a news story on social media, it is because you believe the story is accurate and you want others to become aware of this information as well. So the causal pathway goes from coming into contact with a news story, to believing it is accurate, to thinking it would be good for others to become aware of this information too, to wanting to share it, and finally to actually sharing it.

But in light of findings like the one above, this model is obviously too simplistic. Instead, following the NYU psychologist Jay

Van Bavel and his colleagues, a better picture is more like what they depict in Figure 6.1. The key point is that sometimes the sharing of news on social media appears to bypass belief altogether and instead be driven by other factors.

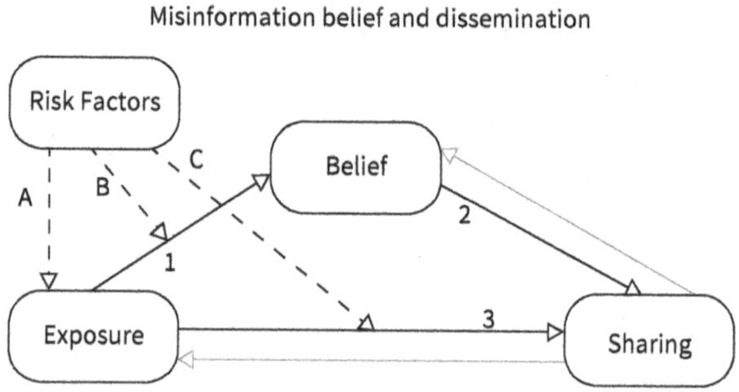

Figure 6.1 A model of misinformation belief and dissemination.[24]

Now to be sure, we should not overstate how prevalent such behavior is. It looks like many people are reticent to share fake news online, whether because they care about accuracy or about the harm to their reputation which might ensue (or both).[25] Indeed, one study found that almost 40% of participants said they would need to be paid at least $1,000 to share fake news stories from their own personal accounts (although almost 25% said they would do it for free).[26] Much of the sharing of fake news is being done, it turns out, by small groups of very active sharers.

For instance, when Twitter behavior for 16,442 accounts in the months leading up to the 2016 US presidential election was examined, researchers found that 0.1% of individuals were responsible for almost 80% of sharing from fake political news websites. These so-called supersharers were doing much of the damage. And for the average Twitter user, only 1.18% of their exposures to political content during this period were from fake news sites, which came to about 10 stories during the month prior to the election.[27]

At the same time, there is also evidence that fake news travels rapidly on social media, and much more so than accurate news stories typically travel. Soroush Vosoughi at MIT and colleagues looked at data from 3 million people on Twitter from 2006 to 2017 and found that "falsehoods were 70% more likely to be retweeted than the truth."[28] In a stunning result, they report that "Whereas the truth rarely diffused to more than 1,000 people, the top 1% of false-news cascades routinely diffused to between 1,000 and 100,000 people."[29] And of the false news, it was the political news that spread the most—to the most people, and at a faster speed. It reached "more than 20,000 people nearly three times faster than all other types of false news reached 10,000 people."[30] So the point is that even small groups of people initially sharing fake news could still lead to it spreading far and wide.

How can we make sense of why people share fake political news when they actually do? I think it is fair to say that researchers do not have a clear answer to this question yet. There are three models out there in the literature, and importantly they are not competing with each other. Each of them surely captures what happens at least some of the time. The question is which better captures what is happening *most* of the time. Here the third model seems to be the leading contender at the moment, but we are still a long way from making any final determination.[31]

First Model: Simple Error. The idea here is that we share fake news because we genuinely do believe it to be true and want others to be aware of the information. We are just ignorant of the facts. We do not realize that we are mistaken and that a given news story is really fake news.

Surely this happens some of the time. But as we just saw with the Pennycook studies, there is a significant disconnect between perceived accuracy and the willingness to share fake news. As Pennycook reports from one of his studies, "of the false headlines that were shared . . . 33% were both believed and shared when participants were asked directly about accuracy—however, this leaves the remaining 67% of sharing unexplained by confusion."[32] And in general, studies find that people are remarkably good at distinguishing between fake and real news.[33]

Second Model: Motivated Reasoning. On the second model, the sharing of fake news is primarily motivated by social and political considerations, regardless of or even despite thinking that a story is not true. For instance, someone could share a fake news story because she wants to advance a particular political cause and get more people to align with it. Or she could be motivated by virtue signaling/moral grandstanding, in which by sharing you aim to boost your social reputation by demonstrating that you hold the 'correct' political views and are aligned with the 'right' people and groups. Or the other way around, she could be motivated to share in order to avoid social penalties from her in-group, like lower social media interactions if she does not share fake news stories that align with what her group endorses.[34] Finally, in some cases her motivation could be more politically destructive, with the aim of trying to stir up chaos and disorder.[35] The key point here is that the perceived accuracy of a story is not an important consideration when it comes to sharing decisions online.[36]

Undoubtedly we should agree that social and political motives drive fake news sharing in some cases. But it turns out that this model also seems to be limited in its applicability. Citing Pennycook's study again, we find that "16% of the headlines were shared despite being identified as inaccurate. Thus, although purposeful sharing occurs, it seems unlikely to explain the bulk of false or misleading content that is shared online."[37] And when asked about what is important to them when sharing on social media, participants overwhelmingly rated accuracy as extremely important, more so than whether the content is surprising, politically aligned, funny, or interesting.[38] In another study, participants also reported that their reputation benefited more from sharing news that they perceived to be *accurate*.[39] All of these results lead naturally to the third model.

Third Model: Inaccuracy. Pennycook and Rand themselves hold that "people have a strong preference to only share [what they perceives as] accurate content, but . . . the social media context distracts them from this preference."[40] Hence engaging with social media can shift users out of an accuracy mindset, which often prevents believing and sharing fake news, into a social media mindset, which can be swayed by other considerations like signaling one's values, boosting one's reputation, and increasing one's following. The key is that accuracy is very important to social media users, but it is also something that they can become distracted from paying attention to.

What did the Pennycook study suggest about this model? The results fit it very well: "Consistent with this account, asking participants to rate the accuracy of each headline before deciding whether to share it decreased sharing of false headlines by 51% relative to the baseline condition [with no accuracy prompt]—suggesting that inattention was responsible for roughly half of the misinformation sharing in the experiment."[41] As we will see in the next section, many other studies have found support for the role of accuracy prompts in reducing rates of sharing (and believing) fake political news online.[42]

One reason it is important to dwell on these models is that they can serve as the basis for thinking about how to *combat* the sharing of fake news and thereby curb the honesty crisis we have in this area. That is the job of the next section. But to end here, we can finally clarify exactly where the honesty crisis is supposed to be.

Consider how often people in America encountered fake news, say, 50 years ago. Pennycook is surely right to note that ". . . we are being exposed to fake news stories with much greater frequency than in the past."[43] The reason for the change is not hard to find: social media. As van Bevel observed in 2021,

> The issue of misinformation is compounded by the rapid growth of social media. Over 3.6 billion people now actively use social media around the world and as social media has become the main source of news for many, it has also become easier to create and spread misinformation.[44]

Our focus has been not on the creating of the fake news, but on willfully spreading it. When someone doubts the accuracy of a story but shares it anyway without any disclaimer, that is dishonest. So too if they do not even consider the story's accuracy but share it with others as if it were accurate.

Hence social media is providing greater opportunities for people to share fake news than they ever had in the past, thereby making it easier to be dishonest. And with anonymous accounts or even personalized accounts where sharing such content is often rewarded by politically aligned followers, there are real questions about how likely it is that someone will be punished for sharing fake news.

Hence, we do have an honesty crisis after all in our political lives today.

What Can Be Done?

So thanks to social media, the sharing of fake political news is on the rise, spurring an honesty crisis. Fortunately, researchers have been working for a while to devise strategies for reigning it in. More specifically, the strategies try to prevent, not the creation of fake news nor the exposure of online users to it, but rather the *choice to share it with others*. Here I will briefly present five strategies, with citations for anyone who is interested in digging into the details.[45]

Pro-Truth Pledge. One group of researchers has encouraged us all to sign and thereby commit ourselves to a formal pledge to be truthful in all that we do. Here is how they word the pledge:[46]

> I Pledge My Earnest Efforts To:
>
> **Share** the truth
>
> - Verify: fact-check information to confirm it is true before accepting and sharing it
> - Balance: share the whole truth, even if some aspects do not support my opinion
> - Cite: share my sources so that others can verify my information
> - Clarify: distinguish between my opinion and the facts
>
> **Honor** the truth
>
> - Acknowledge: acknowledge when others share true information, even when we disagree otherwise

- Reevaluate: reevaluate if my information is challenged, retract it if I cannot verify it
- Defend: defend others when they come under attack for sharing true information, even when we disagree otherwise
- Align: align my opinions and my actions with true information

Encourage the truth

- Fix: ask people to retract information that reliable sources have disproved even if they are my allies
- Educate: compassionately inform those around me to stop using unreliable sources even if these sources support my opinion
- Defer: recognize the opinions of experts as more likely to be accurate when the facts are disputed
- Celebrate: celebrate those who retract incorrect statements and update their beliefs toward the truth

So far, these researchers have succeeded in getting over 21,000 people to commit to signing their pledge, including some prominent figures like the philosopher Peter Singer, psychologists Steven Pinker and Jonathan Haidt, and politician Beto O'Rourke.[47]

Unfortunately, there is not a lot of evidence yet showing that signing such a pledge will actually curb the sharing of fake political news specifically. I also worry about whether there is going to be a significant impact on very momentary decisions about whether to press 'share' or 'retweet' on our phones or computers. As we saw already, in those contexts, accuracy may not even be at the forefront of someone's mind.

Inoculation. Rather than a very general truth pledge, some researchers have supported more targeted inoculations. By analogy with medicine, these inoculations are designed to prevent 'outbreaks' of fake news sharing from happening down the road, by 'vaccinating' users ahead of time and thereby helping to build up their resistance to fake news in the future.

Communication researcher John Cook from George Mason University and his colleagues provide a nice summary of what these inoculations look like:

> There are two elements to an inoculation: (1) an explicit warning of an impending threat and (2) a refutation of an anticipated argument that exposes the imminent fallacy. For example, an inoculation might include (1) a warning that there exist attempts to cast doubt on the scientific consensus regarding climate change, and (2) an explanation that one technique employed is the rhetorical use of a large group of 'fake experts' to feign a lack of consensus. By exposing the fallacy, the misinformation . . . is delivered in a 'weakened' form. Thus, when people subsequently encounter a deceptive argument, the inoculation provides them with a counter-argument to immediately dismiss the misinformation.[48]

Initial studies are encouraging here. In fact, there is even some evidence that fake news inoculations can be *more* effective than fact-checking, which we turn to next. However, caution is recommended for now, as a lot of the studies have to do with coming to *believe* and *react to* fake news, rather than sharing it online.[49]

While promising, the main limitation I see with inoculating people against fake news is that it is practically cumbersome. One inoculation might be effective in reducing someone's likelihood of believing and ultimately sharing subsequent stories *on that very topic*, as in the example above of climate change. But when we scroll through Facebook and Twitter or watch videos on YouTube and TikTok, we are being presented with dozens and dozens of stories on a huge range of topics. To return to the medical analogy, if there were hundreds of new diseases that we were confronted with every day, each requiring its own vaccine, it is hard to see how practically anything could be done to stop the spread of most of them.

To avoid this problem, the inoculation would be better off focusing, not on specific topics in the news, but rather on providing more general warnings and highlighting anticipated techniques used generically in fake news stories. We might think of this as a 'technique-based' or 'broad-spectrum' form of immunization.[50] Or to take the analogy even further, it is analogous to "cross-protection insofar as inoculating people against one strain offers protection against related and different strains of the same misinformation tactic."[51] Current research is exploring precisely such inoculations and how effective they might be.[52]

Fact-Checking. Also known as 'veracity labeling,' fact-checking is certainly a popular strategy for combatting both believing fake news and sharing it. A story can receive a warning message which indicates that it is fake or fabricated or in some way misleading.

This approach is now adopted extensively on Twitter and Facebook, among other social media sites.[53] For instance, Twitter uses Community Notes, which "aims to create a better-informed world, by empowering people on X to collaboratively add helpful notes to posts that might be misleading."[54] Interestingly, these are not paid experts but volunteers on the platform who sign up.

Research so far backs up a fact-checking approach too. For instance, using a similar method we have seen before, Gordon Pennycook and colleagues gave control participants 16 false and 16 true news headlines, but participants in a "warning" group got 16 true headlines, 4 unmarked false ones, and 12 false headlines with a "FALSE" stamped on them. All participants had to say, for each headline, whether they would or would not consider sharing it. Perhaps not surprisingly, the warning made a big difference.

When the 12 stamped headlines were compared to the same ones in the control group (without the stamp), the difference was significant: 29.8% of control participants considered sharing the headline, but only 16.1% did with the warning. Interestingly, the warning made a bigger difference when the stamped headlines were politically *aligned* with the participant's own views. In other words, the warning was more impactful for Republicans if the false headlines leaned *Republican*. Same for Democrats. That is more evidence, by the way, against the motivated reasoning model we saw in the last section.[55]

More generally, across a bunch of studies, it was found that "warning effect estimates range between decreasing belief in false news by 13% to 35% and decreasing sharing of false news by 25% to 46%, relative to control. Warning labels also reduce other forms of positive engagement with false content, such as 'like' or 'love' reactions to posts."[56]

There are, however, some important limitations to fact-checking.[57] The first is that the few professional fact-checkers simply cannot keep pace with the volume of news that is shared on the major platforms. If hours or even days go by before a warning is posted, then a lot of damage could already be done.[58]

Another limitation is that this strategy is impacted by how much social media users trust the reliability of the fact-checkers. If a user thinks that they are politically biased, then she might be more inclined to discount the warning message than she is the original story itself. This can be especially problematic if the fact-checker is attached to one of the traditional media providers. After all, at the time of Donald Trump's election in 2016, only 14% of Republicans said they trusted the media.[59]

But fact-checkers? That's different, right? Surely people trust them. Not necessarily. During the same election, a whopping 88% of people voting for Trump said they did not trust fact-checkers, and even in the case of Hilary Clinton voters, 41% were also skeptical.[60] A Pew Research Center study found that 48% of Americans thought fact-checkers "favor one side," rising to 70% for Republicans.[61]

Thirdly, another limitation—or really more of a danger—is that badly done warnings can be counterproductive by undermining trust in the checker, leading to reduced belief and sharing of *accurate* information. Sometimes misinformation warnings can be used merely as political tools, can be overly vague or broad, or can be deployed in clumsy ways.[62]

Finally, there is the implied truth effect. If I know that Twitter is supposed to be fact-checking stories, and I *do not* see a warning, then I am more likely to trust a particular story I see on social media. But of course I do not have any way of knowing whether that story has already been checked or not. So I could thereby become more confident in a particular fake news story and share it more readily, than I would otherwise do if there were no fact-checking in the first place. There are compelling studies which show that this is a real thing.[63]

Source Labels. Rather than attaching warnings to particular stories, social media sites could flag entire websites and other sources, marking anything that comes from them as potentially unreliable.

For instance, in one study, people in the control condition had to rate their intentions to share a given story after they were presented with the story's headline. In the source-checkers condition, they would get the same headlines, but first they were told: "For some news headlines, you will see a trustworthiness rating of the source of the headline. The rating system goes from 1 to 5 star, where 1 star means that the news outlet is very unreliable, while 5 stars means that the outlet is very reliable. The ratings were created by a set of eight professional fact-checkers."[64] The result was a significant reduction in intentions to share fake headlines in this second group compared to the first. Interestingly, there was also no evidence of an implied truth effect either.

So it seems that a source-labeling approach could do even better than fact-checking when it comes to sharing fake news. It is a lot easier to rate an entire news source than it is individual articles. And if it can avoid an implied truth effect, that is a big plus. There is, though, the continuing worry about trust. Source labels will only be as effective as users trust the judgments being made about whether a source is reliable or not.[65]

Accuracy Prompts. Finally, a strategy I find particularly promising is to nudge users ahead of time in ways to enhance their focus on accuracy. Notably these nudges are not telling users whether a particular political story is accurate or not. They are not in the business of fact-checking or source-checking, and do not put the onus on the social media platform to have to police each news story. So there are no trust issues that arise here. But at the same time, these prompts are not generic one-time pledges either.

Here are some examples of accuracy prompts, taken from a helpful summary by Pennycook and Rand:[66]

- Participants are asked to rate the accuracy of a neutral (non-political, non-COVID-19) headline.
- Participants are asked how important it is to them to only share accurate news or to not share inaccurate news.
- Participants are told that most other survey respondents think it is very important to only share accurate news.
- Participants are shown a 30s video (in the format of a "Public Service Announcement", although these words are not explicitly mentioned) reminding them to think about accuracy before sharing.
- Participants are asked how important it is to them to only share news that they have thought about in a reasoned, rather than emotional, way.
- Participants are shown a set of minimal digital literacy tips.

Surprisingly, using any of these prompts seems to make a big difference.

For instance, in their systematic review of the results of 20 experiments with a total of 26,863 participants, Pennycook and Rand found that accuracy prompts decreased participants' intentions to share fake news by roughly 10% as compared to control participants who did not see an accuracy prompt.[67] Or to take a specific example of a study on accuracy prompts, the researchers Valerio Capraro and Tatiana Celadin gave participants a series of headlines and for each of them said, "If you were to see the above article on Facebook, would you consider sharing it." In the control group, the choices were "Yes" and "No." In the accuracy group, they were "Yes. I think this news is accurate." and "No." The results—intentions to share fake news went down, *and* intentions to share accurate news went up![68]

What might explain the effectiveness of accuracy prompts? Not surprisingly, the inaccuracy model we saw in the last section has a ready answer. The thought is that when they are browsing social media, users are often not in an accuracy mindset. As such they can be more readily swayed by factors which do not always have to do with truth, such as the emotional content of the story or the reputational consequences of sharing it. Hence the fact that a news story might be inaccurate or fake news is not something that is on their radar screen.

Indeed, a fascinating study suggests that just presenting users with the opportunity to share a story online shifts them into a social media mindset and away from an accuracy mindset. Other considerations besides accuracy become prioritized. In the study, asking participants about whether they would share certain headlines, before asking them whether these headlines were accurate, had a massive effect—35% lower accuracy discernment for headlines having to do with COVID-19 and 28% lower for headings having to do with politics. As the authors note, "the social media context—and the mindset that it produces—actively interferes with accuracy discernment. It is not just that people forget to pay attention to accuracy when deciding what to share; rather their actual underlying accuracy judgments are worse when they also consider what to share."[69]

What an accuracy prompt can do is serve as a nudge to shift someone into an accuracy mindset. As we already said in the last section, people do seem to care a lot about the accuracy of the stories they read and share. By and large we want to share information that is accurate. Now we can add the qualifier—when they are in an accuracy mindset. When they are distracted (something social media is very good at doing), then they may be more prone to share something that is fake, even if they do not believe it is accurate in the first place.[70]

There is one major caveat to the effectiveness of accuracy prompts, though. People who are nudged into an accuracy mindset had better be able to tell that a piece of fake news *really is* fake. As Pennycook and Rand write, "if a group of participants is targeted who have a very difficult time distinguishing between true and false content, or if misinformation is identified that the majority of a particular group believes to be true, then accuracy prompts will not improve sharing discernment."[71] Hence you can give a group of election deniers all the accuracy prompts you want, but if they genuinely believe that the election was stolen, they will continue to share fake news stories.

There is something of value in all of these strategies, I think. Thankfully as many researchers emphasize, they are not exclusive. The best approach of all is going to be multifaceted, combining several strategies in an effort to slow the spread of fake political news.[72]

What About the Politicians?

If we ended here, I fear it would be a bit of a letdown. In a chapter on dishonesty and politics, how can I not talk about politicians? How can I not say something about Trump, or Biden, or Clinton, or take your pick?

So let me end the chapter with the politicians. But my discussion will not be aimed at trying to understand why they lie or BS. It will be aimed at punishing them for their dishonesty.

You might initially expect there to be some reputational damage done to politicians when their lies, deceptions, or BS statements are exposed. Such dishonesty could undermine our trust in a leader, spawn worries about what other things the leader has been dishonest about, and raise doubts about the standing of the leader in the eyes of other politicians and even other world leaders. Hence, it is natural to expect negative blowback for politicians when they are caught being dishonest, including to their overall job performance and their likelihood of being reelected.

The prospect of this reputational damage could incentivize leaders to not be dishonest going forward. Yet while there is some evidence that citizens are willing to punish politicians for their lies,[73] it turns out that what could be a helpful way to reign in dishonesty often does not materialize.

Here political polarization plays a significant role.[74] If a dishonest statement is made by a member of your political camp, then these days it is likely that you will not judge it as harshly as a member of the other camp would. To take a well-known example, consider

President Trump's claim in 2016, repeated by his Press Secretary Sean Spicer, about the size of his inauguration crowd. In a study of reactions to Spicer's claim, London Business School Professor Daniel Effron found that even when they believed that the claim was false, Republicans gave Spicer more of a pass than did Democrats, presumably because they were on the same page politically. Democrats do something similar in other cases.[75]

Another factor affecting our moral condemnation of political dishonesty is imagining alternative realities. Studies have found that if citizens can imagine a world in which the purported falsehood (e.g., "largest inauguration ever") could have been true or might have become true if history had gone a different way, then they are less inclined to judge the person lying harshly.[76] Politicians take advantage of this psychological phenomenon in how they couch their dishonest claims.

A third factor at work is the frequency of exposure to stories about a particular dishonest political act, say on social media. The more a person sees it being shared, the more she is likely to become desensitized to it. The less angry and upset she becomes, the less severe her moral condemnation will be of the initial act of dishonesty by a politician.

In addition to these factors, it also matters how dishonest citizens are *in their own lives* and how they treat dishonesty in their relationships. For instance, two political science researchers found that, "Voters who are more prone to lying in their personal lives . . . are significantly more tolerant of presidents who lie on issues of national security and the use of force (by margins of 10 to 20%, depending on the conditions), and under some circumstances do not punish such presidents at all."[77] How many citizens are we talking about here? According to these researchers, over 40% of the electorate might be disposed in ways that would lead them to be more tolerant of presidents who lie, and this holds across party lines.[78]

In light of the various factors which suppress our negative responses to political dishonesty by political leaders, what can be done to try to hold our leaders responsible and have there be real consequences for their reputations and even reelection prospects? One answer is to call the importance of honesty to mind. As we saw when we looked at honor codes in Chapter 5, honesty is a value that most of us care about and have internalized into our self-concept. In other words, we want to think of ourselves as honest people, and to be thought of as honest by others. When made salient, our honesty values can also lead us to judge and sanction others whom we discover have lied to or deceived us.

Recent research has found that for many politicians, being caught lying inflicts reputational costs on them in a variety of ways when people are primed to think about honesty. These include how well the politician did in dealing with the situation in question, how honest she is as a person, and how her overall job performance should be reevaluated.[79]

There are exceptions, though. For some politicians, people are often entrenched in their evaluation of the politician's overall job performance, regardless of whether they are caught lying or not. Indeed, such politicians can regularly make statements that are of dubious honesty and yet still be regarded as highly authentic by their supporters. They are what the sociologist Oliver Hahl and his colleagues call a 'lying demagogue.'[80] I will not name names, but I imagine some will come to mind.

This is surely paradoxical. For on the one hand, such a politician can make statements which he knows are made up, and he also knows his audience will know are made up. Yet it is *still* the case that this person does not seem to take a political hit for his publicly accepted dishonesty. Instead, his supporters rate him high on authenticity. As Hahl notes, if a "constituency feels its interests are not being served by a political establishment that purports to represent it fairly, a lying demagogue can appear as a distinctively *authentic champion* of its interests."[81]

By so blatantly going against establishment norms, including norms of truth-telling, the lying demagogue is clearly willing to run a significant risk for what he believes, and to champion the interests of those on the outside of the political establishment, even at the cost of acceptance by that very establishment. He thereby demonstrates his authenticity.[82] As Hahl remarks, "this very need by the establishment to distance itself from the lying demagogue lends credibility to his claim to be an authentic champion for those who feel disenfranchised by that establishment."[83]

Thankfully, lying demagogues appear to be few in number. Ideally by punishing most politicians who are found to act dishonestly, citizens can incentivize their leaders to be more honest in the future. One can only hope.

Notes

1. Agiesta and Edwards-Levy 2023.
2. Kaiser 2024.
3. The next several paragraphs are drawn from Miller 2021b, with permission from Alessandra Tanesini and the *Open for Debate Blog*.
4. You can visit the society at https://theflatearthsociety.org/home/index.php.
5. I first developed these examples in Miller 2021a: 36–37.
6. For helpful discussion of this issue, see Webber 2018.
7. Some of these issues are discussed in Heffer 2018.
8. The next few paragraphs draw from Miller 2022b, reprinted with permission from *Scientia et Fides* under a Creative Commons Attribution-NoDerivatives 4.0 International License.
9. This list and some of the wording are adapted from Mele 2001: 26–27.
10. And the relevance of the different possibilities could change from case to case. It could be, for example, that most flat Earthers' are in the self-deception category, having to irresponsibly deny the evidence of a round Earth because—for whatever reason—they want to believe that it is flat.
11. Both statistics are reported in Tsipursky et al. 2018: 48.
12. Lazer et al. 2018: 1094.
13. Here I am following Rogers 2020.
14. van der Linden 2022: 461.
15. Gibbs 2017.
16. Kang 2016.
17. See Pennycook and Rand 2021: 393 and especially Pennycook et al. 2018.
18. Pennycook and Rand 2019.
19. Ibid.
20. Pennycook and Rand 2021: 389–390.
21. For more see Pennycook and Rand 2019, 2021, 2022 and Pennycook et al. 2021.
22. Pennycook and Rand 2019, 2021 and Bago et al. 2020.
23. Pennycook et al. 2021: 591.
24. Van Bavel et al. 2021: 86, reprinted with permission of Wiley-Blackwell.

25. See, in particular, Altay et al. 2022.
26. Ibid., 1316.
27. These statistics are from Grinberg et al. 2019. For additional relevant data, see Altay et al. 2022: 1304.
28. Vosoughi et al. 2018: 1149.
29. Ibid., 1148. Similarly van der Linden reports that, "Twitter has found that false news is about 70% more likely to be shared than true news, and it takes true news 6 times longer than false stories to reach 1,500 people" (2022: 463).
30. Vosoughi et al. 2018: 1148.
31. In what follows I have been helped by Pennycook and Rand 2021 and Pennycook et al. 2021.
32. Pennycook and Rand 2021: 394.
33. Pennycook and Rand 2019 and Bago et al. 2020.
34. For research finding this motivation does play a role, see Lawson et al. 2023.
35. For more details about these different proposals, as well as empirical support for at least one of them, see Pennycook and Rand 2021: 394–395, Osmundsen et al. 2021, van Bavel et al. 2021, and Altay et al. 2022: 1319–1320.
36. Although perceived *inaccuracy* could be in some cases, since as Ghezae and colleagues note, "partisans are often willing to share content that aligns with the beliefs and preferences of their political ingroup, regardless of its accuracy—or even *because* of its *inaccuracy*, insofar as sharing *false* partisan news is a particularly effective way to signal one's partisan commitment" (2024: 3, emphasis theirs).
37. Pennycook and Rand 2021: 395.
38. Pennycook et al. 2021: 591. See also relevant findings in Altay et al. 2022. For overviews of the empirical support and challenges for the motivated reasoning model, see Osmundsen et al. 2021 and van der Linden 2022: 462.
39. Ghezae et al. 2024.
40. Pennycook and Rand 2021: 395.
41. Ibid.
42. For an overview of the empirical support and challenges for the inaccuracy model, see van der Linden 2022: 462. For additional empirical support, see Pennycook and Rand 2019.
43. Pennycook et al. 2018: 1866. For a similar claim, see van der Linden 2022.
44. Van Bavel et al. 2021: 85. Similarly Pennycook and Rand note that fake news, "seems to have gained an unprecedented level of prominence through the rise of social media" (2019: 39). And as Osmundsen and colleagues note, "The emergence of the internet, and particularly of social media, has fundamentally changed the relationship between media and audience. Whereas once audiences were more or less passive consumers, they are now actively participating in the distribution and, sometimes, even the production of news" (2021: 1000).
45. For overviews of different strategies, see Pennycook and Rand 2021, van Bavel et al. 2021, and especially the impressive toolbox provided by

A. Kozyreva et al. 2024. For additional ideas related to misinformation more generally, see Lewandowsky et al. 2012.

46. Tsipursky et al. 2018: 54.
47. More can be found at https://www.protruthpledge.org/.
48. Cook et al. 2017. For another helpful summary, see van der Linden 2022: 464–465.
49. For a few of the only exceptions, see Cook et al. 2017 and McPhedran et al. 2023: 5780.
50. van der Linden 2022: 464.
51. Ibid.
52. One intriguing approach is the use of free online games to provide technique-based inoculations. Two such games—*Bad News* and *Harmony Square*—have been developed to combat fake news, and so far measures of their effectiveness look promising, including with respect to willingness to share fake news. See Roozenbeek and van der Linden 2020 and Roozenbeek et al. 2022.
53. For a thorough discussion of content labeling that goes into more detail than I can here, see Morrow et al. 2022.
54. https://communitynotes.x.com/guide/en/about/introduction, accessed on July 15, 2025.
55. Pennycook et al. 2020: 4947–4948. In another study, Ziv Epstein and colleagues found that fact-checking warnings from human-AI systems reduced sharing intentions online, including when there is an explanation of how this kind of fact-checking works (see Epstein et al. 2022). Porter and Wood 2022 used an online environment which simulated Facebook, and had participants rate the degree to which they believed various headlines inclining ones with "False Information. Checked by independent fact-checkers" labels. These labels "provoked large gains in accuracy" (1813), although they didn't assess sharing tendencies in this study.
56. Martel and Rand 2023.
57. Here I have been helped by Celadin et al. 2023. See also Pennycook and Rand 2021: 396, van Bavel et al. 2021: 98–99, van der Linden 2022: 464, and Martel and Rand 2023.
58. An alternative approach is to go with the 'wisdom of crowds' rather than professional fact-checkers. See Celadin et al. 2023: 2. There is also an AI/human crowd generated approach too (see Epstein et al. 2022).
59. Swift 2016.
60. Rasmussen Reports 2016.
61. Walker and Gottfried 2019. See also van Bavel et al. 2021: 90–91. Even with this skepticism, though, fact-checking can still have a significant impact. While the skepticism might reduce the impact of fact-checking on sharing fake news, it is unlikely to negate that impact completely. Indeed, a recent study backs this up. The researchers, Cameron Martel and David Rand at MIT, found that "Participants in our treatment condition were less believing (27.6% reduction)

and less willing to share (24.6% reduction) labeled false headlines relative to the control condition—and importantly, this warning effect persisted even for those low on TFC [trust in fact-checkers]. Fact-checker warnings reduced belief in (12.19%) and sharing of (16.7%) labeled false headlines even for those most distrusting of fact-checkers" (Martel and Rand 2024).

62. Here I have been helped by Freeze et al. 2021 and Martel and Rand 2023.
63. For a good starting place, see Pennycook et al. 2020.
64. Celadin et al. 2023: 4.
65. For more about this approach, see Morrow et al. 2022 and Celadin et al. 2023.
66. What follows is reproduced from Table 1 in Pennycook and Rand 2022.
67. Pennycook and Rand 2022.
68. Capraro and Celadin 2023: 1637. For additional studies supporting the role of accuracy prompts, see Pennycook et al. 2021.
69. Epstein et al. 2023.
70. For more discussion of how accuracy prompts might work in combatting inattention, see Pennycook and Rand 2022.
71. Pennycook and Rand 2022.
72. Note that these are all strategies that focus on how to influence individual social media users to act better. This is to say nothing of system-level strategies, such as "platform design, content moderation, communities of fact-checkers and journalists, and high-level regulatory and policy interventions (such as investing in public broadcasters and establishing regulatory frameworks that promote a diverse media landscape)" (Kozyreva et al. 2024: 1049).
73. See Yarhi-Milo and Ribar 2023.
74. In this and the next two paragraphs I have been helped by Effron and Helgason 2022.
75. Ibid.
76. Effron 2018.
77. Yarhi-Milo and Ribar 2023: 562.
78. Ibid. For individual differences in Right-Wing Authoritarianism and in Social Dominance Orientation predicting moral assessments of imaginary politicians being dishonest, see De keersmaecker and Roets 2019.
79. Croco et al. 2021. See also Maxey 2021, which used additional hypothetical scenarios involving foreign policy decisions by a nameless US president, and found reduced support of the president's election when the president's statement was found by experts to be spin or deceitful.
80. Hahl et al. 2018.
81. Ibid., 3, emphasis theirs.
82. Ibid., 6.
83. Ibid., 8.

7

Fame, Lying, and the Honesty Crisis for Celebrities

Khabane "Khaby" Lame is one of the biggest celebrities in the world. If you are over 40 years old, chances are you have never heard of him. Khaby is a TikTok celebrity. And not just any TikTok celebrity. As I write this in 2025, he is the most followed person on TikTok in the world with 162.2 million followers, beating out Charli D'Amelio.[1] His videos have earned over 2.4 billion likes.

Born in Senegal in 2000, Khaby was working as a machine operator in northern Italy until as recently as 2020 when he lost his job at the start of the pandemic. That is when he started posting regularly on TikTok. A mere two years later, he took over the top spot from D'Amelio, and now is reported to earn as much as $750K for each online post.[2]

Khaby's rise was sparked by videos in which he does not say anything. He is simply responding non-verbally to other people whom he sees making their jobs way harder than they need to be. His response is to demonstrate how they could have done things in a simpler and more straightforward manner. For example, in one video he shows someone cutting a banana using a clever. Khaby just peels the banana.

A big reason for Khaby's success is his extremely expressive facial reactions and hand gestures, especially when he gives his trademark "duh" or "obviously" after showing how something can be done easily. Part of his charm is that he can communicate in a way that everyone can understand, even though he is not using words. He comes across as a person we can all relate to. As a *New York Times*

The Honesty Crisis. Christian B. Miller, Oxford University Press. © Oxford University Press 2026.
DOI: 10.1093/9780197840801.003.0007

profile noted, "He didn't find success through joining a collab house with other 20-somethings, or by relying on artificial growth like buying followers or views. His rise has been entirely organic."[3]

Five years ago, TikTok celebrities did not exist. Now there are tens of thousands of them, joining big crowds of celebrities from YouTube and Instagram. But with the rise of these new platforms for manufacturing and sustaining fame comes an honesty crisis.[4]

What Is Celebrity?

First, though, we need to say something more about what it is to be a celebrity. Celebrities can be found in all walks of life, and not because of anything having to do with TikTok. There are literary celebrities (e.g., J. K. Rowling, Tom Wolfe), musical celebrities (e.g., Taylor Swift, Bono), athletic celebrities (e.g., Tom Brady, LeBron James), political celebrities (e.g., Prince William, Monica Lewinsky), financial celebrities (e.g., Elon Musk, Bill Gates), and many more.

What is it to be a celebrity, period? How would you define it? It is actually surprisingly hard to come up with a good definition. It is kind of like 'pornography'—good luck coming up with a perfect definition of that. But in both cases, we know it when we see it.

For our purposes, the following characterization by philosophers Alfred Archer and Catherine Robb at Tilburg University works well enough. They understand, "a celebrity as someone whose life is subject to high levels of public attention in ways that go beyond their specific talents, expertise, or professional role."[5] Importantly, a celebrity does not have to be responsible for any great accomplishments in their past which account for their celebrity status. If an example would help, the Kardashians come to mind.

To be sure, even if a celebrity may not have any significant past accomplishments herself, it does not follow that she is without remarkable *abilities*.[6] The Kardashians are incredibly talented in creatively maintaining their celebrity status and adapting to changing cultural and social trends. There might be some luck involved in becoming a celebrity in the first place, but actively maintaining one's celebrity status often takes skill.

Thanks to social media sites like TikTok, the allure of celebrity is arguably stronger than it has ever been. Also thanks to those same sites, it is easier to become a celebrity than it has ever been in human history. But fame comes with a huge danger. For fame can lead to greater dishonesty. Hence the stars are in alignment for another honesty crisis.

Are Celebrity and Dishonesty Related?

To be sure, celebrity is one thing, and dishonesty is another. They could be completely unrelated to each other. And I should confess upfront that we do not have any rigorous studies to help clarify what their relationship is. So, I will instead offer some conjectures for us to consider. I do not think they are very hard to accept.

Here is my first conjecture: there is a correlation between celebrity and dishonesty. Compared to those who are not (as) well-known, celebrities seem on average to act more dishonestly.

Take all the celebrities who have been found to be cheating on their spouses and partners. Or take all the cases of financial wrongdoing like tax evasion. Or take using performance-enhancing drugs. It is natural to come away with the impression that dishonesty is prevalent in celebrity culture, and more so than is found in the lives of those of us who are not well-known.

That is just a hypothesis about how two things are correlated with each other. We all know the slogan—correlation does not equal causation. So here comes the second conjecture—there is a *causal* relationship too. Indeed, it is a causal relationship that runs in both directions. Here is one direction:

Dishonest behavior tends to lead to greater celebrity.

For instance, Sam Bankman-Fried might have been well-known in the financial world prior to the collapse of the cryptocurrency exchange FTX. But when his allegedly dishonest scheme was exposed, his celebrity status skyrocketed. For a while he became something of a household name, at least in the United States, and his face was on the cover of *New York Magazine* with the title "The Virtue Was the Con."

But in this chapter, I want to look closely at the other causal relationship:

Celebrity tends to lead to greater dishonest behavior.

Again, I just advance this as a conjecture. But I would be very surprised if it does not turn out to be true.

In fact, I can think of at least *four* reasons for why we should expect greater celebrity to lead to greater dishonesty.

Celebrity Is Insatiable. Once we get a taste of fame, we tend to want more of it. The spotlight burned bright the first time, but it could burn even brighter. The first television appearance was great; now how do we get more? I just reached 5,000 Twitter followers, but Taylor Swift has over 93 million.

In extreme cases, celebrity recognition and attention can feel like a drug. In numerous testimonials, celebrities report how their fame has been, in their own words, "addictive" and "insatiable." Hence Robin Williams once said, "I think celebrity is a drug [. . .] And now with tweeting and Facebook, it's like cybercrack."[7] Another celebrity anonymously reported that, "I've been addicted to almost every substance known to man at one point or another, and the most addicting of them all is *fame*."[8]

For those eager to grow their celebrity status, what is one tempting strategy? Dishonest actions, at least if the celebrity thinks that he can get away with them without getting caught, and they would help to garner more attention.[9] Also, it is not just celebrity for its own sake that can become insatiable. Celebrity status affords greater opportunities to get things for oneself, whether that be money, material possessions, or power. If dishonesty can help increase one's fame, and increased fame can help to achieve a more luxurious lifestyle, well then we can all connect the dots.

Celebrity Is Worth Protecting. Celebrities typically do not want to just grow their celebrity status. They also want to protect it. For some of them, the thought of going back to what might now appear to be a life of relative obscurity or drudgery can be a frightening prospect. Yet there will be times in their careers when celebrities will slip up, just like the rest of us. So rather than risk losing their celebrity status, they might be willing to cover up the problematic behavior by lying, misleading, cheating, or the like. As Rebecca DeYong at Calvin University has noted, "When image is everything, truthfulness is often the first sacrifice on the altar of reputation."[10]

Lance Armstrong is a famous example of exactly this. He was known not only as a legendary cyclist for winning the Tour de France seven times, but also for having batted cancer and founding the Livestrong Foundation. Yet Armstrong is reported to have used lies, misleading statements, and manipulation to cover up his participation in a very sophisticated doping operation for over a decade, something he eventually admitted to in 2013 on the Oprah Winfrey show. Fear of losing endorsement deals, celebrity status, cycling fame, and an inspirational reputation may have all played a role in his allegedly choosing to go down the path of increasing deception rather than honesty as the years went by.

The celebrity has the weight of the gaze of hundreds, thousands, or sometimes even millions of viewers to satisfy. Having one's misdeeds exposed in front of this many eyes can seem crushing. Covering up, even if dishonestly, is better than the destruction of one's public image. Or so the celebrity might think.

Celebrity Erodes Moral Safeguards. Celebrities report that at times it can be challenging for them to behave ethically because they are surrounded by people who tend to affirm everything they do. In other words, there can be a lot of "yes men." Hence they are not going to get as much pushback when doing dishonest things. As Justin Bieber once confessed in a moment of brutal transparency, "Everyone did everything for me so I never even learned the fundamentals of responsibility. So by this point I was 18 with no skills in the real world, with millions of dollars and access to whatever I wanted. This is a very scary concept for anyone."[11]

When it comes to lying, cheating, or stealing, the celebrity might worry less about doing these things if he thinks that people are going to admire him no matter what he does. And after the fact, he might quickly assuage his guilt when his admirers assure him that it was not a big deal. Thus, celebrity can erode moral safeguards.

Potential examples might include some of the political and historical claims made by Kanye West, or Bill Clinton's cheating scandal with Monica Lewinsky, or former NBC news anchor Brian Williams' seemingly questionable reporting on his own experiences covering wars and disasters. I say 'potential' because we would need to dive into the psychology of each of these celebrities to see what was actually behind their apparently dishonest behavior.

In extreme cases, celebrity might even encourage the thought that the moral rules *do not apply*. Here a celebrity might think that she is somehow exempt from or above the moral standards. In such cases, what is the big deal with doing something dishonest, if it will benefit her in some way?

Celebrity Facilitates Greater Opportunities to Be Dishonest. When you are a celebrity, it might seem like more chances come along in life to be dishonest. And compared to the rest of us, acting dishonestly just seems—easier.

Obviously, infidelity is the easy example. Fame makes opportunities for sexual liaisons abound, in a way that they usually do not for ordinary folks. As one celebrity anonymously reported, "I live in Hollywood and I'm a middle-aged man, and Miss September keeps throwing herself at me. That wouldn't happen if I wasn't famous. Believe me . . ."[12] This isn't the only example, though. Opportunities to participate in shady financial transactions, for instance, could come along more frequently, and similarly for opportunities to cut academic corners.

A few years back, several celebrities were part of a college admissions scandal. Hollywood stars Felicity Huffman and William H. Macy allegedly paid someone to "arrange for their daughter's

SAT proctor to secretly correct her wrong answers and boost her score."[13] And the actress Lori Loughlin (most well-known from the TV show "Full House") was accused of helping her daughter Olivia by "paying $500,000 to have Olivia and her sister classified as crew recruits for U.S.C. despite never having participated in the sport."[14] In cases like these, it seems as if celebrity status (and wealth) afforded opportunities to cheat the system that would not be available to most other college applicants.

Unless the celebrity has a strong moral character to begin with, there will be many temptations that do not normally exist in a person's life. The more such temptations, the more difficult it can be to keep acting honestly.

So those are my four best attempts to explain why celebrity and dishonesty are linked to each other.[15] Whether any of these is *correct* is ultimately an empirical matter that has been almost completely neglected by researchers. For what it is worth, my suspicion is that *all four* of the reasons above have something to do with why celebrity and dishonesty are linked. In other words, we do not have to pick and choose.

To be sure, we should not get carried away here. There is the possibility that some celebrities do not do dishonest things at all, or only rarely. I am proposing a general tendency, and not a universal claim.

An Honesty Crisis?

So where are we at this point? I want to suggest that there is plenty of reason to expect that fame can threaten someone's honesty. But what does this have to do with an *honesty crisis* today? After all, celebrities have been around forever, and philosophers have always warned us to avoid the dangers of fame.

Remember that an honesty crisis does not have to involve brand new ways of being dishonest. Already familiar forms of dishonest behavior just need to become much more appealing and easier to pull off. How would this work in the case of celebrities?

Suppose I am right that fame does give rise to increased dishonesty. And suppose let's add the second key point, which is that celebrity status has, in recent years, become even more appealing and easier to attain. Then we have a clear path ahead of us to an honesty crisis.

Thanks to social media, it is undeniable that celebrity status has become more appealing and easier to attain. There are of course different ways to measure fame, and perhaps the number of followers you have on your social media platforms is one of the crudest ways. Still, there is no doubt that people with large followings are celebrities in their own right.

In 2023, analytics data found that there were over 39,000 accounts on TikTok with at least 1 million followers. On YouTube, there were over 32,000 accounts; on Instagram, there were at least 23,000 accounts.[16] With this level of fame comes all kinds of perks—thousands of dollars for a product promotion post, product lines, appearance fees, free travel and accommodations, and so on. Without the visibility provided by social media, many of these influencers and internet celebrities would never have found an audience.

It is no surprise, then, that half of Gen Zers, "would quit their current jobs if they could become an influencer if it was enough to pay for their lifestyle. Three in 10 young people would even pay to become an influencer."[17] A 2021 survey of American teens found that the top dream job was not becoming a doctor or nurse (8%), a professional athlete (7%), or a lawyer (3%)—it was becoming a fulltime Vlogger/YouTuber/Professional streamer (9%).[18]

Of course there are plenty of other ways to become famous besides posting content online. But there is no doubt that even in the past five to ten years, celebrity status has become easier to attain and even more appealing. Hence, we should expect to find another honesty crisis staring us in the face.

"Hold on, Miller," someone might say. "Aren't you overlooking an obvious point? If anything, greater celebrity should lead to greater *honest* behavior. You have things exactly backwards!"

> "Celebrities know that their lives will come under much greater scrutiny from the public. In extreme cases this might even include the

ever-watchful eyes of the paparazzi. Even leaving them aside, with the ubiquity of smartphones and screen shots, everything a celebrity does is at risk of being photographed or recorded. Hence they should realize that it is better to be as honest as possible in public, since there is too great a risk of any lying, cheating, stealing, and the other forms of dishonest behavior being exposed."

"Miller, what you really should have proposed is a *celebrity-honesty* relationship. There goes your argument."

Avoiding public shame and exposure is an understandable and very human motivation. As a result, I agree that celebrities will want to be as honest as possible in public. But how about *in private*? To explore this, we need to think more about the split between the private self of a celebrity and her public image or self.[19] Along the way, we will discover three additional and more subtle ways in which fame can lead to greater dishonest behavior.

The Public/Private Split in the Life of the Celebrity

Let us start with the public image. This is what fans are drawn to, what animates their attention, and what in some cases they even obsess about or fall in love with.

A celebrity's public image is typically shaped at least in part by forces beyond the celebrity herself. The media can construct a narrative around a famous person. Fans also shape who they want this person to be (at least to them). So do detractors of the celebrity.[20]

At the same time, a celebrity is often not entirely passive either.[21] She can use social media platforms to engage with the public, and can attend high publicity events that provide a platform for her to shape how she wishes to be perceived. As time goes by, the celebrity can exercise agency over changes to her public image by updating it or correcting mistakes that others have made about her. She can even attempt to develop so-called para-social relationships with her fans, whereby "members of the public form a non-reciprocal attachment to a celebrity they do not know, believing that they do indeed know the celebrity intimately based on interactions with the celebrity's public persona."[22]

Alongside a celebrity's public image or self is her private one. This is who she takes herself to really be, her authentic self. It does not have to be kept entirely private from everyone else—she may let those she loves, for instance, share in who she really is.

Why believe there is a public/private split in the lives of celebrities? The main reason is because they tell us that there is, and we should take them at their word. For instance, the author Brett Easton Ellis claimed that, "In a sense there were now two Brets—the private and the public—and 1987 was the year I realized they coexisted, which was how unusual my life as a twenty-three-year-old celebrity seemed to me."[23]

Why do celebrities tend to find themselves with this public/private split? As already mentioned, part of the reason is that the celebrity is not the only one involved here. To some extent who she is, at least publicly, is controlled by others. Another part of the story is that having a public/private split can serve as a defense mechanism. As the psychologists Donna Rockwell and David Giles report from their interviews with celebrities,

> The celebrity copes with intense public scrutiny through character-splitting. He or she divides into two identities by contriving a celebrity entity, a new self-presentation in the "public sphere." This "individuating construction of the public personality" allows the famous person to hold his or her more personal "true self" in abeyance, sequestered from all but a trusted inner circle of confidants. "The only way I think you can really handle it is to say, 'That's not really me . . . it's this working part of me, or the celebrity part of me.'. . . So, I am a toy in a shop window."[24]

Summarizing, they write that "The person adapts to fame by crafting, servicing, and protecting the celebrity self. Every move must be considered. A duality between the celebrity's public persona and private self is experienced as a necessary adaptation."[25]

What does any of this have to do with honesty? First of all, even if celebrities will probably try to act as honest as possible in public, it does not follow that the same applies to their private lives. And *that* is where celebrity being insatiable, celebrity being worth protecting, celebrity eroding moral safeguards, and celebrity facilitating greater opportunities to be dishonest mainly come into play.

We can go further than this. The split between a celebrity's public and private images allows at least three additional kinds of dishonest behavior to emerge that we have not seen up to this point: not correcting misinformation about oneself, hypocrisy, and self-deception. Let us consider each of them.

Not Correcting Misinformation. Suppose some misinformation starts to spread about a celebrity, in a way that enhances her status even more. She had nothing to do with creating this misinformation. But now she is aware of it and how much uptake it is getting. She does not see much chance of anyone ever finding out the truth. So, she lets it slide.

There have been many examples of this kind of thing allegedly happening with Hollywood celebrities, but I do not want to get into trouble by calling someone out for it. Suffice it to say that not responding to false allegations of an affair with another celebrity, or of faking a pregnancy, or of cheating financially can be very effective in generating media buzz and boosting one's celebrity status. Is a person in such a case being dishonest? My initial inclination is to say yes.

"Now wait a minute, Miller, it would be crazy to expect an honest person to have to try to correct *all* the misinformation in the world, whenever she comes across it. For instance, suppose you are at a restaurant and you overhear someone at the next table saying that Tom Brady has 6 Super Bowl rings, when you know he really has 7. Only a philosopher would even think that it is dishonest to not say something to correct the mistake."

"Or if you don't like that example, consider that when scrolling Twitter for a few minutes you might come across 10 tweets which you think are misinformed. But you do not stop each time and comment in an effort to correct them. Is that a failure of honesty on your part? Surely not. If it were, then all of us are massively dishonest much of the time, not just on social media but in our interactions with people everyday. Unless, that is, we are spending all of our time correcting the misinformation in the world. And who has time for that?"

I think this challenge is basically right. When it comes to misinformation in general, the celebrity does not have to get her hands dirty all the time in order to be an honest person. But the case we started with is more specific. It is the case of the celebrity who knows about misinformation others have put out there *about her*. Yet she does nothing about it because the misinformation is enhancing her celebrity status.

Again, I think this is dishonest. Suppose a famous person is being interviewed on a podcast and the host happens to mention something about impactful environmental work the celebrity did as a teenager. It would be dishonest to not set the record straight, given that she never actually did this work.

I confess that I do have a lingering worry about my own approach. Imagine that while scrolling through Twitter, our celebrity discovers multiple instances of clearly mistaken claims about her that, nevertheless, enhance her reputation and bring additional attention to her. According to my way of thinking, she would be acting dishonestly if she does nothing to correct them. This has the big downside that it makes living an honest life extremely time-consuming for a celebrity.

Related to this, her honesty is now dependent on having to clean up the mess that others have made. Why, in order to count as honest, should the bad actions of others place an unfair burden on the celebrity to have to fix their mistakes?

To be honest, I am not sure what to think about these problems. Saying that honesty *requires you to correct* any misinformation you come across about yourself seems too burdensome. Saying that honesty *allows you to always ignore* any misinformation you come across about yourself seems too lenient. Where the middle ground is, I do not know.

Hypocrisy. Here is another kind of dishonesty that can threaten celebrities when there is a split between their public and private images. It is hypocrisy.

Publicly a famous person might take a stand on a certain issue, say by coming out against meat-eating. But later he is discovered to be a frequent visitor to Burger King. We would naturally accuse him of hypocrisy. Furthermore, his hypocrisy is dishonest. If a self-described vegan often praises not eating meat-based products, then part of his public image is the expectation that his behavior will harmonize with that praise.[26] By eating at Burger King, his behavior intentionally distorts the facts. He has created certain expectations in the public which admires him, but without having an appropriate excuse to offer, his meat-eating ends up distorting those expectations.

Petter Stordalen has been accused of hypocrisy for precisely these reasons. He is a Norwegian celebrity who is reported to have over $1 billion in net worth, thanks to owning a bunch of hotels and other real estate investments. Over the years he has very publicly contributed millions to the cause of reducing global meat consumption. But in 2019, he posted a picture on Instagram of a visit to the Heart Attack Grill in Las Vegas, where he was about to eat a 20,000-calorie beef burger (8 patties and 20 pieces of bacon!). He commented that, "Must admit that I felt better after eating wifey's burger than this one. But hey, what happens in Vegas . . . ."[27] In doing so, he distorted the expectations he had created in the public about how best to eat.

There is another way in which hypocrisy, and so dishonesty, can make an appearance here. In our imaginary example, by publicly condemning meat-eating a celebrity is aiming to create a certain impression in his audience as to the *depth of his moral values and commitments*. In turn, the audience can come away convinced that this person is deeply committed to the wrongness of eating meat, when in fact he is not. This is a failure of honesty, involving intentionally distorting the facts about the depth of his own commitments. He cares very little about veganism, but because of his strong talk, he hopes his audience gets a different impression. This is the impression one is left with in Stordalen's case too, since by joking about what happened in Vegas, he appears to signal that he did not really care that much about reducing meat consumption after all.

The threat of hypocrisy for famous people gets even worse from here. It turns out that outward behavior is not necessary for hypocrisy. So long as the celebrity's *private thoughts* are out of alignment with his publicly avowed values and commitments, hypocrisy and so dishonesty are a threat.

For example, unlike in the case of Stordalen, consider a famous person who never eats meat and publicly condemns doing so, even though he thinks privately to himself that meat-eating is actually fine and craves it on the inside. Given this disconnect, he is still being hypocritical.

A specific manifestation of this hypocrisy comes in the form of moral grandstanding (or virtue signaling[28]). Suppose someone asks me at a party:

> Do you think it is okay for people to find companionship with AI avatars online?

I really have no idea. I have not looked into the research, nor even tried out one of the websites which markets such relationships. But I have seen some people in my circles say that they are great, and I want to make sure I am playing for the right team here. So, I confidently say:

> Of course that's perfectly fine to do.

I am grandstanding.

A person morally grandstands when he says things about moral issues in public, not because he necessarily thinks that they are true or correct, but because he is trying to impress other people about his own moral qualities.[29] In other words, the moral grandstander is trying to show off. We are perhaps more familiar with someone showing off how smart or rich or famous he is, but in this case, it is a matter of showing off what a good person one is who has all of the "acceptable" moral opinions.

Celebrities would seem to be especially vulnerable to moral grandstanding. They are often pressured to take a public stand on controversial moral issues in society, as well as to make moral pronouncements about specific events that unfold like school shootings or the Ukraine/Russia war. There can be a lot at stake for them depending on what side they endorse (and also if they do not take a side at all). Publicly coming out on the side which aligns best with their admirers is a means to satisfy their desire to enhance and/or preserve their celebrity status.

I would like to give an example of a celebrity grandstanding. But grandstanding is actually very hard to detect. It is a matter of motivation, and we cannot peer into peoples' heads to see their motives. When it really is grandstanding, though, it is also hypocritical. You are publicly communicating your moral stance on AI companionship or immigration, for instance, in a way that conveys that you are genuinely committed to that stance. But as a matter of fact, you are only committed to the stance, provided it serves to boost your moral reputation. As we saw, when there is a disconnect between publicly conveyed and privately held commitments, there is hypocrisy. And where there is hypocrisy, there is also dishonesty.

All moral grandstanding, on this way of thinking, is dishonest. If celebrities are more prone to grandstanding than the rest of us are, which they certainly seem to be, then they are also more prone to being dishonest in this way as well.

Self-Deception. Finally let us turn to fame and self-deception. As a general matter, self-deception is clearly a form of dishonest behavior, as we have seen in previous chapters. A person wants a belief to be true, and is prepared to intentionally distort the facts as she sees them to convince herself that it is true.

With the public/private split that celebrities experience, the threat of self-deception looms larger. A famous person might like what the public is saying about her, even though she has ample evidence that it is not accurate. So, she can come to believe something about herself that she adopts from her public image, which does not correspond to what her private self is really like. Elizabeth Holmes, the disgraced former head of Theranos which promised revolutionary blood testing, is sometimes described in these terms.[30]

Something similar can happen in the opposite direction. Suppose a celebrity has a negative public image, and it is deserved. He has plenty of evidence, indeed, that it is deserved. But he does not want to confront the truth about himself. So, he self-deceptively rejects what the public says about him. Charlie Sheen might fit this profile, when he said things like this at a time in 2011 when there was a lot going wrong in his life that was not exactly a secret: "I'm tired of pretending like I'm not special. I'm tired of pretending like I'm not a total bitchin' rock star from Mars. . . . You can't process me with a normal brain."[31]

Finally, another route to self-deception can come from actively deceiving others. Initially, a famous person might knowingly fabricate part of her own public image. But as Rebecca DeYoung has noted,

> If we project an image of ourselves long enough, our personas begin to feel like the real deal. Far enough into such a life, it might be difficult for the actor herself to tell what is true, because the lines between the self she consistently displays and her inner self have become blurred. Has she become the self outwardly shown, or is she so deceived or confused about her own motives that she can no longer distinguish the two? What begins as a deception of others becomes self-deception.[32]

In this way, the celebrity's dishonesty toward others can spawn still further dishonesty toward herself.

Summing up, we have seen that dishonesty can take at least three additional forms in the life of a famous person due to the public/private split: not correcting helpful misinformation, hypocrisy, and self-deception. Given these problems, perhaps celebrities would be better off if they did not have to deal with the public/private split in the first place. Let's look at that suggestion a bit further.

Avoiding the Public/Private Split

In the extreme, there are two ways to avoid having to deal with the split. One way is to eliminate the split entirely, by the celebrity making her entire self available for the public to view. What you see is what you get. Her life is an open book, and she simply becomes what her public image dictates that she is. Some might claim that Kim Kardashian fit this description early in her career, which was based on extreme visibility ranging from sex tapes to reality shows (*Keeping Up with the Kardashians* aired for 14 years) to endless social media posts.

This approach would have the advantage of eliminating any hypocrisy and self-deception. At the same time, because the celebrity cannot completely control her image, there would still be situations where she would have a chance to correct misinformation. Still, though, it seems progress would be made in curbing the dishonesty in her life.

Yet as the philosophers Archer and Robb argue quite persuasively, such a life is incredibly costly.[33] Your autonomy and freedom are sacrificed if who you are is dictated by the public, and they can control and redefine you as they see fit. This might not seem so bad as long as the public is approving and laudatory. But it rarely stays that way. There is always criticism, jealousy, and hatred to be had. As Taylor Swift once noted, "When you're living for the approval of strangers, and that is where you derive all of your joy and fulfillment, one bad thing can cause everything to crumble . . . When people decided I was wicked and evil and conniving and not a good person, that was the one I couldn't bounce back from because my whole life was centered around it."[34]

The second way to try to avoid having to deal with the public/private split is to drive a hard and fast wedge between them. The famous person will thereby have nothing to do with her public image anymore. It can be shaped by others however they like to. At the same time, she is highly protective of her private self, perhaps letting only a few know who she really is. Similar to the previous strategy, worries about hypocrisy and self-deception would diminish, while there would still be questions about correcting public misinformation.

The actor Joaquin Phoenix might be a good example of someone who has gone down this road, but a particularly striking example is J. D. Salinger, author of *The Catcher in the Rye*, who completely cut off public contact after the book became successful. He retreated to rural New Hampshire and had no interaction with the public, thereby letting others completely control his public image.

How promising does this strategy look? Again, not very. Is it really plausible to think that celebrities will detach themselves completely from their public image and just not care what happens to it? Apart from rare cases like Salinger's, I am skeptical.[35]

So what we are left with is what most celebrities actually experience—constantly having to navigate the relationship between their private and public images.[36] With that comes having to confront head-on the various challenges to behaving honestly.

What About Us?

Now while celebrities might have to face these challenges, what about you and I? You may have been reading this chapter in a detached way, as if it were talking about *them* or *those people*. Are we spared from having to deal with the challenges that come with fame?

The answer, most likely, is no. Fame is not all-or-nothing. Rather it is a matter of degree, and you and I are celebrities to *some* extent, even if it is a minor one (at least speaking for myself!).[37] That means that what celebrity status we do have could foster dishonesty in our lives too. We might be motivated to increase or at least protect our current level of fame, and be willing to cut corners to do so.

In fact, I bet we have all experienced the public/private split to some degree. Our public life might not have any paparazzi in it, but it could include a group of co-workers, or classmates, or religious practitioners. With this split comes the need to navigate it. Hypocrisy and self-deception are real concerns in our lives, and I suspect we have all had a chance to correct positive misinformation about ourselves, but did not.

Now take all these points and magnify them with social media. TikTok, Facebook, Instagram, Twitter, and even LinkedIn enable us to craft a public image. That image can be carefully tailored to create certain impressions and avoid others. And these platforms can fuel a desire to have a greater number of followers, or connections, or likes, or re-tweets. Through our own social media network, we can become a bit more of a celebrity.

The takeaway, then, is that the dangers of dishonest behavior associated with fame are not just dangers for the Taylor Swifts of the world. Granted, they might be *more* of a danger for the really prominent celebrities. But they are dangers for all of us.

Confronting These Dangers

What can we do to help address these dangers? Here are five suggestions.

Become More Aware of Them. Just calling out these ways of being dishonest is already a start. Perhaps you have never given much thought to how not correcting misinformation or engaging in self-deceptive thinking about your public image are ways of being dishonest. Hopefully this chapter can help to promote greater awareness.

But we cannot just keep this at the intellectual level. It is not a matter of *those* people dealing with *their* celebrity status. The point is to look inwards into our own lives, and especially our hearts, to discover the places we need to grow. Where are you projecting one message to your public audience and thinking or doing the exact opposite in private? Where are you inflating your public image or using dishonesty to protect it from being compromised? Where are you turning a blind eye to how others see you, or to how you really are? Without identifying the areas where we each fall short, it is hard to go about trying to repair them.

Correcting Misinformation. We saw that while it is a complicated matter, we cannot just allow misinformation about ourselves to go unchecked if we want to be honest people. Now if the misinformation is negative (it makes us look bad, it damages our job performance, etc.), then it probably won't be hard to get people motivated to do something about it. The more challenging case is when the misinformation actually helps us out. Then there is some cost attached to trying to correct the record. This is a very practical and tangible thing we can do to become more honest.

Look to Exemplars. There are people who do a good job of navigating these dangerous waters of fame and honesty, and we should look to them for inspiration. They can come from all walks of life, and do not need to be instantly recognizable as famous. In fact, it would probably be better if they were *not* famous. For we know that exemplars and role models are more impactful to the extent that they are seen as both *relatable* and *attainable*. "Relatable," in the sense that what they are going through is similar to what I am going through. They can speak to my life. "Attainable," in the sense that I do not get discouraged trying to become more like them, as I would if they were so far superior to me. Finding role models of honesty who are famous to some extent and yet are relatable and attainable can make a huge difference.[38]

Accountability Partners. Perhaps overlapping with the idea of role models is having close friends who can call you out and also be there to share with in times of need.

As Justin Bieber reminded us, one of the dangers of celebrity is being surrounded by people who simply affirm everything you do. That is why it is so important to have people in your life who can make sure that moral safeguards are not being eroded. Because they care about you and want what is best for you, genuine friends are willing to tell the truth. This includes when you are making a mistake or not seeing things clearly, even if you are not going to like what you hear from them.

In my life, my wife helps me here all the time. Despite being an ethics professor and writing books about honesty, I mess up a lot and sometimes do not even realize that I am messing up. As I say half-jokingly, "I only teach ethics." I am so grateful that she is willing to tell me the truth and, very lovingly, not let me ignore my slipups.

The best forms of accountability work in both directions. In other words, accountability is also a matter of being able to *go to someone* I trust and share what I have done that no one else has seen. This is especially important if it is embarrassing and makes me vulnerable.

Grounding Our Worth and Value. The final suggestion is the least tangible, but perhaps the most important. It is to ground our worth and value as people in what really matters.

Philosophers and religious leaders have always cautioned us about becoming too enamored with fame and celebrity status. Fame is alluring, perhaps now more than ever before, but it is also fleeting and fickle. It can build up but also destroy a person. It is not worth paying the price of dishonesty in order to accumulate or preserve.

The thought here, then, is that a lot of the temptation to be dishonest that comes with fame can be tempered if we stay grounded in things that really *do* matter—friends, family, love, truth, kindness, justice, and—for the religious—the sacred and divine. If celebrity happens to come our way, then so be it. But it cannot be allowed to crowd out other things in life that actually matter, and which keep us grounded.

Notes

1. Wikipedia 2025a.
2. Sternlicht 2022.
3. Horowitz and Lorenz 2021.
4. The remainder of this chapter is adapted from Miller 2024, and is used with permission of Bloomsbury Press.
5. Archer and Robb forthcoming: 2. As Robb and Archer note in another article, "a common theme is that celebrities are those whose lives are well-known by the public, but who may not possess any special talents that are worthy of fame" (2022: 37).
6. See Robb and Archer 2022.
7. Quoted in DeYoung 2014: 83. See also 33.
8. Quoted in Rockwell and Giles 2009: 184, emphasis in original.
9. For related discussion, see DeYoung 2014: 33.
10. DeYoung 2014: 57.
11. Quoted in Archer and Sie 2023: 350. Rockwell and Giles note that, "fame changes the way the world responds to the celebrity, who is no longer hearing intimately related others' honest appraisals" (2009: 189, see also 204).
12. Rockwell and Giles 2009: 192.
13. Deb 2019.
14. Ibid.
15. Yet another reason could be that celebrities might be motivated in certain circumstances to be dishonest for *altruistic* reasons. For instance, we can imagine a celebrity couple in the political world putting on a good front that their marriage is healthy even when it is not. They do this for what they take to be

the good of the country. I suspect readers can come up with plenty of recent examples that fit this description.

16. Espada 2023.
17. Liu 2023.
18. Bruce 2021.
19. In what follows, I have been helped by the discussion in Rockwell and Giles 2009 and Archer and Robb forthcoming.
20. Archer and Robb forthcoming: 3–4, 10.
21. Robb and Archer 2022: 47 and Archer and Robb forthcoming: 4.
22. Robb and Archer 2022: 47. See also Archer and Robb forthcoming 3.
23. Quoted in Archer and Robb forthcoming: 5. See also Rockwell and Giles 2009: 195–196, 202–205 and Archer and Robb forthcoming: 4.
24. Rockwell and Giles 2009: 187–188.
25. Ibid., 196. See also 202–203.
26. This paragraph and the paragraph two down both draw upon Miller 2021a: 55, with permission from Oxford University Press.
27. Shakhnazarova and Carter 2019.
28. For potential differences between the two labels, see Tosi and Warmke 2020: 37–40.
29. Here I am following the philosophers Justin Tosi and Brandon Warmke. See Ibid., 15.
30. See, for example, Ethics Unwrapped 2022.
31. Bosch 2011.
32. DeYoung 2014: 66. See also 72–73.
33. Archer and Robb forthcoming: 11.
34. Quoted in Parr 2020.
35. Here I join Archer and Robb forthcoming: 11–12.
36. As Rockwell and Giles write, "The celebrity, left to reconcile self as 'image' and self as 'person,' finds that being-in-the-world is an existential juggling act" (2009: 203).
37. As Archer and Robb note, "We are all, to a certain extent, limited and defined by our environments and others around us, experiencing the objectifying look of the 'other' and the force of their expectations. The celebrity's experience of having a public self that is defined by others is therefore only different by degree and intensity because they are more often in the public eye" (Archer and Robb forthcoming: 6).
38. For more, see Han et al. 2017.

8
Pastors and the Honesty Crisis in Religion

A 2023 Gallup poll showed that Americans' perception of the ethics of religious leaders continues to decline. With respect to the "honesty and ethical standards" of clergy, only 32% of participants gave this group a "high" or "very high" score. This marked a dramatic decrease compared to just a few decades ago. In the 1970s and 1980s, the percentage was consistently over 60%.[1]

High-profile cases of dishonesty involving sermon plagiarism, financial misappropriation, and sexual wrongdoing have no doubt contributed to this decline in perceived honesty. As this list suggests, it is not that there is one particular kind of dishonesty that has been prominent with religious leaders. Rather, a variety of different forces are at work, many of which we have already highlighted in previous chapters.

To take one example, sermon plagiarism has been getting a lot of attention in recent years, perhaps most notably with Ed Litton, who was elected president of the Southern Baptist Convention in 2021. Some of his sermons were reportedly found to contain identical passages from the sermons of J. D. Greear, who was his predecessor in the same position (yes, it is hard to make this stuff up!). Discussion of this case even found its way into *The New York Times*. As their article notes, "the dust-up has revealed a dirty little secret of the preaching life: Many pastors borrow from one another in the pulpit, and the norms around the practice are fuzzy at best."[2]

Sermon plagiarism is a failure of honesty. The pastor is intentionally distorting the facts by knowingly presenting certain material as

The Honesty Crisis. Christian B. Miller, Oxford University Press. © Oxford University Press 2026.
DOI: 10.1093/9780197840801.003.0008

if it were his or her own work, when it actually belongs to someone else. With the availability of sermons on the Internet, sermon plagiarism became much easier than it ever had been in the past. Now with AI, a sermon can be ready to go in a matter of seconds, with little chance of detection and plenty of benefits in terms of time and effort.

Temptations to view pornography and cheat sexually obviously exist for the pastor just as they do for everyone else. These temptations are now stronger, and the prospects of getting away with them are much higher, thanks to online resources. In a *Leadership Journal* survey conducted in 2005, 50% of pastors admitted to viewing pornography in the previous year, and 30% admitted to infidelity since beginning their ministry.[3]

Hence as our honesty crises continue to accelerate dishonest behavior, they will likely catch pastors in their net at an increasingly alarming rate. Given the positions that pastors occupy with respect to their congregations, many will be tempted to cover up their dishonesty with more dishonesty. So honesty crises can also accelerate dishonest behavior designed to mask the pastor's own initial dishonest behavior.

But we are getting ahead of ourselves. Let us first look at how plagiarism plays out in the pastoral context with sermons. Then we will briefly consider infidelity. We will also throw in the celebrity status of pastors, and see how that makes a difference too in covering up dishonesty and promoting moral hypocrisy.

As this suggests, our focus in this chapter will not be on *new* honesty crises. Rather this chapter is an exercise in application—we will see how the very same person can be confronted by pressures to be dishonest that arise, not just from one source like AI, but from multiple different sources in different areas of their lives. In a way, then, the previous chapters have been overly artificial by rigidly compartmentalizing the discussion. This chapter blends things together.

A final note before we dive in. My focus will be on a Christian context here, and specifically a Western Protestant context. This is to keep the discussion focused. Trying to talk about 'religion' in general risks being too superficial and painting over the radical differences in the religious practices of different religions. Having said this, the observations which follow will straightforwardly generalize to other branches of Christianity. They apply to other world religions too, in cases where there are corresponding values and practices in place, such as a leader who is supposed to be giving an original message to an audience, or who is not permitted to engage in infidelity.

For readers who are just not interested in issues at the intersection of dishonesty and religion, they can simply pass this chapter by.

Sermon Plagiarism

> Plagiarize!
> Let no one else's work evade your eyes.
> Remember why the good Lord made your eyes.
> So don't shade your eyes,
> But plagiarize, plagiarize, plagiarize,
> Only be sure always to call it, please—research
>
> —Lobachevsky, A song by Tom Lehrer[4]

Like most Sundays, Colleen Reese was attending Franklin Christian Church in Tennessee, but this particular Sunday in 2016 was one she would never forget. The sermon that day, delivered by her regular pastor Zach Stewart, really bugged her, especially a joke about mental illness being passed from mothers to their children. Later Colleen Googled the sermon title, and reportedly found that Stewart had basically copied and pasted his sermon from another church's online materials. That is when her investigation took off.[5]

According to reports, it turned out that Stewart had been fooling his congregation for years. He had not just plagiarized a small handful of sermons. And he had not just taken some Biblical lessons from other pastors' sermons. There were *hundreds* of sermons which he had allegedly stolen and presented as his own. Plus these sermons were complete with the original personal anecdotes and stories, which Stewart had seemingly co-opted to make them sound like they were from his life.

Reese reported her findings to the church elders, and eventually Stewart left the church, although he never confessed to plagiarizing. Understandably, members of the church were hurt and confused. Said one, "Every story he told was somebody else's story. The hard part is that nobody knows Zach Stewart. When somebody lies all the time, what do you do?"[6]

Sadly, the story does not end there. Somehow Stewart was able to land a new job at Twin Oaks Christian Church in Michigan. Sure enough, according to reports he started plagiarizing again. After this church was alerted to what was apparently happening, videos of Stewart's sermons started immediately disappearing from their website. Today Stewart is no longer with Twin Oaks.

Zach Stewart's story is extreme. But alleged cases of sermon plagiarism are being reported all the time. Here are a few other, memorable examples:[7]

> Ernest T. Campbell was once invited to fill the pulpit of a church in a distant city, and he chose to preach "Adam's Other Son," a creative sermon . . . which Campbell had published in a sermon collection. As he preached that Sunday, however, he had a sense that something was awry. "My sermon," he said later, "was landing like marbles on a tile floor." After the service, he was told that a young associate pastor had preached the same sermon nearly word for word the week before.[8]

> Several years ago my father-in-law returned home from a trip to South Carolina and said, "Funny thing, when I went to my church on Sunday, I heard the same sermon I heard in South Carolina."[9]

> Reba Cobb . . . was accused of preaching someone else's sermon. Cobb, in turn, confronted the research assistant she hired to help write the sermon. She discovered the researcher had plagiarized the entire message. When Cobb went to the researcher's source for the sermon, she discovered that he, too, admitted to lifting the sermon from yet another. Cobb finally tracked her twice-plagiarized sermon back to a 1979 message delivered by a Methodist pastor from Indianapolis.[10]

> As a young staff pastor at a church in the Pacific Northwest, Jesse Holcomb said that he and his colleague would be constantly on the lookout for good ideas at other churches. They even had an inside joke about it: "If you have eyes, plagiarize."[11]

Sometimes these stories even gain national prominence, as in the case of Ed Litton who we mentioned already for allegedly plagiarizing from his own predecessor as President of the Southern Baptist Convention.

What makes these cases of sermon plagiarism? Obviously, sermon plagiarism is plagiarism involving the content of another person's sermon. Sermons are, in part, addresses to people which convey a message that the pastor is trying to communicate to his or her audience. They can be verbal or written, long or short, delivered to Christians in the church or a mixed audience, interesting or boring, orthodox or heretical, and many other things besides. We won't worry about all these variations.

In a more theological vein, sermons are often understood by Christians as much more than just speeches or talks. They are a means of communicating God's word to an audience. Indeed as one writer puts it, "When we listen to the Word preached, we are hearing not just a word about God but a word from God."[12]

As such, sermons are a tremendously important part of the role of the pastor. The pastor may have many other roles as well—spiritual counseling, visiting the sick and poor, administration, and so forth—but preaching a sermon has often been considered central. Hence if, in doing so, a pastor ends up acting in a way that is dishonest—as I will suggest that sermon plagiarism is—then the pastor will be guilty of a serious wrong. Or, in theological language, the pastor is grievously sinning.

Indeed, this wrongdoing is arguably *worse* than academic plagiarism. For there is added moral and theological weight, from a Christian perspective, to the pastor's role in teaching what is considered by Christians to be the Word of God. As the book of James says in the New Testament, "Not many of you should become teachers, my fellow believers, because you know that we who teach will be judged with more strictly."[13]

That is the sermon side. What about the plagiarism side? Fortunately, we already spent a lot of time in Chapter 5 clarifying what plagiarism is. There we said that plagiarism is the presentation of someone else's work—including their words, ideas, or images—as if it were your own work without suitable acknowledgment. In the case of sermons, the most blatant and egregious kind of plagiarism is simply cutting and pasting text from someone else without quotation marks and citations. Parishioners who do not know any better will think that the pastor is the one who came up with these words on his own. That is what reportedly got Zach Stewart into such hot water.

Another form sermon plagiarism can take is to borrow someone else's ideas and use them as your own, without giving credit to the person who thought of them in the first place. Someone's book, for instance, might have a new insight about Jesus's feeding the five thousand. That insight shows up in the sermon, but without any credit given to the author of the book. This will almost certainly mislead the audience into thinking that the pastor was the one who had the insight.

Still other forms of sermon plagiarism include making use of another author's example, illustration, or analogy, and presenting it as one's own without giving credit. The same is true for coopting someone else's personal testimony or experience and presenting it as if it were one's lived experience. Just borrowing the structure of a sermon from someone else, even though the content is different, would still count as plagiarism.[14]

These examples serve to highlight three features of sermon plagiarism.[15] The first is that it is presenting *someone else's work* in your own sermon. The material came from elsewhere, and it is dependent on the actual work that someone else did—they came up with the idea/argument/writing/example/illustration/title or whatever else it happens to be. You did not.

That by itself is no problem, of course, so long as you *acknowledge* the source. If credit is given where credit is due, then plagiarism disappears. That is the second feature of sermon plagiarism—the credit is missing.

Now a pastor can rightly worry about what a ton of acknowledgments would do to a sermon. No one wants to hear an endless stream of "As Tim Keller said in . . ." followed by "John Calvin illustrates this point with . . . ."

But as many writers have noted, there are ways to get around this practical problem.[16] You can put citations in the bulletin or online. You can keep them very brief in the spoken version, like "One author observed that . . . ." And frankly, if the sermon is riddled with tons of acknowledgments to the work of others, then that might indicate a larger problem anyway.

The third thing to highlight here is that it does not matter if the source has given permission for other pastors to use his or her materials in a sermon. Yes, it is great that Chuck Swindoll or Tim Keller told you that you can use one of their main sermon illustrations or central ideas. When his father asked about using some of his son's sermon material in his own sermons, Josh Howerton, who led a 15,000 person per week megachurch in Texas at the time, told his father: "Dad, you don't need to ask. If my bullet fits your gun then shoot it."[17]

But if the father goes ahead and uses this material in a sermon without any acknowledgement, then that *still* counts as plagiarism. He is presenting his son's work as his own without giving the source credit. Consent does not excuse in this case.

So that is a bit about what sermon plagiarism is. I hope at this point that I do not need to convince you that it is dishonest. When a pastor does it, he is intentionally distorting the facts. In what way? By intentionally presenting certain material as if it were his own work, when it actually belongs to someone else.[18]

The 'intentionally' is important, as we said in Chapter 5. If someone is diligent about acknowledging her sources, but in one case just forgets to include a citation, then that is negligent and sloppy, perhaps, and still counts as plagiarism. But it is not a failure of honesty. It was not done on purpose to make it seem like she was the one who came up with the material. From now on we will just focus on the intentional cases of sermon plagiarism.

What emerges is something of a test that a pastor can use to check for dishonesty in the form of sermon plagiarism. The pastor can ask, if she is worried about a particular passage, whether using it without acknowledging the source would be a case of intentionally distorting the facts by misleading the audience into thinking that the material in question is her own creation and not derivative from another source.

Admittedly, there will likely be borderline cases. What about someone who develops an example that was initially inspired by something she had read, but she changes it in certain ways to try to make it more her own? Without knowing the details of the case, it is hard to make any blanket judgments. Still, even if there are fuzzy or difficult cases, the test is still helpful. If it were followed regularly, dishonesty in sermons would plummet.

Whether sermon plagiarism is dishonest does not seem to be very controversial. What is more interesting (and disturbing) is *all the ways in which it ends up being dishonest* that we probably do not pay attention to. Here are four that I spotted.

So that I don't get into trouble with any real people, let's create a fictional pastor named Roberts who used a lot of material from the prominent Protestant minister Tim Keller's work over the course of many of his sermons, without any attribution to Keller. Then it seems to me that:

> He is dishonest to his congregation. The people in the pews are assuming that, unless the pastor tells them otherwise, this material originated with Pastor Roberts. Originality is the default assumption of the audience. When Roberts offers some profound insight about, say, Jesus feeding the five thousand, he is hopefully saying something true. But he is saying it in such a way as to make it seem like *he* was the one who came up with the insight. He did not. This is not lying, because he is saying things which he thinks are true. But it is misleading, since he is hoping that his audience will assume that he was the source of the insight. And being misleading is dishonest. It is intentionally distorting the facts, in this case about who came up with the idea.

> He is dishonest to his source. By not acknowledging Keller's work, Pastor Roberts is being dishonest to Keller too. Assuming that Keller came up with the material in the first place, he was the one who put in the hard work to discover the ideas. To then take those ideas and espouse them as your own, as Pastor Roberts does, is to steal them. And stealing is dishonest.
>
> He is dishonest to the church. In his role as a pastor, Roberts is expected to preach the Word of God to his congregation using his own abilities and talents, and in so doing uphold the norms and standards of his role. By plagiarizing, he is intentionally violating one of the ethical expectations of his job, and so he is thereby cheating. And cheating is dishonest.
>
> He is dishonest to himself and to God. This depends on whether Pastor Roberts also rationalizes what he is doing. Excuses like "I didn't have enough time to prepare for Sunday" or "Nothing is original anyway" or "Every pastor does it" or "What does it matter so long as it advances the Kingdom of God?" are often BS rationalizations. They are not made with an eye to the truth, but rather with an eye to making the person feel better and assuage his guilt. And BSing is dishonest.

All this dishonesty is bred just by the act of preparing and delivering the plagiarized sermons. We have not said anything yet about what he might do to cover up his dishonesty if Roberts is accused of plagiarism. Nor have we said anything about Roberts' dishonest hypocrisy if he condemns the plagiarism of other pastors while engaging in it himself.

Now the Bible does not specifically address these different manifestations of dishonesty. But, no surprise, there are many passages in the Bible which do not take too kindly to dishonesty in general. It is clear that, from a Judeo-Christian perspective, God is someone who is deeply opposed to our intentionally distorting the facts in our lives, and wants us to exhibit behavior that accurately represents the world as we see it. Thus, in Proverbs, we find that with respect to lying:

> Whoever speaks the truth gives honest evidence, but a false witness utters deceit. (12:17, ESV)

And in Colossians:

> Do not lie to one another, seeing that you have put off the old self with its practices. (3:9, ESV)

The same applies to distorting the facts, not to others, but rather to ourselves. Hence, we find in James that:

> Those who consider themselves religious and yet do not keep a tight rein on their tongues deceive themselves, and their religion is worthless. (1:26, NIV)

And in Romans:

> Because of the privilege and authority God has given me, I give each of you this warning: Don't think you are better than you really are. Be honest in your evaluation of yourselves, measuring yourselves by the faith God has given us. (12:3)

Shifting to stealing, in 2 Kings we find:

> They did not require an accounting from those to whom they gave the money to pay the workers, because they acted with complete honesty. (12:15 ESV)

There are dozens of other passages which speak to matters of honesty and dishonesty, and which fit very well with my dishonesty framework of intentionally distorting the facts. It is hard to see how these passages would permit any of the forms of sermon dishonesty we saw above.

Some leading Christian thinkers have been outspoken against the dishonesty of sermon plagiarism. As Trinity Evangelical Divinity School Professor D. A. Carson forcefully argues:

> Taking over another sermon and preaching it as if it were yours is always and unequivocally wrong, and if you do it you should resign or be fired immediately. The wickedness is along at least three axes: (1) You are stealing. (2) You are deceiving the people to whom you are preaching. (3) Perhaps worst, you are not devoting yourself to the study of the Bible to the end that God's truth captures you, molds you, makes you a man of God and equips you to speak for him.[19]

This seems exactly right.

I say "some" Christian thinkers, but not all. For instance, the publication *Preaching Today* ran a survey of its subscribers, with 1,450 responding to the following:

> "Of the following sermon elements, which do you believe can ethically be used from the sermons of others without giving credit?"

Percentage of participants who said these could be used without giving credit:[20]

Theological/scriptural principles	62%
The main idea	53%
Illustrations	53%
Sermon titles	34%
Metaphors	32%
Main outline points	26%
Well-worded sentences or phrases	17%
Sub-points and developing ideas	15%
Nothing should be used without giving credit	19%

Alas, I am with the 19% here—nothing should be used without giving credit.

Common justifications for sermon plagiarism include that "All truth is God's truth" or "God is the ultimate source anyway" or "It's all for the good of advancing God's kingdom." Sometimes these justifications seem like they are calling into question whether sermon plagiarism is really *dishonest*. Other times they seem as if they acknowledge that sermon plagiarism is dishonest, but still want to make the case that it is *ethical*. Perhaps by analogy with white lies and lies that save innocent lives, the thought might be that sermon plagiarism can be dishonest but right. Either way, I think these justifications have little chance at being successful.

Take the point about it's all God's truth. Here is one way someone put the idea:

> There is not a sermon preached that belongs to the one who received it. If they are truly a man of God, preaching his Word, believing in Jesus as Lord and Savior, and the gospel, nothing they preach belongs to them. It all belongs to God. 'Freely you received, freely give.'[21]

But even if it is true, as Christians believe, that God is the ultimate basis for reality and the source of all truth, there has always been an acknowledgment of human accomplishments too.[22] It is not as if humans do not deserve credit for feeding the poor or saving drowning children. So too, they deserve credit for the work they put into their scholarship, writing, and speaking. To then take that work by someone else and pass it off as your own, without acknowledgment, is dishonest. As philosopher Jordan Steffaniak puts it, "It matters not that all truth is God's truth. It matters more that we submit in humility to the God of all truth, acknowledging our debt to others."[23]

What about advancing God's kingdom, even if it involves plagiarism? Here is Rick Howerton making this argument:

> Sometimes the wise pastor utilizes the outline that was seen or heard. Sometimes the preacher is grabbing a mind-boggling turn of a phrase that will stick in the minds of his congregation. Some weeks the pastor is plucking from the online sermon an undeniably effective illustration. The wise pastor longs to be the best preacher he can be for the betterment of and spiritual growth of his congregation. He realizes that bringing the best sermon he can to his people for the sake of their spiritual transformation is more important than originality. He's humble enough to realize that learning from and embracing the ideas of others

> is the way he can bring his best sacrifice to the altar each and every Sunday.[24]

But wait, this is a false dichotomy. *Of course*, go ahead and make use of someone else's outline or turn of phrase or illustration, if they would be effective in your sermon. But just *give credit to the source*, that's all.

Indeed, Howerton's approach can backfire dramatically. If the pastor were to get caught plagiarizing, then whatever "betterment" and "spiritual growth" there might have been from the improved sermons will be dramatically undercut by all the damage that ensues, potentially leading to the dismissal of the pastor.[25] After all, "Almost every community has a story of a church torn apart and a pastor embarrassed, if not dismissed, over 'borrowing' sermons."[26]

Let us suppose that the right thing to say is that sermon plagiarism is dishonest and a serious wrong. Now consider a pastor who is scrupulous and does *not* plagiarize any sermons in the ways outlined above. Would that make the pastor honest in this area of her life? I hate to say it, because I know this is going to come across as harsh. But the answer is no. Why not? Surely if the pastor preaches a sermon with material that is entirely of her own creation, then that is not plagiarism, and so it cannot be a failure of honesty in that respect.

That is right, but just because it would be a form of honest *behavior* does not mean it is coming from the *virtue of honesty*. Think back to Chapter 1. There we said that honest behavior is only one part of the equation of honesty. Motivation matters too. So we have to ask questions like, why did the pastor carefully cite and acknowledge all of her sources, rather than omitting some of them and making it seem like they were her ideas? Some answers to this question are virtuous ones, but some answers are not.

If the answer is one of the following—because it would be the honest thing to do to cite, or because it is the right thing to do to cite, or because the original author deserves credit for coming up with the idea—then those are perfectly good motivations to have. They are just what you would expect an honest person to say. But if instead the answers are more like one of these—because I don't want to get into trouble if the plagiarism were discovered, or because I don't want to feel guilty if I plagiarized, or because God will reward me in the afterlife for not plagiarizing—then these are hardly going to count as virtuous reasons that an honest person would have.

What is the difference between the two groups? The second is egoistic—the focus is just on benefiting oneself. As we said in Chapter 1, that kind of motivation does not count as virtuously honest motivation.

The upshot is that exhibiting the virtue of honesty on Sundays when preaching a sermon is *hard to do*. It not only requires that the spoken words be honest words, honestly acquired, but that they also be spoken with one's heart in the right place. As two pastors put it, "[k]eep your motives pure, and communicate truth by making your sources clear."[27] I suspect many Christians would say that here is another place where God's help is needed.

Okay, so we have talked about what sermon plagiarism is and why it is dishonest. I have made the case for why Christian pastors should stay away from it. What we have not seen is why—today—we are in the midst of an honesty crisis.

Sermon plagiarism is not anything new, and there are all kinds of interesting anecdotes about plagiarism throughout the history of Christianity. For instance, apparently King James of England "was so outraged by the plagiarism of preachers that he made a law requiring preachers to give at least one original sermon a month."[28] What then has changed recently to spark an honesty crisis?

The answer is strikingly similar to what happened with student plagiarism. In both cases, "there is plenty of evidence that the practice is spreading and that the kerosene on the fire is the Internet. Not only are thousands of sermons available for the snatching on church Web pages, but scores of commercial sites hawk complete sermons, illustrations, outlines, images, and PowerPoint accompaniments for a fee."[29]

As we saw, this is what allegedly happened with Stewart. He was able to view sermons online and reportedly copied them so closely that he even used the same body movements as some on the original speakers.[30]

Interestingly, all this mirrors what we have already seen happening with students in the last few decades. Material from the Internet was suddenly showing up in student papers, sometimes subtly, sometimes copied and pasted.

So the availability of Internet resources certainly ramped up sermon plagiarism. Yet if you are a pastor trying to not get caught plagiarizing, enlisting the Internet for sermon material still has some big drawbacks. The most significant is that there is a digital record out there for people to find. If you found the material, then other people in your congregation can find it too. Another drawback is that you will still have to put in *some* time to prepare the sermon. A sermon illustration plagiarized from one source, an idea plagiarized from another source—that still leaves text that needs to be written to fill up 20, 30, or even 40 minutes each week.

Alas, we know that the story about the Internet and plagiarism does not end here. Along came the next big dishonesty step, and once again it parallels the student case—AI. An AI like ChatGPT can take care of all these problems with Internet sermon plagiarism.

For instance, there won't be a digital record of the sermon anymore. Google won't spot it. If someone is really suspicious, they can try running the sermon through an AI checker, but as we noted in Chapter 5, there are no completely reliable ones out there now. Plus, with AI there is no time needed to spend doing research, reading commentaries, finding material on the Internet, and so on. All you have to do is guide the AI a bit—how long should the sermon be, what passage should it focus on, what style should it have, how many practical applications do you want—and voila! The AI does the rest of the work for you.

Don't believe me? Just go to Claude or ChatGPT or Gemini, ask it to prepare a 1,000-word sermon on Jesus feeding the five thousand written in the style of Tim Keller, and see what it comes up with. I bet you will be impressed. If you have ever attended church, it might even sound better than what you heard on Sundays.

If the Internet "is like having a drug dealer on every corner,"[31] then AI is like being connected directly to an IV.

Some say that AI is missing "human warmth," that it can't "convincingly sympathize with the human plight," that it "lacks specificity," or that it "cannot understand community and inclusivity."[32] But I just don't see this, at least in the context of producing sermons. AI is not a church counselor or a greeter or a comforter. It is just delivering text to be preached in a sermon to the congregation. The pastor can add whatever energy and emotion and sympathy he likes.

Plus, AI is evolving rapidly. Newer models are accomplishing what older models could not. And of course the pastor is welcome to throw in a few sentences referencing specific details about the church community. After all, that would only help to mask what is going on in the rest of the sermon.

So the real question, it seems to me, is this one raised by the former editor of *Christianity Today*, Russell Moore: "What if everywhere-accessible AI could write completely orthodox, biblically anchored, and compellingly argued sermons for pastors every week?"[33] Surely at least some pastors would make use of these sermons. An honesty crisis is now looming, to be sure. Pastors could get away with using this technology and not get caught. And it is very enticing, since the AI does a job in seconds that would normally take hours and hours of work.

What can be done to try to address this crisis? When we consider the options in the case of student cheating, we see right away that they are even more limited in the case of sermons.

The first option was to get rid of student papers and shift to in-class assessments only. But that is not going to fly in the case of churches—the sermon is not going away anytime soon.

A second option was to just embrace AI. But that is a bad idea in the student case, and I would argue it is an even worse idea in the pastor case. The pastor's role in the pulpit would be reduced to just reading some text prepared by a machine. That is not going to fly either. As one pastor said, "When I habitually use somebody else's material, I don't allow the Spirit the opportunity to speak into my church, through my personality, out of my walk with God. I lose what a growing number of people are looking for in a preacher: authenticity. They want to know that I'm for real."[34] You are not for real if you are just reading what the AI wrote.

The remaining path with students was to still have writing assignments, but to be strict in trying to do what one can as a professor in limiting their use of AI in producing the paper. In parallel fashion, then, pastors should be expected to not consult AI for any substantive help with their sermons, or if they do receive such help, it has to be acknowledged just like any other source is acknowledged.

The challenge becomes how to help pastors resist the temptation to make use of this shiny new technological toy which, in some ways, would make their job tremendously easier each week. We will return to this topic in the final section.

Pastors and Internet Infidelity

John Gibson was a beloved husband, father, friend, and seminary professor. For 17 years, he taught at New Orleans Baptist Theological Seminary, and was also a pastor at First Southern Baptist Church in Mississippi. "Students loved his approach to teaching," the president of the seminary said. "His smile and outgoing personality could light up a room."[35] They also loved him for another reason—as an act of charity, he would fix the cars of students and friends alike for free.

"It was unbelievable," said Bob Stewart, a fellow professor. "It took a while when I moved across the street from him to get used to the number of cars that were in his driveway and down the street and in front of my house."[36]

But in 2015, the Ashley Madison website breach happened, and Gibson's name was on the list of people who were discovered to have an account. It was natural to assume at the time that he had been seeking out an affair, unbeknownst to anyone else. Such a breach of ethics would mean that he would lose his job at the seminary. But that never happened, as six days after the records were published, Gibson took his life in his garage.

In an interview with CNN, his wife disclosed that there was a suicide note: "He talked about depression. He talked about having his name on there, and he said he was just very, very sorry," she said. "He offered grace and mercy and forgiveness to everyone else, but somehow he couldn't extend that to himself."[37]

Gibson's story vividly illustrates what we already know, which is that pastors are hardly immune from infidelity. Just like the rest of us, some pastors give into temptation. No surprise there. For instance, an early survey from 1988 found in response to the question, "Have you ever had sexual intercourse with someone other than your spouse since you've been in local church ministry?" Yes: 12%. No: 88%.[38] Similarly, a 1986 study had the percentage of 'Yes' at 16.66%.[39] A 1998 study found that 15.6% confessed to extramarital sexual behavior.[40]

That same 1998 study found a starling 45% of pastors they surveyed admitting to using pornography.[41] A 2001 *Leadership Journal* survey found that "half of the pastors (51%) say Internet pornography is a possible temptation for them, while 37 percent admit it is a current struggle."[42] A 2015 Barna study found that 57% of pastors admit to having struggled in the past, while 14% currently struggle; an updated 2024 version of this study has the numbers at 67% having struggled and 14% currently struggling.[43]

Since we have discussed infidelity at length in Chapter 4 and saw how the rise of the Internet has fostered an honesty crisis, there is no need to retread this ground again. Rather, I only want to highlight here how being a pastor may make someone *more susceptible* to temptation in ways that people in other careers and fields may not be. Indeed, pastors themselves tell us as much. According to one study, 70% of pastors say they are especially vulnerable to sexual temptation.[44] Here are some possible reasons for why this might be:[45]

- Pastors are highly visible in their communities, and are expected by their congregations (and by God) to be a role model for how to live a Christian life. Hence while there is great risk of going to a strip club or buying pornographic magazines from a store, the Internet provides a place where the pastor can hide behind the cloak of anonymity.
- Because pastors often do not have normal work hours and can be alone for large blocks of time during the week, there is ample opportunity to partake of morally forbidden pleasures

without others—even their families—being aware of what they are doing.

- Sexual pleasure can become a 'forbidden fruit.' As one pastor said, "I believe ministers have a special degree of 'forbidden fruit' temptation simply because expectations of purity of thought and action by themselves and others are much higher, and, not having the exposure to the raw side of life, they have a stronger tendency to fantasize, instead of realistically rejecting immorality. Thus porn movies or videos or magazines have a stronger appeal purely because they are forbidden."[46]
- Accountability can be difficult, since if a pastor confesses to others in the church about what he is doing online, he might fear that he could lose his job and be ostracized by the very community he has been shepherding. Hence two pastors admitted:

> "We have no one to turn to," wrote one pastor. "We are afraid to go to a counselor for fear that word of our problems will somehow leak out."
>
> Wrote another: "I wouldn't dare tell a fellow minister my problems in this area. My denomination would forgive murder, but not impurity of thought!"[47]

In one study, 96% of pastors who were engaged in infidelity did not tell anyone else about it.[48]

- The week of a pastor can be filled with problems—the challenges, pain, sin, and death facing members of their congregation. Uniquely as compared to many other professions, pastors bear the burden of listening to, counseling, praying for, and trying to help people move forward with their lives. As such, they may in turn look for a release, a source of pleasure without the burdens of responsibility. Cheating with another person can be seen as providing such a release. Hence one pastor noted, "A minister longs for positive feedback in a world filled with problems and tragedy. Sex can seem an easy and accessible route to find that affirmation."[49]
- Put simply, "Isolation and loneliness are inherent to the position. And many pastors neglect their personal relationships for

> the sake of ministry."[50] Isolation and loneliness in turn can lead to searching for pleasurable experiences and companionship online.[51]

Given these general observations about the life of a contemporary Protestant pastor, is it really so surprising that they might face greater temptation to engage in online infidelity as opposed to those in more secular professions?[52]

Of course, one major factor that is supposed to be reining in such temptation is the moral teaching of their own faith. Viewing pornography or engaging in sexual conversations in anonymous chatrooms is clearly antithetical from a Christian perspective to what it is to be honest and loyal to one's significant other. So at some intellectual level pastors are aware that there is no support for such behaviors. In addition, there are religious practices like prayer and confession which are supposed to rein in temptation at both the cognitive but also the emotional and habitual levels. Not to mention senior pastors, bishops, or other church leaders who can hold pastors accountable. Finally, there is meant to be, from a more theological perspective, the internal working of the Holy Spirit in the life of the pastor (and indeed, in the life of all Christians) to work gradually toward the cultivation of a good and virtuous character. Thus the Holy Spirit is also meant to play a part in helping to curb acts of infidelity on the part of the pastor.

And yet, despite all these resources, the percentages of pastors using and struggling with pornography was in the 30–40% range according to multiple studies. One wonders what the percentages would be without these resources. Pastors, I conclude, especially feel the force of the honesty crisis surrounding infidelity.

Pastors and Celebrity

We have already seen how pastors today can be under pressure to be dishonest from multiple directions. Now let's throw into the mix that pastors are also celebrities to varying degrees, and that there are currently more opportunities to amplify their platforms than perhaps ever before in the history of the Christian church.

If nothing else, pastors are celebrities with respect to the high levels of attention they receive from their congregations. But as a matter of fact, the attention rarely stops there. They are often present in other spaces like hospitals, weddings, nursing homes, and funerals. They frequently become leaders in their communities, and their written and spoken voices can be found far beyond the confines of the pulpit on Sunday morning. Many pastors write articles and books, and sometimes those find a home with publications and presses that have a broad reach. All of this has been amplified with the Internet. Now a number of pastors put recordings of their sermons online, or have a blog, or post/tweet/upload content regularly (or all of the above).

Given their position as celebrities, even if it is just with respect to their congregation, pastors will confront some version of the divide between their public and private lives. As we said in the previous chapter, a public image is the object of attention by a celebrity's admirers, while a private image is who she takes herself to really be. In the case of pastors, publicly they project an image of virtue and morally praiseworthy behavior. They prescribe that behavior to others and aim to live it out in their own lives as well. But privately, they mess up just like the rest of us. For instance, they could give into temptation to be dishonest by plagiarizing, viewing pornography, or using the Ashley Madison website.

The writer Katelyn Beaty, author of *Celebrities for Jesus: How Persons, Platforms, and Profits are Hurting the Church*, describes this phenomenon well when she writes,

> We think we know our favorite ministry heads, worship leaders, authors, activists, and evangelists, because we follow them on social media or hear them preach from a stage or read their words on a page. But we are engaging with a presented, medicated self. And the absence of true knowledge, and true accountability, leaves abundant opportunity for their social power to be misused and abused. To have immense social power and little proximity is a spiritually dangerous place for any of us to be.[53]

To make this less abstract, consider the case of Ted Haggard and how stark the split between a public image and someone's private life can become.[54]

Haggard started out his career in Christian ministry with just 22 people meeting in his home. Twenty-two years later, his New Life Church in Colorado Springs had over 14,000 people regularly attending. Haggard became a Christian celebrity, and *Time* magazine at one point put him on its list of the 25 most influential evangelical Christians.

Beaty describes what can happen to Christian celebrities using words that seem to fit well with the case of Ted Haggard:

> Over time, a chasm grew between who they were behind closed doors and who they were on stage or in their own sermons and anecdotes. They had started to believe their own hype. And adoring churchgoers, staff members, book publishers, and social media fans were at the ready to feed the hype, because they derived their *own* meaning and identity from a simulated connection to the celebrity Christian. These celebrities had amazing 'platforms,' and we, their fans and followers, had put them there.[55]

But in 2006, things began to publicly unravel for Haggard. This was the year that Colorado Amendment 43 was on the ballet, which sought to legally forbid same-sex marriage. Haggard was outspoken in his support of it.

At the same time, a male prostitute by the name of Mike Jones went public with allegations that Haggard had been hiring him for several years, as well as regularly using crystal meth. According to Jones, Haggard was very careful, going by an alias named 'Art,' using a pay phone to set up meetings, parking a block away from Jones's apartment, and always paying with hundred-dollar bills. But eventually Jones saw Haggard's face on TV, and discovered who this guy really was. According to reports, Jones felt that he needed to do something to let the world know what was happening. Says Jones: "I had to expose the hypocrisy. He is in the position of influence of millions of followers, and he's preaching against gay marriage. But behind everybody's back [he's] doing what he's preached against."[56] The public/private split was indeed stark.

Eventually that year Haggard was fired from New Life Church, and moved to Phoenix. But in 2010 he was back in Colorado Springs again, founding a new church called Saint James. Guess what happened. New allegations of inappropriate sexual relations and drug use emerged, and Saint James was shut down. That did not keep Haggard away from Christian ministry, though. By 2022, he founded yet another church, this time one that operated out of his home.

As a celebrity, Haggard had sharply distinguished his public image from his private life. In private, he was allegedly living a life of dishonesty, including cheating on his wife. No doubt his life as a celebrity, with the money and power that came with it, could have contributed to Haggard's going down this path. It may have also eroded moral safeguards, too. As Beaty notes, "Celebrity deceives. It whispers to the celebrity leader that they are above the rules, the morals, or the law."[57]

So fame can contribute directly to acts of dishonesty, as we saw in the previous chapter. But what I am especially interested in here is how celebrity can also be used to *coverup* wrongdoing. Given their celebrity status and the need to preserve their public image as people trying to follow a Christian life, it is no surprise that pastors would coverup bad behavior through acts of dishonesty. Lies of commission, lies of omission, and misleading statements can all be put to use to try to hide what would be considered in Christian terms to be sin, such as acts of infidelity, and preserve the pastor's public image of virtue.

Haggard himself apparently took this route initially. It is not as if, when Mike Jones accused him, he immediately confessed to hiring a male prostitute and using illegal drugs. First, he denied everything, saying that, "I did not have a homosexual relationship with a man in Denver . . . I am steady with my wife. I'm faithful to my wife." And about the alleged drug use, "I have never done drugs—ever. Not even in high school. I didn't smoke pot. I didn't do anything like that. I'm not a drug man. We're not a drinking family. I don't smoke cigarettes. I don't socially drink. We don't socially drink. We don't have wine in our house. We don't do that kind of thing."[58]

These defenses did not hold up. There was a voicemail that was released with Haggard requesting drugs. After this, Haggard's story evolved into his buying the drugs but then throwing them away. He also said initially that he never met Jones. But then the story evolved into his receiving a massage from Jones but nothing sexual. Eventually, according to reports, the truth was revealed about the actual drug use and extramarital homosexual behavior.

Hence we said at the start of this chapter that as honesty crises accelerate dishonest behavior, they will increasingly catch pastors in their net, and those pastors will face the temptation to cover up their wronging with dishonesty. We have dishonesty compounding dishonesty.

But things are even worse than this. For while dishonesty in the form of lying and misleading can be used to cover up wrongdoing, *that wrongdoing itself has already created its own dishonesty.* What do I mean by this? Hypocrisy. As we saw in the last chapter, the danger of hypocrisy arises when the public image crafted by a celebrity comes apart from his private self. The same is true for pastors. Haggard preached against homosexual behavior. All the while he was reportedly paying a male prostitute. It does not get much more hypocritical than that.

Also, by publicly condemning certain behaviors, the celebrity pastor is aiming to create a certain impression in his audience as to the depth of his moral values. In turn, the audience can come away convinced that this man is deeply committed to his stance on, say, sexual ethics, when in fact he is not. This is a failure of honesty, involving intentionally distorting the facts *about the depth of his own commitments.* It is also a case of misleading, rather than lying, since he does believe that the sexual behavior in question is wrong, but cares very little about its being wrong. Because of his strong talk, though, he hopes his audience comes away with a different impression.

So the other honesty crises can accelerate dishonest behavior by pastors (like plagiarism and infidelity), which in turn can accelerate the use of dishonest behavior to cover up the transgressions. Yet it would be too late to prevent the dishonesty of hypocrisy. One sin of dishonesty can give rise to many more.

Preserving Honesty

What can be done to help promote honesty here? Given the work of previous chapters, we do not need to start from scratch. Many of the practical suggestions carry over to this context. The key to a discussion of strategies, though, is not to treat them as vanilla recommendations that generically apply to everyone in the same way. Rather, they need to be adapted to the specific individuals in question and their values and circumstances. In this case, they need to be tailored to the religious commitments and contexts of particular pastors.

Here I won't return to all the suggestions that were made with respect to infidelity, plagiarism, and celebrity. Rather I will just highlight a few ideas that seem particularly applicable in this context:

Clarity About Wrongness. When it comes to the wrongness of infidelity, sermon plagiarism, or hypocrisy, most pastors should already have moral clarity that these behaviors are wrong, even if they end up doing them anyway. Developing this moral clarity about what is morally wrong, and indeed a serious form of dishonesty, can hopefully help to reign in temptation to engage in it.

Awareness of Expectations and Consequences. Related to the first point is that the congregational leadership needs to make it clear what the expectations are for honest behavior and what the consequences, including dismissal, are for dishonest behavior. Then there is no excuse when it comes to "not realizing" that, say, borrowing a sermon illustration from another pastor or from ChatGPT without suitable acknowledgment is in fact wrong.

Accountability. Not only should the congregational leadership make expectations clear for the pastor, but they need to hold the pastor accountable to those expectations. This is easy to say but hard to implement. Notoriously those who abuse power in churches often have little accountability in their lives. They may have even handpicked the very people who are supposed to keep them accountable, knowing who they can control or manipulate. Abusive pastors can also create a culture of fear and intimidation.

Fame can complicate accountability as well. For instance, a report about the well-known but later disgraced pastor of Willow Creek Community Church, Bill Hybels, found that, "the senior pastor was larger than life for many. Most board members gave deference to him. This made it difficult for some elders to challenge him in a meeting . . . They felt like they were sitting in board meetings with a celebrity."[59]

But genuine accountability cannot involve deference and servitude. Those in leadership around the pastor need to be able to see what is really going on in that person's life, including sermon preparation, the treatment of those in vulnerable positions, financial management, and signs of public behavior that is not matching private thoughts and practices.

This is especially important with famous pastors, who can push back against allowing others in a church to see into their life. As Beaty notes,

> celebrity isolates. Many celebrity leaders find themselves disconnected from people who really know them. Without true proximity, celebrity leaders can get away with behavior that they'd never consider if others could find out. The space beyond the spotlight can be a dark place indeed. It can be lonely and disorienting. Needless to say, a travel schedule that takes someone from hotel to hotel, in towns with many adoring followers but no real friends, surrounded by an entourage, creates a breeding ground for deception and abuse.[60]

And remember, all pastors are celebrities to some degree.

Again, I do not mean to suggest that any of this is easy. Real accountability can be painful, and few will want to seek it out, least of all from the very people who might be responsible for hiring and firing. But the dangers of isolation, loneliness, narcissism, and deception are worse, and real accountability and accessibility can effectively push back against them.

Moral Reminders. Just as the honor code can be a helpful moral reminder for students, so too can there be honesty reminders for pastors which can be helpful to counter temptation to cheat on their sermons. These reminders can come from regularly reading the Bible, from having a visible message displayed in their office, or even from congregational leaders regularly checking in.

In the case of pornography, chatrooms, and infidelity websites, perspective-taking can function as a kind of moral reminder as well. Whose perspective? Well, we could start with the pastor's spouse or significant other, where applicable, and include the perspective of their children too if they have any. There is also the perspective of the congregation, and what those who stare back at the pastor on any given Sunday would feel. Ultimately, though, in this context there is God's perspective (or perhaps specifically in a Christian context, the perspective of Jesus).

The pastor can step out of his own contemplated (or actual) pursuit of sexual desire, and consider what these others would think and feel. By considering their hurt, anger, disappointment, or heartbreak, the pastor's desire to continue the pursuit of sexual or emotional gratification in morally problematic ways can hopefully diminish.

Exemplars. We know from a number of studies that moral exemplars are often effective in inspiring others to act better.[61] With respect to hypocrisy in the church specifically, the pastor's most important exemplar is Jesus. And Jesus famously reserved some of his harshest condemnation for hypocrites.[62] Instead, his focus was on what is in one's heart and on truly becoming someone of faith, hope, and love, regardless of whether good works are exhibited in front of others or not. So too, the thought is, Jesus can inspire pastors to look to their own hearts and see if they align with how they are acting in front of their congregations and the public at large. Here the focus is meant to be on doing morally good things, where God is the only audience that ultimately matters, out of a heart that is not trying to impress others with how virtuous one is.

I do not envy pastors today who have to confront these honesty crises. We should all have great respect and admiration for those who manage to still live lives of genuine honesty and integrity while following in the footsteps of their God.

Appendix—The Church Sexual Abuse Scandals

Strikingly absent from this chapter is dishonest behavior by Christians that could have been the main focus of the chapter. I have looked at the honesty and dishonesty of individual pastors. But at the institutional level, Christian churches in America have exhibited dishonest behavior in response to a number of cases of sexual abuse. To be sure, instances of sexual abuse themselves often are wrapped up with various forms of dishonesty at the individual level, such as lying, misleading, and hypocrisy. But in some cases, they have also given rise to dishonesty on the part of larger institutions, such as the Southern Baptist Convention and the Catholic Church, which reportedly took steps to ignore, hide, deny, or minimize what was done by individual pastors and priests.

Perhaps the leading approach to better understanding institutional coverups, such as what happened with the sexual abuse crisis in the church, is the theory of institutional betrayal developed by psychologist Jennifer Freyd.[63] Institutions are concerned to preserve their own reputation and the trust of the public. They also are concerned many times to protect themselves financially, and to maintain their authority and power. These motives can foster what Freyd calls 'betrayal blindness.' In the case of a church, for instance, the leaders might engage in willful ignorance concerning the harms that are being perpetrated by abusers in the church. This is a form of dishonesty, akin to self-deception in the individual case. In some instances, institutions go further and actively engage in acts of intentional deception to try to maintain the standing of the institution. Well-documented cases are familiar in the church context.

Given the church's institutional dishonesty in the face of sexual abuse by certain pastors and priests, measures have been developed to prevent future dishonesty and intentionally foster a more honest institutional culture. These measures include promoting greater transparency about and taking greater responsibility for past abuses, making the reporting of abuse something that is protected, providing channels for such reporting which do not involve having to go through church officials, having better screening of individuals for leadership positions, using independent investigators in cases of reported abuse, and more generally empowering and supporting truth-tellers. Ultimately these measures will require what Freyd calls 'institutional courage,' which "involves actively seeking the truth and engaging in moral actions, even when it is difficult or when it may cause discomfort or self-harm to the institution."[64]

So why then wasn't institutional dishonesty by the church a central topic of this chapter? I have a reason, but I also acknowledge that whatever I say here can come across as downplaying the severity of what has transpired. Please know that that is not my intention.

The reason is that I do not know whether the church's institutional dishonesty in recent decades counts, strictly speaking, as an honesty crisis. As I have been understanding honesty crises, they have two elements: (i) dishonesty becoming easier to get away with than it was before, and (ii) dishonesty becoming more enticing or appealing to engage in than it was before. Starting with the second condition, is institutional betrayal by the church more enticing today than it was, say, 25 or 50 years ago? I really don't know. It seems to me that there has been a persistent drive to engage in willful ignorance or intentional deception throughout this period.

And consider the first condition. Is it easier for a church to get away with institutional dishonesty today than it was in past decades when there was much less awareness of sexual abuse in the church? Maybe I am being overly optimistic here, but I would like to think that with greater awareness there has also been a greater focus on detection and prevention.

Again, being unsure about whether the church's institutional coverup of sexual abuse is an honesty crisis today can come across as insensitive. But none of what I say here is meant to detract in any way from the horrors of the sexual abuse itself, nor from the wrongness of the institutional dishonesty involved in covering it up. It only bears on whether there is currently an *honesty crisis* going on in this area, as I have defined those terms.

We should all hope that the answer is no.

Notes

1. Brenan and Jones 2024.
2. Graham 2021.
3. Leadership Journal 2005.
4. Quoted in Gibson 2008.
5. All the details about this story are from Smietana 2021a.
6. Smietana 2021a.
7. For many more examples, see Gibson 2008.
8. Long 2008.
9. Larson 2024.
10. Woodruff and Moore 2003.
11. Smietana 2021b.
12. Moore 2023.
13. James 3:1. I have been helped here by Steffaniak 2021.
14. For more on different forms of sermon plagiarism, see Larson 2024.
15. For helpful discussion of sermon plagiarism that has shaped my thinking here, see Long 2008, Steffaniak 2021, and Larson 2024.
16. See, for example, Woodruff and Moore 2003, Steffaniak 2021, and especially Stinnett 2000.
17. Howerton 2020.
18. See also Larson 2024.
19. The Gospel Coalition Editors 2010.
20. Larson 2024.
21. Quoted in Larson 2024.

22. See, for example, Proverbs 31, Luke 10:7, 2 Corinthians 5:10, and 1 Timothy 5:17.
23. Steffaniak 2021.
24. Howerton 2020.
25. For more, see Larson 2024.
26. Long 2008.
27. Woodruff and Moore 2003. For more on motivation and preaching, see Gibson 2008: 46, 82–83.
28. Gibson 2008: 26.
29. Long 2008.
30. Smietana 2021a.
31. Long 2008.
32. These observations are all from Homiletics Team 2023.
33. Moore 2023.
34. Dash 2023. For a much more positive take, see Lin 2023.
35. Vargas 2015.
36. Ibid.
37. Kumar 2024.
38. *Christianity Today* Editors 1988.
39. Thoburn and Balswick 1998: 450.
40. Ibid., 452.
41. Ibid., 453.
42. *Christianity Today* Editors 2001.
43. Barna Group 2024.
44. *Christianity Today* Editors 1988.
45. What follows has been informed by Laaser and Gregoire 2003 and Ahmad et al. 2015.
46. Thoburn and Balswick 1994: 289.
47. *Christianity Today* Editors 1988.
48. Ibid.
49. Thoburn and Whitman 2004: 504–505.
50. *Christianity Today* Editors 2001.
51. See also Thoburn and Balswick 1994: 288.
52. There is a further discussion to be had about *which* pastors are more likely to engage in infidelity. For instance, pastors who are low on self-esteem or high on shame or rejection sensitivity are more susceptible to give into temptation. See, for example, Thoburn and Balswick 1993 and 1994. There are certainly important issues here, but my focus is on why pastors *as a group* are more susceptible to disloyalty than members of other groups might be.
53. Beaty 2022: 18–19.
54. What follows about Haggard draws upon ABC News 2008, Quintero 2006, and Wikipedia 2025b.
55. Ibid., 22, emphasis hers.

56. Wikipedia 2025b.
57. Beaty 2022: 88.
58. Ibid.
59. Quoted in Beaty 2022: 59.
60. Ibid., 88–89. See also her helpful discussion of the paradox of loneliness for celebrities in chapter 6.
61. See, for example, Han et al. 2017.
62. See, for example, Matthew 6:1–8 and Matthew 23.
63. See, for example, Smith and Freyd 2014.
64. Johnson et al. 2018.

9

If Honesty Is Under Attack, Why Bother Trying to Protect It?

> Honesty is the first chapter in the book of wisdom.
>
> —Thomas Jefferson

In our search for honesty, we have found some hopeful signs. Many people do not lie regularly. Students seem to recognize that cheating is wrong. Some parts of social media are more honest than we might have thought.

But at the same time, we have also found many areas of life where honesty is under a great deal of pressure. These range from students' academic work to fidelity to our significant others to political communication.

Suppose my assessment of where things are these days is roughly correct. You might still say, who cares whether we are in the midst of these honesty crises? Maybe honesty is under pressure. But why should we bother to do anything about it? Sure, we might lie from time to time, exhibit some hypocrisy, mislead others on occasion, maybe cheat here and there. And perhaps it is easier to do these things today, not to mention more tempting too, in light of the developments we have seen in the past 30 years. But so what?

In this final chapter, we will look to see if a case can be made for why honesty is important and worth spending our time trying to foster. I think a powerful case can indeed be made for why we should care.

The easiest way to make this case is to show why promoting honesty *in society* is important. That is where we will begin. Things get more challenging, though, when we turn to our own lives. Yes, it might be

The Honesty Crisis. Christian B. Miller, Oxford University Press. © Oxford University Press 2026.
DOI: 10.1093/9780197840801.003.0009

good for society if there were more honest people. Not to mention that it will make my life better too if the people around me are honest. But how is that supposed to inspire *me* to become more honest as well and resist the forces that are pulling me toward cheating, lying, stealing, and all the rest? So long as I can do these things for my own benefit and not get caught, isn't that living the best life of all?

This is a difficult question. But I will try to make the case that the answer is no.

Does this mean that I am going to go so far as to suggest that we should *always* be honest? What about white lies? Do we really have to tell the truth all the time about how this new outfit looks or this dinner tastes?

I am going to raise some doubts about white lies. There are all kinds of reasons to avoid them, and the empirical literature suggests we overestimate how much harm we are really preventing by telling them. Still, I do not think we can go all the way and make the case that honesty is an absolute requirement with no exceptions. There are important situations where a great deal is at stake, and lying or misleading might be the only way to protect innocent lives. As we will see with the famous case of the Nazi-at-the-door, honesty is important, but it is not the only thing that matters in life. Honesty can be outweighed.

Why Bother with Honesty in Society?

Consider the society you happen to live in right now. Draw the boundaries of that society however you wish (so long as it is more than just you!). In my case, one frame of reference is the United States, although it would work fine to focus more locally on my city of Winston-Salem.

Now with your society firmly in mind, imagine two ways it might look:

<u>Version 1</u>: For the most part, people in your society tell the truth to each other, and do not cheat or steal even when they can get away with it. They rarely act in a hypocritical manner, and

there is little BSing or misleading going on. Furthermore, most people in your society know that this is what is going on with other people in that society.

Version 2: For the most part, people in your society lie to each other regularly, and try to cheat and steal whenever they think they can get away with it. They say things in public that make them sound like upstanding citizens, but in private they routinely act the opposite. There is little hesitancy to engage in BSing or misleading if someone thinks it is to his or her advantage. Furthermore, most people in your society know that this is going on.

Which version would you prefer? It is obvious that I would much rather live in Version 1.

There are many reasons for why the honest version of my society is better than the dishonest one. Here I just highlight four, so that we can get to the more challenging and controversial topics still to come. I know this is selling the case for honesty a bit short, but I am hoping it does not really have to be made that thoroughly in the first place.

Trust. In a dishonest society where most people are aware of what is going on, trust will be hard to come by. Politicians tell me things about what is good for the country. Why should I trust them? Teachers tell me about history, science, or economics. Why should I trust them? My doctors advise me about the best course of treatment. Why should I trust them?

Without trust, there is little hope for team sports, or financial investing, or academic assessments. Business will fail, and productive communication will be difficult. If I doubt much of what you say because I know there is a very good chance you are being dishonest, it is hard to see what the point is in having an extended conversation.

I assume we do not want to live in a society where people cannot trust each other.

Relationships. A lack of trust naturally calls into question whether we could even have meaningful relationships in our lives. We will consider spouses and other family members a bit later. But for now, just think about what the prospects would be of having meaningful friendships. Call to mind some of your closest friends for a moment. Now suppose that you came to discover they are all dishonest, not just with strangers but also with *you*. What hope is there for those friendships going forward?

Try as you might, there could not even be a genuine friendship here. You can do your best on your end, but if the other person is being consistently dishonest toward you for their own selfish benefit, they are not really friends with you. True friendship only exists when both parties are concerned with what is good for each other *for his or her own sake*. There has to be selflessness and genuine caring at the heart of friendship for it to actually matter. But a dishonest person whose interaction with you is infused with lies, BSing, cheating, and stealing only cares about himself.

I assume we do not want to live in a society where there are no genuine friendships, including with you.

Respect. Friendships will be off the table because dishonest people instrumentalize others. They treat people merely as means to their own benefit. The opposite of this is to treat others with respect as people with dignity and worth.

When dishonest people steal from others, they are disrespecting them by taking away what is rightfully theirs. When dishonest people cheat, they are disrespecting the game they are playing, or their teacher, or the legal authorities. When dishonest people lie, they are disrespecting the autonomy of others by not presenting them with the facts of the case and letting them make up their own minds.

I assume we do not want to live in a society in which people are not treated with respect as beings with dignity and worth.

Fear. Perhaps the most straightforward reason of all why a dishonest society is to be avoided is that it spawns fear. Knowing that most of those around you are dishonest means that you know they will try to take advantage of you if they see it as worthwhile and attainable. They will try to steal or cheat from you, for instance.

I assume we do not want to live in a society where we are always afraid.

These points are all about our society. But let's not stop there. Let's bring things closer to home, or literally into our home, to see that they apply even more forcefully to those who are nearest and dearest to our hearts.

The first place my mind goes is to my children. As I write this, they are 13, 11, and 9 years old. They do not pay too much attention to me working away on this book. Their minds are much more focused on Legos, books, and sports (as they should be!). But when I think about my children, it is frightening to consider what it would mean for them to be consistently dishonest:

> Suppose I discover that my oldest son has been lying repeatedly to me about things at school and his personal life.
>
> Suppose I discover that my middle child has been stealing from school and from our things at home.
>
> Suppose I discover that my daughter has been cheating on her tests, homework, and the games we play around the house.

I do not know for sure how I would react. But I strongly suspect that it would be devastating.

My wife and I would know that we cannot trust our children anymore, at least in these areas of their lives and for the forceable future. We would realize that we do not know them very well. We do not have a genuine friendship with them. They do not respect us very much. And depending on what form the dishonesty took, we might even be afraid. In short, the people we have spent so much of our lives with, do not love their mother and father as much as we had thought they did. If you are a parent to whom this has actually happened, I cannot imagine what it must be like to live through.

Of course, children are not the only ones in a family where we can see what dishonesty can do. Sadly, it can happen in the reverse too, where parents are the guilty party in being dishonest toward their children. I saw this happen with another boy I knew growing up. I rarely ran into his father because, I was told, he was a lawyer and had to travel a lot for work. I never gave it a moment's thought.

But after we went off to different high schools and drifted apart, I learned what was really going on. My friend's father had been living a secret double life. Not as a spy or anything exciting like that. Rather, he was able to keep it hidden for many years that he had a second family—a woman with whom he had also had children who were being raised in parallel with my friend's family. The reason he was not with my friend on some Christmasses, for instance, was that he was spending time with family #2.

So not only was he cheating on his wife for many years, but he also had to weave an elaborate web of lies and half-truths to cover up this second family. It was all patently dishonest. It also meant that he did not respect his wife, and whether she knew what was going on or not, he could not truly be friends with her or genuinely love her.

These points about parents and children generalize to other relationships in families, such as those between siblings and between grandparents and grandchildren. In the context of one's family, just as in larger contexts like organizations and societies, there is a powerful case for promoting the virtue of honesty.

So far, we have been talking about the case for honesty when it comes to groups like families and larger societies. Let me end by highlighting an important point that emphasizes how vital it is to promote honesty *just in the case of one individual.* It is that a single dishonest person can leave a path of destruction in his or her wake. For instance, think of Bernie Madoff and his Ponzi scheme. Or Elizabeth Holmes and her company Theranos which reportedly ran fraudulent blood tests. Or even Lance Armstrong, who admitted to dishonestly covering up his doping and to defrauding sponsors and fans while also tarnishing the sport of cycling.[1]

By reinforcing how destructive the opposite of honesty can be, we can hopefully appreciate even more the value of promoting honesty in everyone's life. This is not some academic exercise we are going through. A great deal is at stake.

Honesty in My Own Life

I can hear the challenge already. "Hey, Miller, you might have made a strong case for promoting honesty in the lives of *other people*. But none of what you said speaks to *me*. Why should I care about becoming more honest myself? Indeed, so long as I am careful about it, the best thing for me to do is to be *dishonest* when it would benefit me and I can get away with it, while at the same time appearing to be upstanding. What do you have to say about that?"

This is a really serious challenge. To make it more vivid, consider the case of Judah, the main character in Woody Allen's best film, *Crimes and Misdemeanors*. Judah is a highly respected eye doctor who, as the movie opens, is receiving an award from the community. He lives a comfortable life with his wife and children, and is greatly admired by others. Soon enough, though, we discover that he has been leading a double life. He has been visiting a mistress on the side, and has also been involved in some fraudulent money dealings. Yet at the end of the movie, he has his mistress killed and all evidence of his dishonesty buried with her. He was able to enjoy the fruits of his cheating for a while, and then moved on with his life.

Judah checks a lot of dishonesty boxes—he is a liar, cheater, misleader, thief, and hypocrite. Yet he also seems to be doing just fine for himself. If we were able to live a double life like his, why not do it?

This question goes all the way back to the beginning of Western philosophy. In arguably the most famous work of philosophy ever written, Plato's *Republic*, the main character Socrates is challenged by Glaucon and Adeimantus to make the case for why we should live a virtuous life. As it applies here, their challenge is to find fault with the dishonest person who is publicly honest. If anything, this person looks to be doubly blessed—esteemed by others in public, while indulging in his own dishonest pleasures in private. Indeed, the inspiration for Judah's character in *Crimes and Misdemeanors* came straight from Plato.

To make the challenge especially difficult, Glaucon appeals to a mythical story about a shepherd who finds a ring which, when he turns it a certain way, makes him completely invisible.[2] Knowing this, what does the shepherd do with the ring? Note that there is nothing preventing him from still being honest. But he goes in the opposite direction. Among other bad stuff, he steals the throne of the land for himself. The suggestion is that dishonesty enables the shepherd to live a far better life for himself, and that for the rest of us what is often holding us back is just the fear of getting caught. Otherwise, we too would be dishonest with abandon if it served our interests.

Now admittedly we are working with some extreme examples. There are no invisibility rings last time I checked. And how many people can really have a lover on the side, have her killed when she starts causing problems, and completely get away with it?

But that is not the point. The point is—wouldn't that be a better way to live, *if* we could pull it off? If we are acting honestly only because we are afraid of what would happen if we were caught doing dishonest things, then that is hardly a rousing endorsement of honesty.

Plus, unlike taking over the throne or killing a lover, there are plenty of dishonest things we can do that are very likely to go unnoticed. This book has been full of examples, ranging from cheating on graded assignments, to secretly viewing pornography while in an exclusive relationship, to sharing misinformation. More mundane examples include stealing supplies from the company, leaving out small sources of income from an income tax filing, and cheating at cards with novice players who won't be able to notice.

So here we are. I said that it is important to develop the virtue of honesty in our lives. The challenge suggests instead that honesty can be useful as window dressing, to help keep up good appearances, but deep down the carefully curated dishonest life is the way to go. Who is right?

It is true that there is a real risk you might be caught and exposed if you try to live the secretly dishonest life. That is what happened to

Tiger Wood when all of his reported affairs came to light. In *Crimes and Misdemeanors*, Judah got away with the murder, but in real life he would have been apprehended by the police right away (there was plenty of evidence to trace him back to the crime).

Yes, this is a fair point. Of course, we do not actually know how many people were successful in living their double lives, so it could be that the number of times someone gets away with it vastly outweighs the times they get caught. But even if you *are* caught, plenty of people are able to recover after being exposed for their dishonesty. Tiger Woods is a good illustration here too. He quickly reestablished himself in the golfing world, and in the court of public opinion.

Here is another angle, though. What about the *fear* of getting caught? How rewarding of a life would it be to be consumed with worry that, if you slip up just once, the whole charade will come crashing down?

There is certainly something to this point too. But alas, I think it only goes so far. If you are clever about your dishonesty, then there is little reason to fear getting caught. Do spouses who view pornography or people who cut corners on their taxes really worry that much about getting caught? Also, as time goes on and one keeps getting away with it, the fear will likely dissipate. Indeed, in some cases, there is almost no risk from the start. For instance, we noted that students can turn in AI-generated work that successfully hides the fact that it was written by an AI.

Hold on, you might say. Fear of being caught is not the only emotional response that can erode the secretly dishonest life. When viewing pornography or cheating on school work, I might experience feelings of guilt. I might also be ashamed of myself. After he had his mistress killed, Judah could not sleep at night because he was wracked with both guilt and fear of being caught, in his case because he thought the "eyes of God" were watching him.

Again, there is something to this point as well. If the alternative is a life without guilt, shame, and fear, then I would gladly take that alternative, even if I had to miss out on a few tempting pleasures or benefits in the process. Yet there is a response here too. It all depends on how you view dishonesty in the first place. If you are already convinced that the best life for you to live includes secret acts of dishonesty, then why feel guilty when you watch the pornography or cheat on your school work? You are just doing what you personally think is the right thing to do!

This just goes to show that, *if* the only thing that matters to a person is how he can squeeze the most benefit for himself out of life, it is really hard to convince someone to not live a double life. Philosophers call such people ethical egoists. If they are clever about avoiding detection and if they think that being dishonest is sometimes beneficial for them, then they should hardly have any qualms about doing so.

I am not sure how to convince someone who is already a diehard egoist to care about becoming an authentically honest person. So I won't try to do that here. But leaving the diehard egoist aside, there is a powerful reason for the rest of us to not even begin to go down the path of being secretly dishonest. The reason is that you will sacrifice the love and friendships you have in your life.

Think about what is involved in really loving someone. I cannot love another person if I only care about what is good for me. To love someone is, fundamentally, to care about what is good *for that person for his or her own sake*. I may benefit or I may not. But that is not what love is all about.

Now of course I am not talking about lust or infatuation or romantic interest or what used to be called *eros*. I am talking about the kind of love that grounds the best relationships between spouses or between parents and their children or between friends.

To see the point, consider a father who routinely takes his children to sports practice. When asked why, he admits that he does it so that he can look good in front of the other parents. Or take the mother who helps her children with their homework every day after school. Why? So that she does not feel guilty if they do not do well in school.

These are not expressions of love. The best parents sacrifice their time, resources, energy, health, and opportunities for their children because they care about them and want what is best for them. Sure, they might get some satisfaction as well from seeing their children flourish, and their reputation might get a boost too. But those are not what primarily motivate a loving parent. They are nice byproducts or side-effects of their love.

Now take this back to the secretly dishonest person. When he covertly watches pornography, hiding it from his wife, he is not doing what is ultimately good for her. He is eroding the love between them. Generally speaking, the more you try to live a secretly dishonest life, the less you will be in a loving relationship with another person. And these points carry over to *friendships* as well. As we have already seen, true friends are concerned with the good of the friend, not their own personal benefit.

Recently a friend of mine was in a pinch. He had to be out of his rental house and on the road in the morning to drive his U-Haul van two states away to his new home. He did not have anyone helping him, and there were tons of jobs still to do—patching drywall, painting, sweeping, vacuuming, getting all the backyard cleaned up, and so forth. He was not going to make it, even if he pulled an all-nighter. So we worked together until after midnight and got most everything done.

What if he asked me why I was helping, and I said things like:

> I didn't want to feel guilty if I didn't.
> I was bored.
> God will reward me for this.
> It will help me out with my new book.

He would probably still appreciate the help, but start to wonder if I really cared about him and our friendship. Instead, if I had said:

> You're my friend!
> I care about you.
> I didn't want you to have to do all this by yourself.
> It was the right thing to do.

Then I am sure he would have been comforted by those responses.

What's the point? True friends aren't motivated the way the secretly dishonest person is. They are motivated to treat others in ways that reflect something other than their own benefit. Hence when guided mainly by trying to benefit himself, the secretly dishonest person would not have any true friends.

People can indeed live a life of fake honesty in public and real dishonesty in secret. But it comes at a tremendous cost. It is essentially lonely.

What about White Lies?

Here comes the next challenge: "Miller, you have gotten carried away here by making *too* strong of a case for honesty. Do you really want to go so far as to say that we can *never* be dishonest? That seems a little much. For example, do you think that it is always wrong to tell a white lie to keep the peace and not hurt someone else's feelings?"

This is another completely fair concern. As we will see later on, I *do* think it would go too far to just declare that all forms of dishonesty are wrong. There need to be some exceptions.

But I am not convinced that white lies are the place to look for those exceptions. First, though, what are 'white lies,' especially since many cultures do not have that expression?

Here are some examples I suspect we may be able to relate to:

> "How does this outfit look on me?"
> "It looks great!"
> "Does this make me look fat?"
> "No not at all."
> "How did you like the new dessert I made?"
> "It was delicious."
> "Didn't I do a good job on this craft project?"
> "It turned out great!"
> "You have such a lovely house."
> "I love what you've done with the place."

Now for these to be *lies*, you cannot actually believe what you say. You need to believe the opposite. And for these to be *white* lies, they need to be relatively small or minor.

What about the motivation behind the lie? There could be white lies which are self-interested. You might say the dessert was delicious because you do not want to get in a fight if you told the truth. But let us focus on white lies which are altruistic. In other words, you are lying because you worry that the truth will hurt the other person's feelings.

The challenge can now be sharpened: "Yes, altruistic white lies! That is a great clarification. What can be so bad about those? Surely it is okay if I tell them once in a while. And what is the alternative—to crush the other person's spirits?"

I do not want to come down too hard on white lies, and to be honest I have said dozens of them myself in my life. The goal of trying to spare someone from hurt feelings is surely admirable. Still, I think we should be cautious.

What we have here is a conflict between two values:

> Honesty, which favors not telling the white lie.
> Compassion, which favors telling the white lie.[3]

Which one of these gets the upper hand?

Remember that these are relatively minor lies we are talking about. Matters of serious harm are not at stake. For instance, if I know that someone is in a very precarious mental state, where one negative comment could send them spiraling into depression or suicidal thoughts, then that radically changes the equation.

Also, we are not talking about the "Hey, how are you?" "Good!" exchanges, where we all know that there is no expectation of truth-telling when passing each other in the hall. Sometimes "You have such a lovely house" can be interpreted in that way, as just being polite.

In fact, some couples have an understanding between themselves that when one of them says, "How does this outfit look on me?" or "How do you like the dessert I made?," that person is *not* asking for an honest answer. He is just seeking positive affirmation. In that case, you would not be lying if you offered praise, since you do not have an intention to deceive your significant other. You are just playing along.

Still, there are plenty of cases where a question is asked, the person is looking for an honest answer, and he is emotionally vulnerable. Nor should we minimize the fact that feelings are involved. My wife, children, friends, and colleagues could get angry, disappointed, resentful, annoyed, sad, or deflated depending on what I say. What then is the morally right thing to do? Typically, it is to *not* tell a white lie. Or at least I think a strong case can be made that this is what is required of us.

Take the example of my wife asking about the new dessert she has made. Suppose she has been working on it for several hours, and she is happy with how it turned out. She is asking for my reaction, yet privately I think it is not nearly as good as the other desserts she has made in the past. I could say, "It was delicious." But I am also thinking about saying this: "I really appreciate how hard you worked on this dessert! It was okay, but I'm afraid I liked the last dessert a bit better." The first statement is a lie. The second is the polite truth.

Here is one reason to avoid lying. If I say the dessert is delicious, she will likely make it regularly. To be consistent, I will need to eat it again and again, with enthusiasm. I have just made things worse for myself. Suppose she responds to my lie with, "Great, since it turned out so well, I will make it again for the party next week." Now I have just made things worse for other people, too. So it continues. For if other people share my opinion and think the dessert is not great too, then they will think less well of my wife and her cooking. I have made things worse for her too.

Also, I probably cannot get away with just one lie. Lies tend to compound. So, the next time and the time after when we have the dessert again, I will need to lie again. This puts a burden on me. For now, I have to remember my lie, and later on recall the lie. I also need to take steps to maintain the lie, which can take effort.

Of course, I might get caught, too. I might confess to the kids that I did not really like the cake, and then they sell me out to mommy. Or I forget next time we have the dessert and say that it was not my favorite. She rightly can complain, "But you told me last time it was delicious!"

If my white lie is exposed, it undermines my wife's trust. She was expecting me to give an honest evaluation because she trusts my opinion. Remember, this is not a case where she is just looking for positive affirmation. If I do not give her my honest opinion, then she may not ask for it on other subjects too, or start to doubt my truthfulness when I do offer other opinions. Trust is easy to erode, but hard to build up.

Suppose she never finds out my true reaction to the dessert. Still, by assuming that I know it is better for her that I lie rather than tell her the truth, I am being paternalistic. I am not valuing what she wants, and instead imposing what I think is better onto her. It could very well be that, if I had instead politely told her the truth, she would have been appreciative and grateful to learn this.

A last reason for caution about telling white lies is that we tend to erroneously predict what will happen if we are honest with other people. Emma Levine from the University of Chicago along with one of my fellow Honesty Project leaders, Taya Cohen from Carnegie Mellon University, demonstrated this empirically. They had some participants focus on being honest in every one of their communications for three days, while others focused on being kind, and still others focused on being conscious about their communication. The results were striking; it turned out that, "[f]ocusing on honesty (but not kindness or communication-consciousness) is more pleasurable, socially connecting, and does less relational harm than individuals expect."[4]

To sum up, we can see why we might want to think twice before telling a white lie. There are a lot of reasons to be cautious. I am not saying that there isn't *ever* a situation where a white lie might be better than an honest response. But the burden of proof is high, and it is clearly on the side of those telling white lies.

Is Always Being Honest Going Too Far?

Some of the giants of Western philosophy would agree with me that white lies are wrong. But people like Augustine, Aquinas, and Kant went much farther than this. They maintained that *all lies* are wrong. Here I am afraid I have to join most contemporary philosophers in parting ways with them.

Kant himself provided a famous example that actually led many people away from his own conclusion. In Kant's story, a murderer is searching for your friend, and asks you where your friend is. You know the answer.[5] Today the updated version of Kant's story is the so-called 'Nazi-at-the-door.' Here is my version of the example,

> You are hiding a Jewish family in your basement in a Nazi occupied town during World War II. The Nazis do not suspect you in particular, and are doing a routine patrol of the neighborhood trying to find any Jews. At each house they ask if the owner knows where any Jews are, and if the response is no, then the Nazis move on. You know all this, and here is the knock at your door. It's a single Nazi soldier, and he asks, "Do you know where any Jews are?"

What would you do if you were in the position of this homeowner? I strongly suspect you would lie and say that you do not know where any Jews are. That is what the overwhelming majority of my students always say. It is my own position as well.

Let me quickly get rid of some distracting possibilities. To avoid lying, you might just not answer the Nazi's question. But then he will get suspicious and have his fellow soldiers search your house. You and the Jewish family will be sent to a concentration camp (or just executed).

To avoid lying, you might try to distract the soldier, say by inviting him in for a drink and then steering the conversation in another direction. But this will likely make the soldier suspicious, and the same outcome will result.

To avoid lying, you might come up with a misleading answer like "I saw some Jews sneaking around the neighborhood earlier today, but I haven't seen them recently." That is technically true, since it could describe the Jewish family in the basement. It could also hopefully get the soldier to draw the false implication that I do not know where these Jews are now. Note, though, that while not lying, this is still dishonest.

And do not get any thoughts about overpowering the soldier with force and eliminating the danger that way. It won't work.

So it looks like some dishonesty is needed here, with the simplest form being to just lie outright to the Nazi. Indeed, not only does morality allow the homeowner to do this, lying even seems to be *morally required*. The homeowner must be dishonest, or he is doing something wrong.

There have been a couple of more clever attempts to avoid this conclusion. For instance, the medieval theologian Grotius once held that lies can only be told to those who have a right to the truth. You might think that the Nazi has forfeited his right to the truth, and thus saying "I don't know where any Jews are" to the Nazi would not count as lying. If it is not lying, then it cannot be dishonest. But, contrary to what Grotius suggests, I take it to just be *obvious* that the homeowner is lying to the Nazi. Furthermore, it would be very hard to draw a clear line between those who do and those who do not have a right to the truth. Few accept Grotius' approach today.

A rather different and intriguing response has been developed by the Baylor philosopher Alex Pruss. He makes the startling claim that if the homeowner says, "I don't know where any Jews are," he is actually *telling the truth*.[6] How could that be? For clearly he does know where a few Jews are, since he is hiding them.

But Pruss wants us to pay attention to what the Nazi means by 'Jew.' For the Nazi, that word has connotations of being 'sub-human,' or 'animal,' or 'worthless.' Now the homeowner knows how Nazis think about Jews, even though he abhors their viewpoint. So he can adopt the usage of the term by the Nazi-at-the-door, and give it right back to him by saying,

> "I don't know where any Jews [i.e., sub-human animals who are worthless] are."

He is right. He does not know where anyone matching *that* description is. He does know where some human beings with dignity and worth are who practice the Jewish faith. But that is not what the Nazi is asking. The homeowner is giving a literal answer to the literal question, which does not seem like it would be a lie.

This is a very intriguing approach, I have to confess. But as Pruss himself concedes, it does not cover all the bases. After all, we can just change the example so that the Nazi instead asks where a particular family is, while holding up a picture of the people hiding in the basement. Or the Nazi could ask where anyone going by the name 'Jew' is nearby. Now the homeowner is back to needing to lie.

At this point, where we are headed is to the conclusion that it is okay to lie to the Nazi-at-the-door. Indeed, it appears to be morally required. In other words, dishonesty is sometimes morally expected of us, while honesty in certain cases would be wrong.

What is happening is that, while honesty is always important, it sometimes gets outweighed by another thing of even greater value. Earlier for white lies we saw a conflict between two virtues, and here it returns again:

Honesty, which favors telling the truth to the Nazi.
Compassion, which favors telling a lie to the Nazi.

Unlike at least most white lies, though, now compassion outweighs honesty. Hence honesty does not always reign supreme. Sometimes it can be outweighed.

How many times does this happen? That is impossible to say. Every case is different, and the only way to be careful is to spell them each out one-by-one. But as broad categories where we can go to look for more cases of honesty being outweighed, these seem to work pretty well:

Cases involving spying on the enemy for your country.
Cases involving protecting innocent people from serious harm or death at the hands of wrongful aggressors.
Cases involving matters of national security, such as the timing or location of a military operation.
Cases involving protecting an innocent person from receiving information that could seriously damage his or her mental or physical well-being.

Doubtless there are other ones besides these. Extrapolating from these cases, is there any rule we can come up with to help us think about when being dishonest is or is not morally okay?

This is a huge topic that will take us into the world of ethical theory and the task of devising abstract criteria for when actions are morally right and wrong. I am not going to open that Pandora's box now. I will only offer my own opinion, which is that there is no single rule to be found which tells us all the answers to morality, or even just the answers to when dishonesty is morally okay. Morality is far too complex and nuanced to be distilled down into a single rule.

Fortunately, most of the time the honest thing is clearly and straightforwardly the right thing to do, while the dishonest action is wrong. It is only in cases of conflicting values, such as honesty versus compassion, where things can get hairy.

In the case of white lies, I suggested that the conflict always or at least usually can be resolved in favor of honesty. In cases like the Nazi-at-the-door, I suggested it goes in the opposite direction. In between these two extremes, when another virtue like compassion conflicts with honesty in a way that does not immediately suggest which is more important, we need to examine the details of the case closely and try our best to discover what the right thing to do is in this particular instance.

Does this approach open the floodgates to an anything-goes form of moral relativism? Does it all boil down to people having different opinions about what to do in these particular cases which are equally valid?

No, I do not have much hope in the relativist's way of thinking. Moral relativism is an extremely problematic view, and few philosophers working in ethics today actually hold it. For good reason, I might add. It is hard to accept that the person who thinks the homeowner should lie to the Nazi-at-the-door, and the person who thinks the homeowner should be truthful, are holding positions that are both equally valid. Rather, there is one correct answer about what to do in this situation, and our goal should be to figure what that answer is. The consensus now is that the correct answer is to lie to the Nazi.

Having said this, just because there is one correct answer, that does not mean it will be easy to figure out. We have to think carefully about the details of particular cases, and even then our thinking can be biased or distorted in many ways. Just as in science and math, believing there is an objectively correct answer is one thing. Figuring out that answer is something else entirely.

To sum up, we have seen that honesty is an incredibly important virtue in life. But we have also seen that it is not the only thing that matters. In some cases, other things matter more.

Does God Change Anything?

In making the case for the importance of honesty, we have operated at a purely secular level. But billions of people today believe that there is more to reality than just this universe, and in particular that there is a divine being who created us and cares about us. Let us look very briefly at what difference such a being could make to what we have been talking about in this chapter.

Of course we will just be scratching the surface here. Any proper discussion would need to go religion by religion and dive into its teachings. Here we will look at some preliminary ideas from a perspective which claims that there exists an all-powerful, knowledgeable, and perfectly good God who governs our world. This is the perspective shared by Judaism, Christianity, and Islam as well as a few other world religions.

Does believing in such a God provide additional reason to care about honesty in our own lives and to try harder to improve how honest our society is? The answer is clearly 'yes.' According to these religions, God cares about honesty, and expects us to be honest. That gives us reason to care about it too.

How do we know that God cares about honesty? One way is through the teachings of the main religions which believe in such a god. Here are some examples from Judaism:[7]

> You shall not give false testimony against your neighbor. (Exodus 20:16)

> The remnant of Israel
>   will trust in the name of the Lord.
> They will do no wrong;
>   they will tell no lies.

A deceitful tongue
 will not be found in their mouths.
They will eat and lie down
 and no one will make them afraid. (Zephaniah 3:12–13)

Here are two examples from the Christian New Testament:[8]

Therefore each of you must put off falsehood and speak truthfully to your neighbor, for we are all members of one body. (Ephesians 4:25)

Do not lie to each other, since you have taken off your old self with its practices. (Colossians 3:9)

And here are examples from the Koran:[9]

Do not confound Truth by overlaying it with falsehood, nor knowingly conceal the Truth. (2:42)

Believers, fear Allah and speak the truth: Allah will set your deeds right for you and will forgive you your sins. (33:70–71)

Note that it is not just that God cares about whether we are honest with him. God also cares a great deal about whether we are honest with each other.

In fact, honesty is at the very foundation of the Genesis narrative about God, Adam, and Eve. Regardless of whether it was meant to be taken as historically accurate or not, there is embedded in the story all kinds of moral judgments about honesty. The serpent is dishonest in what he tells Eve about the fruit from the tree in the middle of the garden. Adam and Eve dishonestly break their promise to God. Adam is dishonest in putting the blame on Eve, and Eve is dishonest in putting the blame on the serpent. God punishes the serpent for its dishonesty.

So for those who are followers of one of the major Western religions, of which roughly half of the entire world appears to be, there is even more reason to care about trying to become an honest person. What does that reason look like? One answer is that I have reason to become more honest, because that way I will be rewarded by God in the afterlife. Or on the flip side, I can avoid being punished by God in the afterlife.

Rewards and punishments can indeed be powerful reasons which inspire people to become more honest. But if we are talking about the virtue of honesty, then they cannot be the *only* motivator there is. They are entirely self-centered, after all. Becoming more honest becomes all about what I get out of it for myself from God. As we said way back in Chapter 1, an honest person has virtuous motives. These would not count.

This is not to say that such motives cannot be helpful in steering a person in a better direction. It is also not to say that we cannot have more than one motive for honest behavior, which we clearly can. It is just to say that there had better be, *in addition*, some virtuous motives.

What might those virtuous motives be in a religious context? Once again, I think we should look to relationships. We have already seen how dishonesty is an obstacle to genuine friendships and loving relationships. The same is true when it comes to our relationship with God. Again, go back to the Genesis account. What was it that damaged Adam and Eve's relationship with God? It was dishonesty.

The greatest commandment throughout the major Western religions is to love God. Lying to God won't help in that regard. Neither will trying to mislead God, or cheat and steal from God's people. Self-deception about how good we are or how we have everything figured out on our own and do not need God isn't going to do much good either. Needless to say, religious hypocrites who preach their message and then betray it in private are not going to win God's favor.

Being in a loving relationship with God is arguably the greatest good there is for human beings from the perspective of these religions. Growing in honesty helps to foster that relationship; growing in dishonesty undermines that relationship. Religious believers, then, have an additional source of motivation to become more honest people. It is a virtuous source too, aimed at pursuing something that is intrinsically good. This is how we were always meant to be, according to these religions, namely in a loving relationship with God.

Note that relationship with God is an *additional* reason to care about honesty. It is not going to replace the reasons we have already discussed in this chapter. The point is that, for these particular religious believers, the case for honesty becomes even stronger than it already was.

Final Thoughts

We have seen what the virtue of honesty is, and how at its core it involves not intentionally distorting reality as we see it. We have seen that honesty is under pressure in a number of areas in our society today, especially when it comes to matters of manipulated recordings, sexual fidelity, AI-use in education and religion, fame and celebrity, and political information. Finally, we have seen a case be made for why honesty is so important to still preserve in the face of these honesty crises.

What remains is to do our best to preserve our most cherished virtue in an increasingly dishonest world.

Notes

1. Woodall 2018.
2. Plato 359d–360a.
3. Technically it is not compassion but what is called 'non-malevolence,' which has to do with preventing harm. The focus of compassion is on relieving existing suffering. But that's just a pedantic point.
4. Levine and Cohen 2018.
5. Kant 1799.
6. Pruss 1999.
7. NIV translation.
8. NIV translation.
9. From https://www.islamicstudies.info/, accessed on July 15, 2025.

Bibliography

ABC News. (2008). "Haggard Admits Buying Meth." https://abcnews.go.com/GMA/story?id=2626067, accessed on July 15, 2025.

Adams, Richard. (2024). "More than Half of UK Undergraduates Say They Use AI to Help with Essays." *The Guardian*. https://www.theguardian.com/technology/2024/feb/01/more-than-half-uk-undergraduates-ai-essays-artificial-intelligence, accessed on July 15, 2025.

Agiesta, Jennifer and Ariel Edwards-Levy. (2023). "CNN Poll: Percentage of Republicans Who Think Biden's 2020 Win Was Illegitimate Ticks Back Up Near 70%." CNN.com. https://www.cnn.com/2023/08/03/politics/cnn-poll-republicans-think-2020-election-illegitimate/index.html, accessed on July 15, 2025.

Ahmad, Zeba, John Thoburn, Kristen Perry, Meghan McBrearty, Sadie Olson, and Ginger Gunn. (2015). "Prevalence Rates of Online Sexual Addiction Among Christian Clergy." *Sexual Addiction & Compulsivity* 22: 344–356.

Ahmed, F., M. Shafiq, and A. Liu. (2016). "The Internet Is for Porn: Measurement and Analysis of Online Adult Traffic." IEEE *Xplore*. https://ieeexplore.ieee.org/document/7536508, accessed on July 15, 2025.

Al-Khateeb, Zac. (2022). "Manti Te'o's Fake Girlfriend, Explained: How Notre Dame Star Became Victim of Catfishing Hoax." *The Sporting News*. https://www.sportingnews.com/us/ncaa-football/news/manti-teo-catfishing-fake-girlfriend-hoax-notre-dame/sloxrlwu4vweln0nuxtwmpcz, accessed on July 15, 2025.

Altay, S., A.-S. Hacquin, and H. Mercier. (2022). "Why Do So Few People Share Fake News? It Hurts Their Reputation." *New Media & Society* 24: 1303–1324.

Anderman, E. and A. Koenka. (2017). "The Relation Between Academic Motivation and Cheating." *Theory Into Practice* 56: 95–102.

Anderman, E., S. Tilak, A. Perry, J. von Spiegel, and A. Black. (2022). "Academic Motivation and Cheating: A Psychological Perspective," in *Cheating Academic Integrity: Lessons from 30 Years of Research*. Eds. David Rettinger and Tricia Bertram Gallant. Hoboken: Wiley, 65–98.

Archer, Alfred and Catherine Robb. (forthcoming). "Being a Celebrity: Alienation, Integrity, and the Uncanny." *Journal of the American Philosophical Association*. DOI:10.1017/apa.2022.28.

Archer, Alfred and Maureen Sie. (2023). "Using Stars for Moral Navigation: An Ethical Exploration into Celebrity." *Journal of Applied Philosophy* 40: 340–357.

Back, M. D., J. M. Stopfer, S. Vazire, S. Gaddis, S. C. Schmukle, B. Egloff, and S. D. Gosling. (2010). "Facebook Profiles Reflect Actual Personality, Not Self-Idealization." *Psychological Science* 21: 372–374.

Bago, B., D. Rand, and G. Pennycook. (2020). "Fake News, Fast and Slow: Deliberation Reduces Belief in False (but Not True) News Headlines." *Journal of Experimental Psychology: General* 149: 1608–1613.

Ballotpedia. (2025). "Deepfake Policy in the United States, 2019–Present." https://ballotpedia.org/Deepfake_policy_in_the_United_States%2C_2019_-_Present, accessed on July 15, 2025.

Barna Group. (2024). "The Silent Problem of Pornography Use Among Pastors." *Barna.* https://www.barna.com/research/pastors-pornography-use/?utm_source=chatgpt.com, accessed on July 15, 2025.

Barnum, Matt and Deepa Seetharaman. (2025). "There's a Good Chance Your Kid Uses AI to Cheat." *The Wall Street Journal.* https://www.wsj.com/tech/ai/chatgpt-ai-cheating-students-97075d3c, accessed on July 15, 2025.

Beaty, Katelyn. (2022). *Celebrities for Jesus: How Persons, Platforms, and Profits Are Hurting the Church.* Brazos Press.

Belkin, Douglas. (2023). "As AI-Enabled Cheating Roils Colleges, Professors Turn to an Ancient Testing Method." *The Wall Street Journal.* https://www.wsj.com/articles/ai-colleges-cheating-oral-exams-286e0091, accessed on July 15, 2025.

Bilen, Eren and Alexander Matros. (2021). "Online Cheating Amid COVID-19." *Journal of Economic Behavior & Organization* 182: 196–211.

Bing, M., H. Davison, S. Vitell, A. Ammeter, B. Garner, and M. Novicevic. (2012). "An Experimental Investigation of an Interactive Model of Academic Cheating Among Business School Students." *Academy of Management Learning & Education* 11: 28–48.

Birnbaum, G., T. Bachar, G. Levy, K. Zholtack, and H. Reis. (2022). "Put Me in Your Shoes: Does Perspective-Taking Inoculate Against the Appeal of Alternative Partners?" *The Journal of Sex Research* 61: 1–10.

Birnbaum, G., K. Zholtack, and S. Ayal. (2022). "Is Infidelity Contagious? Online Exposure to Norms of Adultery and Its Effect on Expressions of Desire for Current and Alternative Partners." *Archives of Sexual Behavior* 51: 3919–3930.

Bodnick, Maya. (2023). "GPT-4 Can Already Pass Freshman Year at Harvard." *The Chronicle of Higher Education.* https://www.chronicle.com/article/gpt-4-can-already-pass-freshman-year-at-harvard, accessed on July 15, 2025.

Bogost, Ian. (2023). "The First Year of AI College Ends in Ruin." *The Atlantic.* https://www.theatlantic.com/technology/archive/2023/05/chatbot-cheating-college-campuses/674073/, accessed on July 15, 2025.

Bosch, Torie. (2011). "Charlie Sheen Interviews: Tiger Blood, Adonis DNA and Charlie Sheen the Drug." Aolnews.com. https://web.archive.org/web/20120511004437/http://www.aolnews.com/2011/02/28/charlie-sheen-interviews-tiger-blood-adonis-dna-and-charlie-s/, accessed on July 15, 2025.

Brenan, Megan and Jeffrey Jones. (2024). "Ethics Ratings of Nearly All Professions Down in U.S." *Gallup.* https://news.gallup.com/poll/608903/ethics-ratings-nearly-professions-down.aspx, accessed on July 15, 2025.

Bruce, Graeme. (2021). "Doctor, Vet, Esports Star, Influencer: Dream Jobs Among US Teens." YouGov. https://today.yougov.com/technology/articles/39997-influencer-dream-jobs-among-us-teens?, accessed on July 15, 2025.

Bryan, C., G. Adams, and B. Monin. (2013). "When Cheating Would Make You a Cheater: Implicating the Self Prevents Unethical Behavior." *Journal of Experimental Psychology: General* 142: 1001–1005.

Burkhart, Gabrielle. (2020). "Albuquerque Teen Rewarded for Turning in $135K of Cash Found near ATM." *Albuquerque News*. https://www.krqe.com/news/albuquerque-metro/albuquerque-teen-rewarded-for-turning-in-135k-of-cash-found-near-atm/, accessed on July 15, 2025.

Capraro, V. and T. Celadin. (2023). "'I Think This News Is Accurate': Endorsing Accuracy Decreases the Sharing of Fake News and Increases the Sharing of Real News." *Personality and Social Psychology Bulletin* 49: 1635–1645.

Celadin, T., V. Capraro, G. Pennycook, and D. Rand. (2023). "Displaying News Source Trustworthiness Ratings Reduces Sharing Intentions for False News Posts." *Journal of Online Trust and Safety* 1: 1–20.

Chan, J. and D. Ahn. (2023). "Unproctored Online Exams Provide Meaningful Assessment of Student Learning." *Proceedings of the National Academy of Science* 120: e2302020120.

Chen, Angela. (2019). "Forget Fake News—Nearly All Deepfakes Are Being Made for Porn." *MIT Technology Review*. https://www.technologyreview.com/2019/10/07/132735/deepfake-porn-deeptrace-legislation-california-election-disinformation/, accessed on July 15, 2025.

Chesney, Bobby and Danielle Citron. (2019). "Deep Fakes: A Looming Challenge for Privacy, Democracy, and National Security." *California Law Review* 107: 1753–1819.

Childs, Jason. (2013). "Personal Characteristics and Lying: An Experimental Investigation." *Economics Letters* 121: 425–427.

Christianity Today Editors. (1988). "How Common Is Pastoral Indiscretion?" *Christianity Today*. https://www.christianitytoday.com/pastors/1988/winter/88l1012.html, accessed on July 15, 2025.

Christianity Today Editors. (2001). "The Leadership Survey on Pastors and Internet Pornography." *Christianity Today*. https://www.christianitytoday.com/pastors/2001/winter/12.89.html, accessed on July 15, 2025.

Christie, A. N. (2019). "On Religion, Lying, and Social Preferences." *Economics Letters* 174: 161–164.

Cole, Samantha. (2017). "AI-Assisted Fake Porn Is Here and We're All Fucked." *Motherboard* 2017. https://www.vice.com/en_us/article/gydydm/gal-gadot-fake-ai-porn, accessed on July 15, 2025.

Cook J., S. Lewandowsky, and U. Ecker. (2017). "Neutralizing Misinformation Through Inoculation: Exposing Misleading Argumentation Techniques Reduces Their Influence." PLoS ONE 12: e0175799.

Cooper, A. (ed). (2002). *Sex and the Internet: A Guidebook for Clinicians*. New York: Brunner-Routledge.

Cotton, D., P. Cotton, and J. Reuben Shipway. (2024). "Chatting and Cheating: Ensuring Academic Integrity in the Era of ChatGPT." *Innovations in Education and Teaching International* 61: 228–239.

Cravens, J. and J. Whiting. (2016). "Fooling Around on Facebook: The Perceptions of Infidelity Behavior on Social Networking Sites." *Journal of Couple & Relationship Therapy* 15: 213–231.

Croco, S., J. McDonald, and C. Turitto. (2021). "Making Them Pay: Using the Norm of Honesty to Generate Costs for Political Lies." *Electoral Studies* 69: 102250.

Curtis, G. (2022). "Trends in Plagiarism and Cheating Prevalence: 1990–2020 and Beyond," in *Cheating Academic Integrity: Lessons from 30 Years of Research*. Eds. David Rettinger and Tricia Bertram Gallant. Hoboken: Wiley, 11–44.

Dash, Darryl. (2023). "Confessions of a Sermon Thief." *Preaching.com*. https://www.preaching.com/articles/confessions-of-a-sermon-thief/, accessed on July 15, 2025.

Davis, J. (2023). "Happy (?) First Birthday to ChatGPT." *Inside Higher Ed*. https://www.insidehighered.com/opinion/views/2023/11/30/chatgpt-complicates-education-versus-assessment-opinion, accessed on July 15, 2025.

Deb, Sopan. (2019). "Felicity Huffman and Lori Loughlin: How College Admission Scandal Ensnared Stars." *The New York Times*. https://www.nytimes.com/2019/03/12/arts/huffman-loughlin-college-scandal.html, accessed on July 15, 2025.

Debey, E., M. De Schryver, G. D. Logan, K. Suchotzki, and B. Verschuere. (2015). "From Junior to Senior Pinocchio: A Cross-Sectional Lifespan Investigation of Deception." *Acta Psychologica* 160: 58–68.

De keersmaecker, J. and A. Roets. (2019). "Is There an Ideological Asymmetry in the Moral Approval of Spreading Misinformation by Politicians?" *Personality and Individual Differences* 143: 165–169.

DePaulo, B. M., M. E. Ansfield, S. E. Kirkendol, and J. M. Boden. (2004). "Serious Lies." *Basic and Applied Social Psychology* 26: 147–167.

DePaulo, B. M. and D. A. Kashy. (1998). "Everyday Lies in Close and Casual Relationships." *Journal of Personality and Social Psychology* 74: 63–79.

DePaulo, B. M., D. A. Kashy, S. E. Kirkendol, M. M. Wyer, and J. A. Epstein. (1996). "Lying in Everyday Life." *Journal of Personality and Social Psychology* 70: 979–995.

DePaulo, B. M., J. J. Lindsay, B. E. Malone, L. Muhlenbruck, K. Charlton, and H. Cooper. (2003). "Cues to Deception." *Psychological Bulletin* 129: 74–118.

De Ruiter, Adrienne. (2021). "The Distinct Wrong of Deepfakes." *Philosophy & Technology* 34: 1311–1332.

Dey, Sneha. (2021). "Reports of Cheating at Colleges Soar During the Pandemic." *NPR*. https://www.npr.org/2021/08/27/1031255390/reports-of-cheating-at-colleges-soar-during-the-pandemic, accessed on July 15, 2025.

DeYoung, Rebecca K. (2014). *Vainglory: The Forgotten Vice*. Grand Rapids: Eerdmans Publishing Co.

Docan-Morgan, T. and C. Docan. (2007). "Internet Infidelity: Double Standards and the Differing Views of Women and Men." *Communication Quarterly* 55: 317–342.

Drouin, M., D. Miller, S. Wehle, and E. Hernandez. (2016). "Why Do People Lie Online? "Because Everyone Lies on the Internet." *Computers in Human Behavior* 64: 134–142.

Dyreng, S. D., W. J. Mayew, and C. D. Williams. (2012). "Religious Social Norms and Corporate Financial Reporting." *Journal of Business Finance & Accounting* 39: 845–875.

Effron, D. (2018). "It Could Have Been True: How Counterfactual Thoughts Reduce Condemnation of Falsehoods and Increase Political Polarization." *Personality and Social Psychology Bulletin* 44: 729–745.

Effron, D. and B. A. Helgason. (2022). "The Moral Psychology of Misinformation: Why We Excuse Dishonesty in a Post-Truth World." *Current Opinion in Psychology* 47: 101375.

Epstein, Z., N. Foppiani, S. Hilgard, S. Sharma, E. Glassman, and D. Rand. (2022). "Do Explanations Increase the Effectiveness of AI-Crowd Generated Fake News Warnings?" *Proceedings of the International AAAI Conference on Web and Social Media* 16: 183–193.

Epstein, Z., N. Sirlin, A. Arechar, G. Pennycook, and D. Rand. (2023). "The Social Media Context Interferes with Truth Discernment." *Science Advances* 9: eabo6169.

Eshet, Y. (2023). "The Plagiarism Pandemic: Inspection of Academic Dishonesty During the COVID-19 Outbreak Using Originality Software." *Education and Information Technologies* 29: 3279–3299.

Espada, Mariah. (2023). "How TikTok Changed the Meaning of a Million Followers." *Time*. https://time.com/6299379/tiktok-youtube-follow-count/, accessed on July 15, 2025.

Ethics Unwrapped. (2022). "Theranos' Bad Blood." https://ethicsunwrapped.utexas.edu/wp-content/uploads/2022/11/Theranos-Bad-Blood.pdf, accessed on July 15, 2025.

Fallis, Don. (2021). "The Epistemic Threat of Deepfakes." *Philosophy & Technology* 34: 623–643.

Ferron, A., Y. Lussier, S. Sabourin, and A. Brassard. (2017). "The Role of Internet Pornography Use and Cyber Infidelity in the Associations Between Personality, Attachment, and Couple and Sexual Satisfaction." *Social Networking* 6: 1–18.

Fitzsimmons, Emma and Jeffery Mays. (2023). "Since When Does Eric Adams Speak Spanish, Yiddish and Mandarin?" *The New York Times*. https://www.nytimes.com/2023/10/20/nyregion/ai-robocalls-eric-adams.html, accessed on July 15, 2025.

Flattery, Tobias and Christian Miller. (2024). "Deepfakes and Dishonesty." *Philosophy & Technology* 37: 120.

Franklin, Jonathan. (2024). "Carlee Russell Pleads Guilty, Avoids Jail After Falsely Reporting Her Own Kidnapping." *NPR*. https://www.npr.org/2024/03/21/1239983143/carlee-russell-pleads-guilty-avoids-jail-time-kidnapping-hoax, accessed on July 15, 2025.

Freeze, M., M. Baumgartner, P. Bruno, J. R. Gunderson, J. Olin, M. Ross, and J. Szafran. (2021). "Fake Claims of Fake News: Political Misinformation, Warnings, and the Tainted Truth Effect." *Political Behavior* 43: 1433–1465.

Garg, M. and A. Goel. (2022). "A Systematic Literature Review on Online Assessment Security: Current Challenges and Integrity Strategies." *Computer & Security* 113: 102544.

Gerlach, P., K. Teodorescu, and R. Hertwig. (2019). "The Truth About Lies: A Meta-Analysis on Dishonest Behavior." *Psychological Bulletin* 145: 1–44.

Ghezae, I., J. Jordan, I. Gainsburg, M. Mosleh, G. Pennycook, R. Willer, and D. Rand. (2024). "Partisans Neither Expect Nor Receive Reputational Rewards for Sharing Falsehoods over Truth Online." *PNAS Nexus* 3.

Gibbs, Nancy. (2017). "A Note to Our Readers." *Time*. https://time.com/4645541/donald-trump-white-house-oval-office/, accessed on July 15, 2025.

Gibson, Scott. (2008). *Should We Use Someone Else's Sermon? Preaching in a Cut-and-Paste World*. Grand Rapids: Zondervan.

Goldman, J., M. Carson, and J. Simonds. (2022). "It's in the Pedagogy: Evidence-Based Practices to Promote Academic Integrity," in *Cheating Academic Integrity: Lessons from 30 Years of Research*. Eds. David Rettinger and Tricia Bertram Gallant. Hoboken: Wiley, 131–168.

The Gospel Coalition Editors. (2010). "TGC Asks Don Carson: When Has a Preacher Crossed the Line into Plagiarism in His Sermon?" *The Gospel Coalition*. https://www.thegospelcoalition.org/article/tgc-asks-don-carson-when-has-a-preacher-crossed-the-line-into-plagiarism-in/, accessed on July 15, 2025.

Graham, M. A., J. Monday, K. O'Brien, and S. Steffen. (1994). "Cheating at Small Colleges: An Examination of Student and Faculty Attitudes and Behaviors." *Journal of College Student Development* 35: 255–260.

Graham, Ruth. (2021). "'Sermongate' Prompts a Quandary: Should Pastors Borrow Words from One Another?" *The New York Times*. https://www.nytimes.com/2021/07/06/us/sermongate-plagiarism-litton-greear.html, accessed on July 15, 2025.

Grinberg, N., K. Joseph, L. Friedland, B. Swire-Thompson, and D. Lazer. (2019). "Fake News on Twitter During the 2016 U. S. Presidential Election." *Science* 363: 374–378.

Guillory, J. and J. T. Hancock. (2012). "The Effect of LinkedIn on Deception in Resumes." *Cyberpsychology, Behavior, and Social Networking* 15: 135–140.

Hackathorn, Jana and Brien Ashdown. (2021). "The Webs We Weave: Predicting Infidelity Motivations and Extradyadic Relationship Satisfaction." *The Journal of Sex Research* 58: 170–182.

Hahl, O., M. Kim, and E. Zuckerman Sivan. (2018). "The Authentic Appeal of the Lying Demagogue: Proclaiming the Deeper Truth About Political Illegitimacy." *American Sociological Review* 83: 1–33.

Han H., J. Kim, C. Jeong, and G. Cohen. (2017). "Attainable and Relevant Moral Exemplars Are More Effective than Extraordinary Exemplars in Promoting Voluntary Service Engagement." *Frontiers in Psychology* 8: 1–14.

Hancock, J. and J. Guillory. (2015). "Deception with Technology," in *The Handbook of the Psychology of Communication Technology*. Ed. S. S. Sundar. Chichester: John Wiley & Sons, 270–289.

Hancock, J., J. Thom-Santelli, and T. Ritchie. (2004). "Deception and Design: The Impact of Communication Technology on Lying Behavior," in *Proceedings of the SIGCHI Conference on Human Factors in Computing Systems*. New York: Association for Computing Machinery, 129–134.

Harris, Keith Raymond. (2021). "Video on Demand: What Deepfakes Do and How They Harm." *Synthese* 199: 13373–13391.

Hart, Christian and Drew Curtis. (2023). *Big Liars: What Psychological Science Tells Us About Lying and How You Can Avoid Being Duped.* Washington, DC: APA LifeTools.

Hartley, A. G., R. M. Furr, E. G. Helzer, E. Jayawickreme, K. R. Velasquez, and W. Fleeson. (2016). "Morality's Centrality to Liking, Respecting, and Understanding Others." *Social Psychological and Personality Science* 7: 648–657.

Heffer, Chris. (2018). "Poisonous Words: Arrogance, Bullshit and Accusations of Lying in Public Discourse." *Open for Debate Blog.* https://blogs.cardiff.ac.uk/openfordebate/poisonous-words-arrogance-bullshit-and-accusations-of-lying-in-public-discourse/, accessed on July 15, 2025.

Henline, B., L. Lamke, and M. Howard. (2007). "Exploring Perceptions of Online Infidelity." *Personal Relationships* 14: 113–128.

Hern, Alex. (2022). "AI Bot ChatGPT Stuns Academics with Essay Writing Skills and Usability." *The Guardian.* https://www.theguardian.com/technology/2022/dec/04/ai-bot-chatgpt-stuns-academics-with-essay-writing-skills-and-usability, accessed on July 15, 2025.

Hertlein, K. and F. Piercy. (2006). "Internet Infidelity: A Critical Review of the Literature." *The Family Journal* 14: 366–371.

Hertlein, K. and F. Piercy. (2012). "Essential Elements of Internet Infidelity Treatment." *Journal of Marital & Family Therapy* 38: 257–270.

Hertlein, K. and M. Webster. (2008). "Technology, Relationships, and Problems: A Research Synthesis." *Journal of Marital and Family Therapy* 34: 445–460.

Hobbs, Tawnell. (2021). "Cheating at School Is Easier Than Ever—And It's Rampant." *The Wall Street Journal.* https://www.wsj.com/articles/cheating-at-school-is-easier-than-everand-its-rampant-11620828004, accessed on July 15, 2025.

Homiletics Team. (2023). "Using AI to Write Sermons: Is ChatGPT a Solution for Busy Pastors?" *Homiletics.* https://blog.homileticsonline.com/the-back-page/using-ai-to-write-sermons-is-chatgpt-a-solution-for-busy-pastors/, accessed on July 15, 2025.

Horowitch, Rose. (2023). "Here Comes the Second Year of AI College." *The Atlantic.* https://www.theatlantic.com/ideas/archive/2023/08/ai-chatgpt-college-essay-plagiarism/674928/, accessed on July 15, 2025.

Horowitz, Jason and Taylor Lorenz. (2021). "Khaby Lame, the Everyman of the Internet." *The New York Times.* https://www.nytimes.com/2021/06/02/style/khaby-lame-tiktok.html, accessed on July 15, 2025.

Horton, Adrian. (2024). "Inside the Rise and Fall of Ashley Madison: 'People Literally Lost their Lives.'" *The Guardian.* https://www.theguardian.com/tv-and-radio/article/2024/may/14/ashley-madison-netflix-documentary, accessed on July 15, 2025.

Howerton, Rick. (2020). "6 Undeniable Reasons It's Nearly Impossible to Plagiarize a Sermon." *KentuckyToday.* https://www.kentuckytoday.com/downloads/6-undeniable-reasons-it-s-nearly-impossible-to-plagiarize-a-sermon/article_47541bac-905b-53e7-b69a-ac69b3d40522.html, accessed on July 15, 2025.

IBISWorld. (2025). "Adult & Pornographic Websites in the US." https://www.ibisworld.com/united-states/market-size/adult-pornographic-websites/4576/, accessed on July 15, 2025.

Jenkins, B., J. Golding, A. Le Grand, M. Levi, and A. Pals. (2023). "When Opportunity Knocks: College Students' Cheating Amid the COVID-19 Pandemic." *Teaching of Psychology* 50: 407–419.

Johnson, Paula A., Sheila E. Widnall, and Frazier F. Benya (eds.). (2018). *Sexual Harassment of Women: Climate, Culture, and Consequences in Academic Sciences, Engineering, and Medicine*. Consensus Report of the National Academies of Sciences, Engineering, and Medicine. Washington, DC: The National Academies Press. https://doi.org/10.17226/24994.

Kaiser, Jocelyn. (2024). "House Panel Concludes that COVID-19 Pandemic Came from a Lab Leak." *ScienceInsider*. https://www.science.org/content/article/house-panel-concludes-covid-19-pandemic-came-lab-leak, accessed on July 15, 2025.

Kang, Cecilia. (2016). "Fake News Onslaught Targets Pizzeria as Nest of Child-Trafficking." *The New York Times*. https://www.nytimes.com/2016/11/21/technology/fact-check-this-pizzeria-is-not-a-child-trafficking-site.html, accessed on July 15, 2025.

Kant, Immanuel. (1799). "On a Supposed Right to Lie Because of Philanthropy," in *Kant's Critique of Practical Reason and Other Works on the Theory of Ethics*. Trans. T. K. Abbott. London: Longmans, Green and Co.

Kerner, Catherine and Mathias Risse. (2021). "Beyond Porn and Discreditation: Epistemic Promises and Perils of Deepfake Technology in Digital Lifeworlds." *Moral Philosophy and Politics* 8: 81–108.

Klein, H., N. Levenburg, M. McKendall, and W. Mothersell. (2007). "Cheating During the College Years: How Do Business Students Compare?" *Journal of Business Ethics* 72: 197–206.

Kozyreva, A. et al. (2024). "Toolbox of Individual-Level Interventions Against Online Misinformation." *Nature Human Behaviour* 8: 1044–1052.

Kreps, S., R. M. McCain, and M. Brundage. (2022). "All the News That's Fit to Fabricate: AI-Generated Text as a Tool of Media Misinformation." *Journal of Experimental Political Science* 2022: 104–117.

Kumar, Anugrah. (2024). "Netflix 'Ashley Madison' Docu Features Pastor Who Killed Himself After Being Outed as User." *Christian Post*. https://www.christianpost.com/news/netflix-ashley-madison-docu-features-pastor-who-killed-himself.html, accessed on July 15, 2025.

Laas, Oliver. (2023). "Deepfakes and Trust in Technology." *Synthese* 202. https://doi.org/10.1007/s11229-023-04363-4.

Laaser, Mark and Louis Gregoire. (2003). "Pastors and Cybersex Addiction." *Sexual and Relationship Therapy* 18: 395–404.

Lancaster, Thomas. (2022). "The Past and Future of Contract Cheating," in *Cheating Academic Integrity: Lessons from 30 Years of Research*. Eds. David Rettinger and Tricia Bertram Gallant. Hoboken: Wiley, 45–64.

Landers, C. (forthcoming). "ChatGPT, the CUPID Model, and Low-Stakes Writing." *AAPT Studies in Pedagogy*. https://philpapers.org/archive/LANCTC-3.pdf, accessed on July 15, 2025.

Lang, James. (2013). *Cheating Lessons: Learning from Academic Dishonesty.* Cambridge: Harvard University Press.

Lang, James. (2015). "Cheating Inadvertently." *The Chronicle of Higher Education.* https://www.chronicle.com/article/cheating-inadvertently/, accessed on July 15, 2025.

Larson, Craig Brain. (2024). "Plagiarism, Shmagiarism." *Preaching Today.* https://www.preachingtoday.com/skills/2005/august/plagiarism-shmagiarism.html, accessed on July 15, 2025.

Lawson, M., S. Anand, and H. Kakkar. (2023). "Tribalism and Tribulations: The Social Costs of Not Sharing Fake News." *Journal of Experimental Psychology: General* 152: 611–631.

Lazer, D., M. Baum, Y. Benkler, A. Berinsky, K. Greenhill, F. Menczer, M. Metzger, B. Nyhan, G. Pennycook, D. Rothschild, M. Schudson, S. Sloman, C. Sunstein, E. Thorson, D. Watts, and J. Zittrain. (2018). "The Science of Fake News." *Science* 359: 1094–1096.

Leadership Journal. (2005). "Leadership Survey on Pastors and Internet Pornography." *Leadership Journal* 87.

Levine, E. E. and T. R. Cohen. (2018). "You Can Handle the Truth: Mispredicting the Consequences of Honest Communication." *Journal of Experimental Psychology: General* 147: 1400–1429.

Levine, Timothy. (2019). *Duped: Truth-Default Theory and the Social Science of Lying and Deception.* Tuscaloosa: University of Alabama Press.

Lewandowsky, S., U. Ecker, C. Seifert, N. Schwarz, and J. Cook. (2012). "Misinformation and Its Correction: Continued Influence and Successful Debiasing." *Psychological Science in the Public Interest* 13: 106–131.

Lin, Yi-Li. (2023). "I Used ChatGPT for Six Months to Help My Pastoral Ministry. Here's What Worked." *Christianity Today.* https://www.christianitytoday.com/ct/2023/august-web-only/chatgpt-ai-ministry-pastoral-taiwan.html, accessed on July 15, 2025.

Liu, Jennifer. (2023). "More than Half of Gen Zers Think They 'Can Easily Make a Career in Influencing,' Says Branding Expert." CNBC. https://www.cnbc.com/2023/09/20/more-than-half-of-gen-zers-think-they-can-easily-make-a-career-in-influencing.html#, accessed on July 15, 2025.

Long, Thomas. (2008). "Stolen Goods: Tempted to Plagiarize." *Preaching Today.* https://www.preachingtoday.com/skills/2008/april/stolengoods.html, accessed on July 15, 2025.

Maheu, M. M. and R. B. Subotnik. (2001). *Infidelity on the Internet.* Naperville: Sourcebooks.

Malesky, A., C. Grist, K. Poovey, and N. Dennis. (2022). "The Effects of Peer Influence, Honor Codes, and Personality Traits on Cheating Behavior in a University Setting." *Ethics & Behavior* 32: 12–21.

Manning, J. (2006). "The Impact of Internet Pornography on Marriage and the Family: A Review of the Research." *Sexual Addiction & Compulsivity* 13: 131–165.

Markowitz, D. (2022). "Revisiting the Relationship Between Deception and Design: A Replication and Extension of Hancock et al. (2004)." *Human Communication Research* 48: 158–167.

Martel, C. and D. Rand. (2023). "Misinformation Warning Labels Are Widely Effective: A Review of Warning Effects and Their Moderating Features." *Current Opinion in Psychology* 54: 101710.

Martel, C. and D. Rand. (2024). "Fact-Checker Warning Labels Are Effective Even for Those Who Distrust Fact-Checkers." *Nature Human Behaviour* 10: 1957–1967.

Maxey, S. (2021). "Limited Spin: When the Public Punishes Leaders Who Lie About Military Action." *Journal of Conflict Resolution* 65: 283–312.

Mazar, N., O. Amir, and D. Ariely. (2008). "The Dishonesty of Honest People: A Theory of Self-Concept Maintenance." *Journal of Marketing Research* 45: 633–644.

McCabe, D., K. Butterfield, and L. Treviño. (2006). "Academic Dishonesty in Graduate Business Programs: Prevalence, Causes, and Proposed Action." *Academy of Management Learning and Education* 5: 294–305.

McCabe, D. and L. Treviño. (1993). "Academic Dishonesty: Honor Codes and Other Contextual Influences." *The Journal of Higher Education* 64: 522–538.

McCabe, D., L. Treviño, and K. Butterfield. (2001). "Cheating in Academic Institutions: A Decade of Research." *Ethics & Behavior* 11: 219–232.

McGlynn, Clare. (2024). "Deepfake Porn: Why We Need to Make It a Crime to Create It, Not Just Share It." *The Conversation.* https://theconversation.com/deepfake-porn-why-we-need-to-make-it-a-crime-to-create-it-not-just-share-it-227177, accessed on July 15, 2025.

McKeever, Natasha. (2020). "Why, and to What Extent, Is Sexual Infidelity Wrong?" *Pacific Philosophical Quarterly* 101: 515–537.

McPhedran, R., M. Ratajczak, M. Mawby, E. King, Y. Yang, and N. Gold. (2023). "Psychological Inoculation Protects Against the Social Media Infodemic." *Scientific Reports* 13: 5780.

McQueen, Paddy. (2021). "Sexual Interactions and Sexual Infidelity." *The Journal of Ethics* 25: 449–466.

Mele, Alfred. (2001). *Self-Deception Unmasked.* Princeton: Princeton University Press.

Mileham, B. (2007). "Online Infidelity in Internet Chat Rooms: An Ethnographic Exploration." *Computers in Human* Behavior 23: 11–31.

Miller, A., T. Murdock, and M. Grotewiel. (2017). "Addressing Academic Dishonesty Among the Highest Achievers." *Theory Into Practice* 56: 121–128.

Miller, Christian. (2013). *Moral Character: An Empirical Theory.* Oxford: Oxford University Press.

Miller, Christian. (2014). *Character and Moral Psychology.* Oxford: Oxford University Press.

Miller, Christian. (2017a). "Honesty," in *Moral Psychology, Volume V: Virtue and Character*. Eds. Walter Sinnott-Armstrong and Christian B. Miller. Cambridge: MIT Press, 2017, 237–273.

Miller, Christian. (2017b). *The Character Gap: How Good Are We?* New York: Oxford University Press.

Miller, Christian. (2020). "Just How Dishonest Are Most Students?" *The New York Times.* https://www.nytimes.com/2020/11/13/opinion/sunday/online-learning-cheating.html, accessed on July 15, 2025.

Miller, Christian. (2021a). *Honesty: The Philosophy and Psychology of a Neglected Virtue*. New York: Oxford University Press.

Miller, Christian. (2021b). "Honesty and Radically Opposing Views: Flat-Earthers, Apocalyptic Preachers, and 2020 American Election-Deniers." *Open for Debate Blog*. https://blogs.cardiff.ac.uk/openfordebate/honesty-and-radically-opposing-views-flat-earthers-apocalyptic-preachers-and-2020-american-election-deniers/, accessed on July 15, 2025.

Miller, Christian. (2021c). "Is Your Crush on OkCupid Telling You the Truth?" *The New York Times*. https://www.nytimes.com/2021/08/06/opinion/honesty-social-media.html, accessed on July 15, 2025.

Miller, Christian. (2022a). "Are Most People Liars?" *Forbes*. https://www.forbes.com/sites/christianmiller/2022/10/17/are-most-people-liars/, accessed on July 15, 2025.

Miller, Christian. (2022b). "Intellectual Honesty." *Scientia et Fides* 7: 83–98.

Miller, Christian. (2023). "How Often Do You Lie? Deception Researchers Investigate How the Recipient and the Medium Affect Telling the Truth." *The Conversation* 2023. https://theconversation.com/how-often-do-you-lie-deception-researchers-investigate-how-the-recipient-and-the-medium-affect-telling-the-truth-214815, accessed on July 15, 2025.

Miller, Christian. (2024). "Celebrity and Dishonesty: Do They Go Hand in Hand?" in *The Philosophy of Fame and Celebrity*. Eds. Alfred Archer, Catherine Robb, and Matthew Dennis. Bloomsbury, 50–68.

Miller, Christian, Meghan Sullivan, Devin Gouvêa, Gregory Robson, Matthew Frise, and Philip Swenson. (forthcoming). "Advice to Christian Philosophers, 40 Years Later." *Faith and Philosophy*.

Mirsky, Y. and W. Lee. (2020). "The Creation and Detection of Deepfakes: A Survey." *ACM Computing Surveys* 54: 1–41.

Mitchell, Alex. (2022). "Professor Catches Student Cheating with ChatGPT: 'I Feel Abject Terror.'" *New York Post*. https://nypost.com/2022/12/26/students-using-chatgpt-to-cheat-professor-warns/, accessed on July 15, 2025.

Moore, Russell. (2023). "AI Might Teach, But It Can't Preach." *Christianity Today*. https://www.christianitytoday.com/ct/2023/january-web-only/chatgpt-artificial-intelligence-ai-preach-sermons-church.html, accessed on July 15, 2025.

Morales, Christina. (2021). "University of South Carolina President Resigns After Speech Blunders." *The New York Times*. https://www.nytimes.com/2021/05/13/us/usc-president-speech-plagiarism.html, accessed on July 15, 2025.

Morgan, Lucy. (2024). "It's Not Just Taylor Swift—All Women Are at Risk from the Rise of Deepfakes." *Glamour*. https://www.glamour.com/story/taylor-swift-all-women-are-at-risk-from-the-rise-of-deepfakes, accessed on July 15, 2025.

Morrow, G., B. Swire-Thompson, J. Polny, M. Kopec, and J. Wihbey. (2022). "The Emerging Science of Content Labeling: Contextualizing Social Media Content Moderation." *Journal of the Association for Information Science and Technology* 73: 1365–1386.

Muir, Tom. (2023). "Will ChatGPT Change Our Definitions of Cheating?" *Times Higher Education*. https://www.timeshighereducation.com/campus/will-chatgpt-change-our-definitions-cheating, accessed on July 15, 2025.

Nagourney, Adam, David Sanger, and Johanna Barr. (2018). "Hawaii Panics After Alert About Incoming Missile Is Sent in Error." *The New York Times*. https://www.nytimes.com/2018/01/13/us/hawaii-missile.html, accessed on July 15, 2025.

Newton, P. and K. Essex. (2023). "How Common Is Cheating in Online Exams and Did It Increase During the COVID-19 Pandemic? A Systematic Review." *Journal of Academic Ethics* 22: 323–343.

Noorbehbahani, F., A. Mohammadi, and M. Aminazadeh. (2022). "A Systematic Review of Research on Cheating in Online Exams from 2010 to 2021." *Education and Information Technologies* 27: 8413–8460.

Öhman, Carl. (2020). "Introducing the Pervert's Dilemma: A Contribution to the Critique of Deepfake Pornography." *Ethics and Information Technology* 22: 133–140.

Oliveira, C. M. and T. R. Levine. (2008). "Lie Acceptability: A Construct and Measure." *Communication Research Reports* 25: 282–288.

Onu, D., M. Chidi Onyedibe, L. Ugwu, and G. Nche. (2021). "Relationship Between Religious Commitment and Academic Dishonesty: Is Self-Efficacy a Factor?" *Ethics & Behavior* 31: 13–20.

Osmundsen, M., A. Bor, P. Vahlstrup, A. Bechmann, and M. Petersen. (2021). "Partisan Polarization Is the Primary Psychological Motivation Behind Political Fake News Sharing on Twitter." *American Political Science Review* 115: 999–1015.

Padilla 2020 "Teenager, an Aspiring Detective, Returns $135,000 He Found." *The New York Times*. https://www.nytimes.com/2020/05/09/us/atm-cash-135000-albuquerque-police.html, accessed on July 15, 2025.

Park, N. and C. Peterson. (2008). "Positive Psychology and Character Strengths: Application to Strengths-Based School Counseling." *Professional School Counseling* 12: 85–92.

Parr, Annabelle. (2020). "5 Life Lessons from Taylor Swift's Miss Americana and Acceptance and Commitment Therapy." The Center for Stress & Anxiety Management. https://www.csamsandiego.com/blog/five-life-lessons-from-taylor-swifts-miss-americana-and-acceptance-and-commitment-therapy, accessed on July 15, 2025.

Pennycook, G., A. Bear, E. Collins, and D. Rand. (2020). "The Implied Truth Effect: Attaching Warnings to a Subset of Fake News Headlines Increases Perceived Accuracy of Headlines Without Warnings." *Management Science* 66: 4944–4957.

Pennycook, G. and D. Rand. (2019). "Lazy, Not Biased: Susceptibility to Partisan Fake News Is Better Explained by Lack of Reasoning than by Motivated Reasoning." *Cognition* 188: 39–50.

Pennycook, G. and D. Rand. (2021). "The Psychology of Fake News." *Trends in Cognitive Sciences* 25: 388–402.

Pennycook, G. and D. Rand. (2022). "Accuracy Prompts Are a Replicable and Generalizable Approach for Reducing the Spread of Misinformation." *Nature Communications* 13: 2333.

Pennycook, G., T. Cannon, and D. Rand. (2018). "Prior Exposure Increases Perceived Accuracy of Fake News." *Journal of Experimental Psychology: General* 147: 1865–1880.

Pennycook, G., Z. Epstein, M. Mosleh, A. Arechar, D. Eckles, and D. Rand. (2021). "Shifting Attention to Accuracy Can Reduce Misinformation Online." *Nature* 592: 590–595.

Plato. (1968). *The Republic of Plato*. Trans. Allan Bloom. New York: Basic Books.

Porter, E. and T. Wood. (2022). "Political Misinformation and Factual Corrections on the Facebook News Feed: Experimental Evidence." *The Journal of Politics* 84: 1812–1817.

Pruss, Alexander R. (1999). "Lying and Speaking Your Interlocutor's Language." *The Thomist: A Speculative Quarterly Review* 63: 439–453.

Quintero, Fernando. (2006). "Accuser Recounts Trysts with 'Art.'" *Rocky Mountain News*. https://web.archive.org/web/20061120180326/http://www.rockymountainnews.com/drmn/local/article/0%2C1299%2CDRMN_15_5115225%2C00.html, accessed on July 15, 2025.

Rasmussen Reports. (2016). "Voters Don't Trust Media Fact-Checking." https://www.rasmussenreports.com/public_content/politics/general_politics/september_2016/voters_don_t_trust_media_fact_checking#google_vignette, accessed on July 15, 2025.

Reed, Philip. (2024). "Why So Many Plagiarists Are in Denial About What They Did Wrong." *Psyche* 2024. https://psyche.co/ideas/why-so-many-plagiarists-are-in-denial-about-what-they-did-wrong, accessed on July 15, 2025.

Rettinger, D. (2017). "The Role of Emotions and Attitudes in Causing and Preventing Cheating." *Theory Into Practice* 56: 103–110.

Reuters. (2020). "Fact Check: 'Drunk' Nancy Pelosi Video Is Manipulated." *Reuters*. https://www.reuters.com/article/idUSKCN24Z2B1/, accessed on July 15, 2025.

Rini, Regina. (2020). "Deepfakes and the Epistemic Backdrop." *Philosopher's Imprint* 20. https://quod.lib.umich.edu/p/phimp/3521354.0020.024/1.

Rini, Regina and Leah Cohen. (2022). "Deepfakes, Deep Harms." *Journal of Ethics and Social Philosophy* 22. https://doi.org/10.26556/jesp.v22i2.1628.

Robb, Catherine and Alfred Archer. (2022). "Talent, Skill, and Celebrity." *Ethical Perspectives* 29: 33–63.

Roberts, Tom. (2023). "How to Do Things with Deepfakes." *Synthese* 201: 43.

Rockwell, Donna and David Giles. (2009). "Being a Celebrity: A Phenomenology of Fame." *Journal of Phenomenological Psychology* 40: 178–210.

Rogers, R. (2020). "Research Note: The Scale of Facebook's Problem Depends upon How 'Fake News' Is Classified." *Harvard Kennedy School Misinformation Review* 1. https://doi.org/10.37016/mr-2020-43.

Rokovski, C. and E. Levy. (2007). "Academic Dishonesty: Perceptions of Business Students." *College Student Journal* 41: 466–481.

Roozenbeek, J., C. Traberg, and S. van der Linden. (2022). "Technique-Based Inoculation Against Real-World Misinformation." *Royal Society Open Science* 9: 211719.

Roozenbeek, J. and S. van der Linden. (2020). "Breaking *Harmony Square*: A Game that 'Inoculates' Against Political Misinformation." *Misinformation Review*, https://misinforeview.hks.harvard.edu/article/breaking-harmony-square-a-game-that-inoculates-against-political-misinformation/.

ruby Life. (2020). "Report on Customer Statistics 2020." https://lander-cdn.ashleymadison.com/images/2020-Report.pdf, accessed on July 15, 2025.

Scarfe, P., K. Watcham, A. Clarke, and E. Roesch. (2024). "A Real-World Test of Artificial Intelligence Infiltration of a University Examinations System: A 'Turing Test' Case Study." *PLOS One* 19: e0305354.

Schneider, J. (2003). "The Impact of Compulsive Cybersex Behaviours on the Family." *Sexual and Relationship Therapy* 18: 329–354.

Security Hero. (2023). "State of Deepfakes." https://www.homesecurityheroes.com/state-of-deepfakes/#key-findings, accessed on July 15, 2025.

Seitz-Wald, Alex. (2024)." Democratic Operative Admits to Commissioning Fake Biden Robocall that used AI." *NBC News*. https://www.nbcnews.com/politics/2024-election/democratic-operative-admits-commissioning-fake-biden-robocall-used-ai-rcna140402, accessed on July 15, 2025.

Seitz-Wald, Alex and Mike Memoli. (2024). "Fake Joe Biden Robocall Tells New Hampshire Democrats Not to Vote Tuesday." *NBC News*. https://www.nbcnews.com/politics/2024-election/fake-joe-biden-robocall-tells-new-hampshire-democrats-not-vote-tuesday-rcna134984, accessed on July 15, 2025.

Selterman, D., S. Joel, and V. Dale. (2023). "No Remorse: Sexual Infidelity Is Not Clearly Linked with Relationship Satisfaction or Well-Being in Ashley Madison Users." *Archives of Sexual Behavior* 52: 2561–2573.

Serota, K. B., T. R. Levine, and F. J. Boster. (2010). "The Prevalence of Lying in America: Three Studies of Self-Reported Lies." *Human Communication Research* 36: 2–25.

Serota, K. B., T. R. Levine, and T. Docan-Morgan. (2022). "Unpacking Variation in Lie Prevalence: Prolific Liars, Bad Lie Days, or Both?" *Communication Monographs* 89: 307–331.

Serota, K. B., T. R. Levine, L. Zvi, D. M. Markowitz, and T. Docan-Morgan. (2024). "The Ubiquity of Long-Tail Lie Distributions: Seven Studies from Five Continents." *Journal of Communication* 74: 1–11.

Shakhnazarova, Nika and Hana Carter. (2019). "Billionaire Who Funds Campaigns to Make People to Eat Less Meat Is Pictured Scoffing 20,000-Calorie Burger Containing Eight Beef Patties and 20 Rashers of Bacon." *The Sun*. https://www.thesun.co.uk/news/8241884/billionaire-hypocrite-blasts-meat-eaters-burger/, accessed on July 15, 2025.

Shalvi, S. and D. Leiser. (2013). "Moral Firmness." *Journal of Economic Behavior & Organization* 93: 400–407.

Shu, L., F. Gino, and M. Bazerman. (2011). "Dishonest Deed, Clear Conscience: When Cheating Leads to Moral Disengagement and Motivated Forgetting." *Personality and Social Psychology Bulletin* 37: 330–349.

Siele, Martin. (2023). "AI Is Taking the Jobs of Kenyans Who Write Essays for U.S. College Students." *Rest of World*. https://restofworld.org/2023/chatgpt-taking-kenya-ghostwriters-jobs/, accessed on July 15, 2025.

Smietana, Bob. (2021a). "'If You Have Eyes, Plagiarize': When Borrowing a Sermon Goes Too Far." *Religion News Service*. https://religionnews.com/2021/04/27/plagiarism-pastors-sermon-ghostwriters-zach-stewart-driscoll/, accessed on July 15, 2025.

Smietana, Bob. (2021b). "When Pastors Plagiarize Sermons." *Word&Way*. https://wordandway.org/2021/04/27/when-pastors-plagiarize-sermons/, accessed on July 15, 2025.

Smith, C. P. and J. J. Freyd. (2014). "Institutional Betrayal." *American Psychologist* 69: 575–587.

Smith, M., J. Hancock, L. Reynolds, and J. Birnholtz. (2014). "Everyday Deception or a Few Prolific Liars? The Prevalence of Lies in Text Messaging." *Computers in Human Behavior* 41: 220–227.

Sosik, J. J., W. Gentry, and J. Chun. (2012). "The Value of Virtue in the Upper Echelons: A Multisource Examination of Executive Character Strengths and Performance." *Leadership Quarterly* 23: 367–382.

Statista 2024. "Most Popular Pornographic Websites Worldwide as of November 2024, by Total Visits." https://www.statista.com/statistics/1445661/most-visited-porn-websites-worldwide/, accessed on July 15, 2025.

Steffaniak, Jordan. (2021). "Sermon Plagiarism as Vice: A Short Exploration and Defense." *The London Lyceum*. https://thelondonlyceum.com/sermon-plagiarism-as-vice-a-short-exploration-and-defense/, accessed on July 15, 2025.

Stephens, J. (2017). "How to Cheat and Not Feel Guilty: Cognitive Dissonance and Its Amelioration in the Domain of Academic Dishonesty." *Theory into Practice* 56: 111–120.

Sternlicht, Alexandra. (2022). "The World's Most Followed TikToker Gets Paid as much as $750K per Post, but to Reach His Greatest Business Goal Khaby Lame Is Binge-Watching American Cartoons." *Fortune*. https://fortune.com/2022/09/14/how-khaby-lame-plans-expand-business-that-gets-750k-dollars-for-tiktok-post/, accessed on July 15, 2025.

Stinnett, Chris. (2000). "Footnotes in the Pulpit." *Christianity Today*. https://www.christianitytoday.com/pastors/2000/fall/14.89.html, accessed on July 15, 2025.

Story, Daniel and Ryan Jenkins. (2023). "Deepfake Pornography and the Ethics of Non-Veridical Representations." *Philosophy & Technology* 36. https://doi.org/10.1007/s13347-023-00657-0.

Susnjak, T. (2022). "ChatGPT: The End of Online Exam Integrity?" *arXiv.org*. https://doi.org/10.48550/arXiv.2212.09292, accessed on July 15, 2025.

Swift, Art. (2016). "Americans' Trust in Mass Media Sinks to New Low." Gallup. https://news.gallup.com/poll/195542/americans-trust-mass-media-sinks-new-low.aspx, accessed on July 15, 2025.

Tatum, H. (2022). "Honor Codes and Academic Integrity: Three Decades of Research." *Journal of College & Character* 23: 32–47.

Tatum, H. and B. Schwartz. (2017). "Honor Codes: Evidence Based Strategies for Improving Academic Integrity." *Theory Into Practice* 56: 129–135.

Terry, Owen Kichizo. (2023). "I'm a Student. You Have No Idea How Much We're Using ChatGPT." *The Chronicle of Higher Education*. https://www.chronicle.com/article/im-a-student-you-have-no-idea-how-much-were-using-chatgpt, accessed on July 15, 2025.

Thoburn, John and Jack Balswick. (1998). "Demographic Data on Extra-Marital Sexual Behavior in the Ministry." *Pastoral Psychology* 46: 447–457.

Thoburn, John and Jack Balswick. (1993). "A Prevention Approach to Infidelity Among Male Protestant Clergy." *Pastoral Psychology* 42: 45–51.

Thoburn, John and Jack Balswick. (1994). "An Evaluation of Infidelity Among Male Protestant Clergy." *Pastoral Psychology* 42: 285–294.

Thoburn, John and D. Mitchell Whitman. (2004). "Clergy Affairs: Emotional Investment, Longevity of Relationship and Affair Partners." *Pastoral Psychology* 52: 491–506.

Thompson, A. E. and L. F. O'Sullivan. (2016). "I Can But You Can't: Inconsistencies in Judgments of and Experiences with Infidelity." *Journal of Relationships Research* 7: 1–13.

Thorkildsen, T., C. Golant, and L. Richesin. (2007). "Reaping What We Sow: Cheating as a Mechanism of Moral Engagement," in *Psychology of Academic Cheating*. Eds. E. Anderman and T Murdock. Amsterdam: Elsevier Academic Press, 171–202.

Toma, C. L., J. A. Bonus, and L. M. Van Swol. (2019). "Lying Online: Examining the Production, Detection, and Popular Beliefs Surrounding Interpersonal Deception in Technologically-Mediated Environments," in *The Palgrave Handbook of Deceptive Communication*. Ed. T. Docan-Morgan. London: Palgrave Macmillan, 583–601.

Toma, C. L., J. T. Hancock, and N. B. Ellison. (2008). "Separating Fact from Fiction: An Examination of Deceptive Self-Presentation in Online Dating Profiles." *Personality and Social Psychology Bulletin* 34: 1023–1036.

Toma, C. L., L. C. Jiang, and J. T. Hancock. (2018). "Lies in the Eye of the Beholder: Asymmetric Beliefs About One's Own and Others' Deceptiveness in Mediated and Face-to-Face Communication." *Communication Research 45*: 1167–1192.

Tosi, Justin and Brandon Warmke. (2020). *Grandstanding: The Use and Abuse of Moral Talk*. New York: Oxford University Press.

Tsipursky, G., F. Votta, and K. M. Roose. (2018). "Fighting Fake News and Post-Truth Politics with Behavioral Science: The Pro-Truth Pledge." *Behavior and Social Issues* 27: 47–70.

Tyton Partners. (2023). "GenAI in Higher Education: Fall 2023 Update Time for Class Study." 9. https://tytonpartners.com/app/uploads/2023/10/GenAI-IN-HIGHER-EDUCATION-FALL-2023-UPDATE-TIME-FOR-CLASS-STUDY.pdf, accessed on July 15, 2025.

Um, Sungwoo. (2023). "Honesty: Respect for the Right Not to Be Deceived." *Journal of Moral Education* 53: 292–306.

van Bavel, J., E. Harris, P. Pärnamets, S. Rathje, K. Doell, and J. Tucker. (2021). "Political Psychology in the Digital (Mis)Information Age: A Model of News Belief and Sharing." *Social Issues and Policy Review* 15: 84–113.

van der Linden, S. (2022). "Misinformation: Susceptibility, Spread, and Interventions to Immunize the Public." *Nature Medicine* 28: 460–467.

Vargas, Ramon Antonio. (2015). "New Orleans Baptist Pastor Commits Suicide After His Name Appeared on Ashley Madison List." Nola.com. https://www.nola.com/news/new-orleans-baptist-pastor-commits-suicide-after-his-name-appeared-on-ashley-madison-list/article_07ef9b24-0013-5805-a73b-cdc32734ad59.html, accessed on July 15, 2025.

Vosoughi, S., D. Roy, and S. Aral. (2018). "The Spread of True and False News Online." *Science* 359: 1146–1151.

Vossler, A. (2016). "Internet Infidelity 10 Years On: A Critical Review of the Literature." *The Family Journal* 24: 359–366.

Vossler, A. and N. Moller. (2020). "Internet Affairs: Partners' Perceptions and Experiences of Internet Infidelity." *Journal of Sex & Marital Therapy* 46: 67–77.

Walker, M. and J. Gottfried. (2019). "Republicans Far More Likely than Democrats to Say Fact-Checkers Tend to Favor One Side." *Pew Research Center*. https://www.pewresearch.org/short-reads/2019/06/27/republicans-far-more-likely-than-democrats-to-say-fact-checkers-tend-to-favor-one-side/, accessed on July 15, 2025.

Wallbank, Adrian. (2023). "ChatGPT and AI Writers: A Threat to Student Agency and Free Will?" *Times Higher Education*. https://www.timeshighereducation.com/campus/chatgpt-and-ai-writers-threat-student-agency-and-free-will, accessed on July 15, 2025.

Waltzer, T. and A. Dahl. (2022). "The Moral Puzzle of Academic Cheating: Perceptions, Evaluations, and Decisions," in *Cheating Academic Integrity: Lessons from 30 Years of Research*. Eds. David Rettinger and Tricia Bertram Gallant. Hoboken: Wiley, 99–130.

Waltzer, T. and A. Dahl. (2023). "Why Do Students Cheat? Perceptions, Evaluations, and Motivations." *Ethics & Behavior* 33: 130–150.

Webber, Jonathan. (2018). "Bullshit You Can Believe In." *Open for Debate Blog*. https://blogs.cardiff.ac.uk/openfordebate/bullshit-you-can-believe-in/.

Wetzel, Dan. (2022). "A Decade Later, the Real Tragedy of the Manti Te'o story Is How a Victim Was Turned into the Butt of a Joke." *Yahoo Sports*. https://sports.yahoo.com/a-decade-later-the-real-tragedy-of-the-manti-teo-story-is-how-a-victim-was-turned-into-the-butt-of-a-joke-182354889.html, accessed on July 15, 2025.

Wikipedia. (2025a). "List of Most-Followed TikTok Accounts." https://en.wikipedia.org/wiki/List_of_most-followed_TikTok_accounts, accessed on July 15, 2025.

Wikipedia. (2025b). "Ted Haggard." https://en.wikipedia.org/wiki/Ted_Haggard#cite_note-Harris-ABC-14, accessed on July 15, 2025.

Wolken, Dan and Paul Myerberg. (2013). "Manti Te'o's Inspirational Girlfriend Story a Hoax." *USA TODAY*. https://www.usatoday.com/story/sports/ncaaf/2013/01/16/manti-teo-girlfriend-hoax-deadspin/1840415/, accessed on July 15, 2025.

Woodall, Bernie. (2018). "Lance Armstrong Settles U.S. Federal Fraud Case for $5 Million: Attorney." *Reuters*. https://www.reuters.com/article/sports/lance-armstrong-settles-us-federal-fraud-case-for-5-million-attorney-idUSKBN1HQ31W, accessed July 15, 2025.

Woodruff, Mike and Steve Moore. (2003). "An Honest Sermon." *Christianity Today*. https://www.christianitytoday.com/pastors/2003/winter/2.32.html, accessed on July 15, 2025.

Wright, Irene. (2023). "Woman Faked Her Own Kidnapping in Alabama, Cops Say. Now Carlee Russell Is Charged." *Miami Herald*. https://www.miamiherald.com/news/nation-world/national/article277752663.html, accessed on July 15, 2025.

Yaniv, G., Y. Tobol, and E. Siniver. (2019). "Self-Portrayed Honesty and Behavioral Dishonesty." *Ethics & Behavior* 30: 617–627.

Yarhi-Milo, K. and D. Ribar. (2023). "Who Punishes Leaders for Lying About the Use of Force? Evaluating the Microfoundations of Domestic Deception Costs." *Journal of Conflict Resolution* 67: 559–586.

Young, Garry. (2021). *Fictional Immorality and Immoral Fiction*. Lanham: Lexington Books.

Young, K., E. Griffin-Shelley, A. Cooper, J. O'Mara, and J. Buchanan. (2000). "Online Infidelity: A New Dimension in Couple Relationships with Implications for Evaluation and Treatment." *Sexual Addiction and Compulsivity* 7: 59–74.

Young, L., A. Chakroff, and J. Tom. (2012). "Doing Good Leads to More Good: The Reinforcing Power of a Moral Self-Concept." *Review of Philosophy and Psychology* 3: 325–334.

Index

For the benefit of digital users, indexed terms that span two pages (e.g., 52–53) may, on occasion, appear on only one of those pages.

Figures are indicated by an italic *f* following the page number.